THE COLUMBIAN MUSE OF COMEDY

*The Development of a Native Tradition in
Early American Social Comedy, 1787–1845*

DANIEL F. HAVENS

SOUTHERN ILLINOIS UNIVERSITY PRESS
Carbondale and Edwardsville

Feffer & Simons, Inc
London and Amsterdam

Library of Congress Cataloging in Publication Data

Havens, Daniel F   1931–
    The Columbian muse of comedy.

    Bibliography: p.
    1.   American drama (Comedy)—History and criticism.
I.   Title.
PS336.C7H37   812'.052   73–4822
ISBN 0–8093–0609–3

CONTENTS

ACKNOWLEDGMENTS

My thanks to Professor Joe Lee Davis, my wise teacher and counselor at the University of Michigan, for showing me that there was much worth enjoying, and thinking and writing about in early American drama. Thanks as well to another wise teacher, Professor Marvin Felheim, for his humane encouragement throughout this undertaking. Very special thanks to my wife Ellie, without whose patient support the book would not have been possible. Finally, thanks to Royall Tyler and other early American dramatists, whose works inspired me and continue to delight me with their comic energy. May this book in some small way repay them.

DANIEL F. HAVENS

Edwardsville, Illinois
October 1972

The Columbian Muse of Comedy

1

Introduction: The Quest for Literary Independence in Native American Social Comedy, 1787–1845

EVEN though drama comprises an impressive portion of the total literary productions in America to 1850, little scholarly attention of a critical nature has been given to it. The standard histories of the American stage are written by theatre historians, whose interests, understandably, are not always in drama as literature. While providing valuable information of the historical, biographical, and bibliographical sort, these histories generally lack the analytical approach — with clearly defined criteria — of literary criticism.[1] In the interest of filling in some of the critical gap, this book will trace the development of a native tradition in American social comedy from its beginning to the mid-nineteenth century: from Royall Tyler's *The Contrast* (1787) to Anna Cora Mowatt's *Fashion* (1845). The emerging native tradition will be examined in terms of dramatic characters, wit and humor, and structure (dramatic form) and theme.

The appearance in 1787 of Royall Tyler's *The Contrast* marks the beginning of American comedy, in this case of social comedy. As a play written by an American about Americans in America, it obviously qualifies as native drama. Yet, internal evidence suggests that Tyler modeled his play after Sheridan's *The School for Scandal*,[2] an assumption which many theatre historians have taken as proof of a close parallel between the plays. For example, Arthur Hobson Quinn points out the relationship between Tyler's Dimple and Sheridan's Joseph Surface,[3] an opinion echoed without challenge in more recent histories and anthologies. But the question of such a parallel is subordinate to the broader issue of literary independence. Assuming that early American comedy is in some way related to a definable British tradition, and of course that there is such a tradition, several questions arise.

How closely do the American comedies follow the British tradition? But

1

more vital to this search for an emerging native tradition, how widely do they vary from it? In what elements of the plays can such variation be discovered? Is there a sufficiently recognizable pattern of deviation in any element, for example plot, character, or scene, to constitute a native tradition? These questions underlie the larger issue of literary independence in native American social comedy.

Unfortunately, *social comedy* is an elusive term. It is far more convenient than definitive in grouping together a motley assortment of native comedies, largely unsophisticated, that appeared in America prior to the mid-nineteenth century. Playwrights on both sides of the Atlantic tended to label any play a comedy that was not bona fide tragedy, motivated perhaps by an ignorance of or boredom with quibbling critical distinctions — or more likely by the very practical desire to market their productions under a traditionally appealing label. Within such a sweeping classification one finds a gamut ranging from low farce through comic operetta, domestic drama (or dramas of sensibility), sentimental comedy, with an occasional comedy of manners. Although their practice may be disconcerting to scholars, our first playwrights have at least provided some precedent in permitting an elastic definition of social comedy.

Social comedies, particularly today, are related to each other more by subject matter and by their approach to it than by any traditional or classical form. The subject is always contemporary social behavior and the approach satirical — thus more intellectual than emotional. In its fullest sense, "social behavior" includes all actions, whether acceptable or not, in response to codes of behavior founded upon prevailing social values beyond the pale of mere polite manners. But its homogeneity of subject matter and mode does not control the form of social comedy as it does, for example, in the comedy of manners.

Manners comedy always involves ladies and gentlemen of society's upper class engaged in some stage of courtship, whether premarital, marital, or postmarital, and they are governed (or not) in these pursuits by a rigid code of behavior. It is during wooing that men and women exhibit to a greater extent their awareness or ignorance of these social (hence "artificial") codes. Those who can play this social game according to the rules, or are clever enough to break them discretely on occasion are the heroes and heroines. But those who lack such *savoir faire* suffer society's ridicule, in particular at the hands of the bolder, more intelligent people, who can from time to time violate the social code with impunity.

Manners comedy is grounded on the assumption that the judgment of the majority of intelligent men and women is right and will prevail. It accepts society largely as it is, confident that good sense will govern its members. Although it satirizes fashionable foibles, manners comedy does not primarily seek to reform social attitudes. As a result of its goals — the celebration of

good sense in guiding social behavior, and the satire of fashionable folly —
its form is stabilized. With little exception, whether it dates from the Restoration or from contemporary theatre, a manners comedy will be set in the
drawing room (or the contemporary equivalent), a ballroom, bedroom, or
mall; and it will present fashionable men and women in some sort of sexual
relationship. Finally, because character is seen more as social type than individual, and because dialogue is dominated by wit, the appeal of manners
comedy is intellectual.[4]

Thus, comedies of manners are related in both their approach to a common
subject matter and in form. In fact the treatment of subject limits and governs
the form of manners comedy. This is not the case with social comedy, which
is least definitive in form. In his discussion of American comedy types from
1825 to 1860, Quinn suggests that social comedy has a positive sense of social
consciousness that urges it to ridicule false social standards, thereby revealing
its awareness of true standards.[5] But this description fits manners comedy
equally well, and, as Quinn admits, few American comedies before 1860 reveal
such an awareness. While Quinn's description may be inadequate as a definition, it does remind us that social comedy derives from the older tradition of
manners comedy.

Both uphold social standards imposed by common sense, and both ridicule
or otherwise oppose false standards. Likewise, both appeal to the intellect, but
it is here that the parallel breaks down. In pure manners comedy, as Allardyce
Nicoll puts it, disapprobation for violation of the true standard "never passed
beyond a kind of fastidious contempt" for the fools outside the magic social
pale, struggling to get in.[6] Because the comedy of manners is essentially intellectual, it "permits practically no emotion whatsoever": violations of accepted
standards are viewed as folly and rarely as immorality. This suspension of
emotional sensibility, as Nicoll says, "renders innocuous what might otherwise
have been of evil effect."[7] Nicoll's definition of manners is helpful here.

Manners, in the mouths of the Restoration dramatists themselves, meant
something quite apart from the modern meaning of the term. "A Manner?" cries Cynthia in *The Double Dealer* (II.ii), "What's that, Madam?"
and Lady Froth replies, "Some distinguishing Quality, as for example,
the *Bel-air* or *Brilliant* of Mr. Brisk . . . or something of his own, that
should look a little *Jene-scay-quoysh.*" This quotation seems to make the
question easier. When we say that Jonson's comedy is a comedy of manners we are using the word in its ordinary sense of ways of men: when
we say that Congreve's comedy is a comedy of manners we are using the
word in its Congrevian sense, betokening something brilliant about a man
or woman, not a humour, but a grace or a habit of refined culture,
something that "looks a little *Jene-scay-quoysh.*"[8]

Social comedy views folly with more seriousness than the "fastidious contempt" of manners comedy, for its scope is broadened by a reforming spirit and therefore a moral core. It might be that the accepted standard has become anachronistic, mere inhibition existing for no useful social purpose. In such a case common sense defends the right of the individual to challenge that standard, which likens social comedy to the problem play of the late eighteenth century, itself an outgrowth of sentimental drama. Or it might be that the deviation from the accepted social norm is sufficiently widespread to represent a threat to the foundation of common sense upon which social stability is built, in which case social comedy — like the comedy of manners — fights to preserve the accepted norm. Like manners comedy, social comedy is primarily intellectual, although it does not exclude emotion, nor does it rely on character types alone, but on individuals too. As in Restoration comedy feelings are minimized, but not eliminated, for there is a stronger emphasis on realism in both character and plot, as in sentimental drama.

In view of these characteristics, social comedy cannot possibly have as rigid a form as the comedy of manners from which it derives in part. Like its Restoration forebear, its creed includes a faith in the standard of good sense; but the influence of sentimental drama may be seen in the reforming spirit and moral seriousness of social comedy as it satirizes contemporary social folly. Social comedy owes its objectivity and intellectual appeal to the comedy of manners, for it does satirize folly, even though regarding social problems with some seriousness. Moreover, it minimizes or discourages sentiment, but without suspending moral judgment entirely. In this latter respect and in its verisimilitude in creating, as Nicoll says, "scenes of real life . . . displaying a problem of some distinct and more or less poignant nature," [9] social comedy is related to sentimental drama. Anna Cora Mowatt's *Fashion* (1845) reveals both these influences. The themes of this social comedy arise from Mrs. Mowatt's serious concern for certain real problems in mid-nineteenth-century American society: parvenu values, heiress-hunting foreigners, and filial obedience. While the play understandably reflects some of the conventional sentimental attitudes of the age, Mrs. Mowatt's keen comic perception shows in her predominantly intellectual treatment of the social problems essayed. The play's primary appeal is to the intellect and reason of the audience because of her witty approach to subject matter.

If there is a lack of social consciousness in American comedies prior to 1860, it is nonetheless during this period that, out of the bastard forms of native comedy, a native tradition emerges in character, wit, and humor, and, while less distinct, nevertheless evident in dramatic structure and theme. The reason for pairing the last two elements is that theme often limits form. In Restoration comedy of manners, for example, plot and character were secondary to wit, which meant that the playwright, interested in witty exchanges between highly sophisticated, articulate characters — social types rather than individuals — created an illusion of tempo and forward motion in the plot through dialogue. Emphasis was less on a consistent *physical* plot development and more on the brilliant scene, with its rapid interplay of characters upon one another and its repartee. Thus, the eighteenth-century ideal of decorum, central to neoclassical thought and the aristocratic ideal of wit, and the Restoration playwright's low view of man as selfish and pleasure-loving — in other words theme — unite to govern form.

On the other hand, the basic philosophical assumption of the sentimental period following the Restoration was the perfectibility of man, virtually a complete reversal of the Restoration attitude. Therefore, sentimental playwrights, both comic and tragic, governed by this assumption, focused more upon physical action, upon a steady plot progression that gradually unfolded to the inevitable conclusion: the triumph of virtue and goodness in the tearful but joyous reconciliation of estranged lovers, or husband and wife, or father and son, and so forth. In short, the wit comedies of the Restoration were no longer satisfactory thematically, and the sentimental dramatists turned to comedies of sudden reform. Just as in Restoration comedy, then, we can pinpoint the essence of sentimental comedy as a philosophical attitude: theme exercising a significant control over dramatic structure, or form.

There is no need to delineate a tradition of character, and wit and humor in British comedy here because such a definition will emerge inevitably from the extended discussion of Tyler's *The Contrast* and Sheridan's *The School for Scandal* in the following chapter. A superb comedy of manners, *The School for Scandal* stands as a late eighteenth-century revival of the Restoration comic tradition. At the same time, it also reflects the coventional sentimental attitudes of Sheridan's own age. A critical examination of Sheridan's play requires some reference to familiar comedies from both the Restoration and sentimental periods, which will provide a cumulative and detailed delineation of the British tradition of character, and wit and humor. Still, two points remain to be taken up.

First, the distinction between wit and humor that plagued eighteenth-century English writers, and elicited such abundant definition, need not detain us because our interest is in useful critical definitions rather than a detailed history of the controversy. Nicoll says wit

> is opposed to humor and to the absurd in that it is intellectual, conscious, artificial, and refined. It is conscious and intellectual in that the creator of wit, although he may be laughed with, is never laughed at; he is deliberately saying laughable things. It is artificial in that it arises not out of natural buffoonery or unconscious eccentricity. It is refined in that it appears nowhere in primitive nations, having been developed by long

centuries of intellectual pursuits and of cultured conversation. Fundamentally wit arises out of the conflict of two ideas or of an idea and of an object. The *bon mot* is the expression of a clash between two several fancies or ideas, combined for one moment together. In its most obvious form it issues forth as a pun; in its highest moment it appears as a merely implied confusion of two conceptions. It marks an intellectual acumen, the swift juxtaposition of two ideas fundamentally inharmonious.[10]

Nicoll's definition makes some useful distinctions between wit and humor and needs no further elaboration, except to add a statement from the *Oxford Universal Dictionary* (rev. 1955): Wit is "that quality of speech or writing which consists in the apt association of thought and expression, calculated to surprise and delight by its unexpectedness; later always with reference to the utterance of brilliant or sparkling things in an amusing way." Hereafter I will use wit and humor as defined above.

Second, since social comedy has been shown to have roots in the Restoration comedy of manners and also in sentimental comedy — in many ways an aberration of that earlier mode — it seems logical to use the Restoration comedy as a starting point for the British tradition as defined in this book. We can safely assume that early American playwrights were most immediately influenced by productions in contemporary American theatre. A sampling of comedies and farces in the repertoire of the Lewis Hallam Company in 1754, just two years after it had come to the colonies, gives us an idea of that influence. Included were Cibber's *The Careless Husband* (sentimental comedy); Congreve's *Love for Love* (Restoration comedy of manners); Farquhar's *The Beaux's Stratagem, The Constant Couple, The Recruiting Officer,* and *The Twin Rivals* (post-Restoration genteel comedies); Fielding's *The Mock Doctor* (farce) and *Tom Thumb* (dramatic satire, operatic farce); Hoadley's *The Suspicious Husband* (sentimental comedy); Steele's *The Conscious Lovers* (sentimental comedy); and Vanbrugh's *The Provok'd Husband* (sentimental comedy [completed by Cibber]).[11] The comedies and farces of Cibber, Mrs. Centlivre, Garrick, and of course Goldsmith and Sheridan remained perennial favorites on the American stage up to the nineteenth century.

Any dramatic period inherits the tradition of the preceding one, yet modifies it to meet newer tastes, whether intellectual, emotional, aesthetic, moral, or whatever. Thus the comic dramatist of the eighteenth century inherited a successful array of stock comic types from the comedies of the Restoration, but of course many stock types are as old as the Greek comedies of Menander, in whose period (342–291?) the boy-meets-girl situation emerged. The Restoration comedy of manners was, as Nicoll describes it, "a peculiar, intangible sort of thing," but was not an innovation in plot and character, for

Fletcher's *The Wild Goose Chase* . . . contains a good deal of its atmosphere. Jonsonian personages abound in Etherege and in Congreve. The intrigue of the Spanish school is to be marked in every plot. Molière and his companions of the French stage gave merely a touch to the wit and to the theme.[12]

In view of this, using the Restoration manners comedy as a point of departure for the definition of a tradition in British comedy may seem rather arbitrary. It is, however, convenient in limiting what otherwise would be a sprawling task. Furthermore, it seems justified when we consider the influence of Restoration comedy on sentimental comedy, and the apparent influence of the two on early American drama, as seen in the sampling of plays from the Hallam repertoire.

Summing up the importance of Bronson Howard and Clyde Fitch as comic dramatists, Quinn suggests that their example

> perhaps, led their successors to attempt a broader scope of theme and treatment than was permitted by the European comedy of manners. Social drama in America has a wider sphere than the drawing-room comedy of an older day, and while it proceeds most frequently by means of satire, it is not limited to that mode of approach. Its prime essential lies in its employment of social inhibitions to accelerate or to prevent the actions of the characters.[13]

Yet we must not overlook the debt of later nineteenth-century playwrights such as Howard and Fitch to the earlier pioneers — to Tyler, Woodworth, Dunlap, and Mrs. Mowatt — in the search for the genesis of a native tradition in comedy. Granted, few of the early plays are mature social comedies (drama itself was as immature as the new American society), but they are the stuff out of which maturity finally emerged at the end of the nineteenth and beginning of the twentieth centuries.

Enter Jonathan

WHEN, on April 16, 1787, the American Company premiered Royall Tyler's *The Contrast* at the John Street Theatre in New York, American drama was in its infancy. Professional theatre had been born less than forty years before at a Philadelphia warehouse. *The Contrast* was the first American comedy to be professionally produced, but the second native play to reach the boards. The first, Thomas Godfrey's *The Prince of Parthia*, a tragedy, had been produced by the same American Company at Philadelphia on April 24, 1767.[1] But while Godfrey's tragedy was acted only once, *The Contrast* had a remarkably long life on the stage, considering that it was a first play by an amateur. After its initial performance on April 16, 1787, it was repeated in New York three times that year (April 18, May 2, and 12) and once more on June 10, 1789.[2] The four performances of 1787 alone constitute a good run, as any quick look at theatrical annals for the period will show.[3] William Dunlap was probably very close to the truth, however, when he attributed what he felt was at best a poor play's success to the talents of comedian Thomas Wignell in the part of Jonathan and to an audience "gratified by the appearance of home manufacture."[4] But the play was well received in all of the major theatrical cities of the time, having been produced in New York, Baltimore, Philadelphia, Boston, Richmond, and Charleston, with a record of sixteen performances before 1800.[5]

Major Royall Tyler, only two years out of college, had served in August 1778 with General Sullivan in a frustrated attack on the British at Newport late in the Revolution. He had returned to active duty in 1787, this time as General Benjamin Lincoln's aid-de-camp, in pursuit of the insurgents during the Shays Rebellion in Massachusetts. After the rebellion was put down at Petersham, Tyler had been sent to New York to arrange for the capture of Shays himself, who somehow had eluded the soldiers in Vermont. After his arrival on March 12, Tyler, who had never before seen live theatre, became a regular visitor to the playhouse in John Street, intimate with the actors, and particularly Wignell. Tyler was immediately inspired to write his first play in less than a month. The advertisement announces:

> This comedy has many claims to the public indulgence, independent of its intrinsic merits: It is the first essay of American genius in a difficult species of composition; it was written by one who never critically studied the rules of the drama, and, indeed, had seen but few of the exhibitions of the stage; it was undertaken and finished in the course of three weeks.[6]

Thus on these shores is launched the romantic myth of the natural, untrained genius of letters, if only from the pen of comedian Wignell.

Tyler was a talented and charming member of Boston's younger intellectual set. Although he had never expressed any desire to become a professional writer, his friends knew him to have had some literary ambitions. Not unlike many writers of his age, Tyler was first a man of affairs and politics, and only second a man of letters. Writing was for many gentlemen of the eighteenth century a pleasant and stimulating exercise, the pastime of a dilettante — but seldom a livelihood.[7]

Blessed with what Tupper describes as "a handsome face, a volatile wit, great friendliness and the large gift of laughter," Tyler was known as a clever parlor conversationalist in Boston society after his graduation from Harvard in 1776.[8] Although his waggish humor had led him into some pranks at Cambridge, Tyler was nevertheless graduated as his class valedictorian, and simultaneously honored by a B.A. degree from Yale in recognition of his scholarship.[9] During the early years of the Revolution, when he was reading for law in Boston, he had become a member of a lively club of young men who met at the apartment of the painter John Trumbull to discuss "literature, politics and war." [10] Intimate throughout his life with the socially prominent New England society, he had once been engaged to the daughter of John Adams, although the match never materialized.[11] Tyler's New England Puritan conscience may have gasped at the fashionable follies of New York society, just as Manly, the Puritan-turned-Yankee hero of *The Contrast*, did. But while the stage Tyler shuns Dimple's invitation to see the town, the real Tyler evidently responded enthusiastically to the pleasures of New York.

As enthusiastically as Royall Tyler, man of letters, attended the theatre and associated with the players, and as eagerly as Tyler, the Harvard wit, plunged into the social life of Charlotte Manly's dizzy world, Tyler, the respectable man of affairs and politics, was reluctant to link his name professionally with the theatre. Hence, the manuscript *and* the copyright were given to Wignell, who promised Tyler the anonymity he sought. The title page of the first edition of 1790 lists the author merely as a "Citizen of the United States." Yet the authorship was no secret, for in her reminiscences Mary Palmer Tyler (Mrs. Royall Tyler) recalls, with just a hint of Puritan disapproval:

> The winter my grandfather died was the time *The Contrast* was written and had such a wonderful run that winter. *The May-Day in Town* also was brought out as an after piece with unusual success. Like most authors of that day, I expect the honor and reputation was his chief reward, he was petted, caressed, feasted and toasted, and no doubt lived too freely.[12]

May-Day in Town was not, however, an "unusual success" for it was played only once, on May 19, 1787 at the John Street Theatre — and even then for only a benefit. Because none of Tyler's published plays after *The Contrast* have survived, it is difficult to judge their merit. There are reviews, but often less scholarly than entertaining. The following, from a letter by someone who had seen the performance of *May-Day*, indicated that Tyler's second play was, like the first, morally concerned with fashionable folly in New York society.

> [*May-Day*] has plott and incident and is as good as several of the English farces; it has, however, not succeeded well, owing . . . to the author's making his principal character a scold. Some of the New York ladies were alarmed for fear strangers should look upon Mrs. Sanders as the model of the gentle-women of this place.[13]

Mrs. Sanders perpetuated a tradition begun with Manly. That moralist-satirist Tyler failed because his pen touched too sensitive a spot is an interesting hypothesis. But whatever, *May-Day* lacked the saving grace of Yankee Jonathan, whose comic presence tempers the earnest moral tone of *The Contrast*. Ironically, in view of Tyler's ofter stern, Puritan stance, perhaps the most memorable scene from *The Contrast*, in which Jonathan describes his evening at the playhouse, "the shop where the devil hangs out the vanities of the world upon the tenter-hooks of temptation" (3.1), is a satiric thrust at the traditional Puritan attitude toward the stage.

This ambiguous mixture of moralist and wit, of Puritan and man of the world, suggests an ambivalence or dualism in Tyler's comic attitude. The matter will be discussed more fully below, but it warrants some attention here as regards Tyler's style. It is difficult to sympathize with Frederick Tupper's blunt criticism of the highly stylized eighteenth-century diction. He ignores the literary conventions of Tyler's own time. For example, the review of the play in the New York *Daily Advertiser* (April 18, 1787), which is generally enthusiastic, finds Manly's advice to Americans given in high rhetoric "to blame" only because "a man can never be supposed in conversation with himself, to point out examples of imitation to his countrymen."[14] The review never questions the style. Nevertheless, Typper's thesis is essentially accurate: that only Tyler's humor and realism counteracted the "infection" of a "nocuous eighteenth century manner."

> Tyler was ever quick to see the absurdities of pompous and ponderous speech in the mouths of other men; but when his own sense of fun is dormant, as in his moments of stately eloquence or of high morality, his style is straightway vitiated by all the artificialities of the stilted contemporary jargon.[15]

If Tyler is at fault in this respect, and the reference is obviously to Manly's language, in all fairness it must be said that he was in accord with the taste of his age for heroic drama. In the season of 1787 Hallam's company had performed, for example, Addison's *Cato*, Rowe's *Jane Shore*, Hartson's *The Countess of Salisbury*, and Lee's *Alexander the Great (The Rival Queens)* in New York. It would have been impossible for Tyler, while at Harvard, to have escaped the influence of the high political and patriotic oratory of his day. For one thing, on the eve of the Revolution, the Massachusetts General Court was meeting on the Harvard campus in order to escape the mob influence in Boston. A letter from Rev. Andrew Eliot calls attention to the reaction of students.

> The young gentlemen are already taken up with politics. They have caught the spirit of the times. Their declamations and forensic disputes breathe the spirit of liberty. This has always been encouraged, but they have sometimes been wrought up to such a pitch of enthusiasm, that it has been difficult for their Tutors to keep them within due bonds.[16]

For another thing, at that time Harvard had three student speaking clubs, whose activities approaching the Revolution became "more and more classic. Publius Valerius, Hannibal, Pericles, Cicero, Callicrates, and Appius Claudius occupy the rostrum and candlelight." [17] While none of this may justify the passages of inflated, stylized diction in a comedy, it reveals something of the man holding the pen. Tyler was a man of his literary time.

This conflict in Tyler between his wittier and his more serious, patriotic, moral, and grandiloquent self is not simply a chance occurrence in the spring of 1787. It is the fabric of a pattern traceable throughout his literary career — essentially an anonymous one. None of his works were published under his own signature, with the exception of five poems and some legal reports.[18] That Tyler should put his name to legal writings seems to fit the picture of a man not entirely sure of the propriety of the writing profession. Legal writings would be another matter. Futhermore, that so much of his writing was satiric points to Tyler's essential moral seriousness, an earnestness which he shares with the great satirists of any age.

After *May-Day in Town* his next two plays are both lost and neither was published. *The Doctor in Spite of Himself,* (ca. 1795),[19] evidently an adaptation of Molière's *Le Médicin malgré lui,* satirized quackery, one of the themes in Tyler's only novel, *The Algerine Captive* (1797). The second farce, likewise an adaptation, was *The Farm House, or The Female Duellists,* based on Kemble's play with the same title (Drury Lane, May 2, 1789). It was produced only once, at the Haymarket Theatre in Boston on May 6, 1796; the first was never acted. On October 30, 1797, *A Georgia Spec, or Land in the Moon* was produced at the Haymarket, which Colonel John Tyler, Royall's brother, had managed from November 1795 to April 1796. A farce satirizing the Yazoo land frauds, the play was good enough so that William Dunlap, then sole owner and manager of the American Company, produced it twice at the John Street Theatre, on December 20 and 23, 1797, and once on February 12, 1798 at the New Theatre (Park Theatre).[20] Two days before its premier in Boston an amusing advertisement appeared in the *Columbian Sentinel,* October 28, 1797.

> It contains a rich diversity of national character and native humor scarcely to be found in any other drama of the language. Replete with incident, enlivened by wit and amply fraught with harmless mirth, the comedy is entitled to the applause of all without wounding the feelings of any.[21]

One wonders about the "harmless mirth"? Did the company anticipate a sensitive reaction, as that to the satire of *May-Day* ten years before? Important, however, is that Tyler was continuing to work with native types, capitalizing on the earlier success of Jonathan. It is unfortunate that the play has been lost, eliminating any possibility of comparing it to *The Contrast.*

Tyler's last four plays were unpublished and unproduced,[22] of which three, *The Origin of the Feast of Purim, Joseph and His Brethren,* and *The Judgement of Solomon,* are biblical dramas in blank verse. Coming at the end of his playwriting activity, these closet dramas are further evidence of Tyler's moral seriousness, present since the earliest comedies. The remaining play, *The Island of Barrataria,* is a three-act farce based on Sancho Panza's brief term as "governor" of his island, *Don Quixote,* Part 2. While the farce is obviously romantic in setting, Sancho is curiously Yankee-like in his clipped, provincial dialect, and in his fondness for homely sayings. Moreover, two of Tyler's recurring themes are to be seen in Sancho's satirical comments on political corruption and fraudulent medical practices.[23]

The preface to Tyler's novel, *The Algerine Captive* (1797) announces the

same thematic concerns as the prologue of *The Contrast*, although there is a
shift from the attack in the play on manners and social etiquette as corruptive
of American morals to an attack on British literature as the source of moral
decay. In either case his concern arises from a deep sense of moral responsibility and from an anti-British chauvinism. The villain by 1797 was no longer
Lord Chesterfield but Mrs. Ann Radcliffe (1764–1823) and her ilk. Speaking
through his fictitious hero, Dr. Updike Underhill, Tyler says in the preface:

> In no other country [i.e., than in America] are there so many people, who,
> in proportion to its numbers, can read and write; and therefore, no sooner
> was a taste for amusing literature diffused, than all orders of country life,
> with one accord forsook the sober sermons and practical pieties of their
> fathers, for the gay stories and splendid impieties of the traveller and the
> novelist. The worthy farmer no longer fatigued himself with Bunyan's
> Pilgrim up the "hill of difficulty," or through the "slough of despond";
> but quaffed wine with Brydone in the hermitage of Vesuvias, or sported
> with Bruce on the fairy-land Abyssinia: while Dolly the dairy maid, and
> Jonathan the hired man, threw aside the ballad of the cruel step-mother,
> over which they had so often wept in concert, and now amused themselves
> into so agreeable a terror with the haunted houses and hobgoblins of Mrs.
> Ratcliffe, that they were both afraid to sleep alone.
>
> Although a lover of literature, however frivolous, may be pleasing to
> the man of letters, yet there are two things to be deplored in it. The first
> is, that, while so many books are vended, they are not of our own manu-
> facture. If our wives and daughters will wear gauze and ribbands, it is
> a pity they are not wrought in our own looms. The second misfortune
> is, that novels, being the picture of the times, the New England reader
> is insensibly brought to admire the levity, and often the vices of the parent
> country. While the fancy is enchanted, the heart is corrupted. The farm-
> er's daughter, while she pities the misfortune of some modern heroine,
> is exposed to the attacks of vice, from which her ignorance would have
> formed her surest shield. If the English novel does not inculcate vice, it
> at least impresses on the young female mind an erroneous idea of the
> world in which she is to live. It paints the manners, customs, and habits,
> of a strange country; excites a fondness for false splendor; and renders
> the home-spun habits of her own country disgusting.
>
> There are two things wanted, said a friend to the author: that we write
> our own books of amusement, and that they exhibit our own manners.[24]

Tyler's wit does not mask his basic moral concerns. However delightful the
indictment of poor Mrs. Radcliffe and the gothic novelists, there can be no
mistaking his serious plea for a moral, *native* literature.

The novel is a leisurely narrative dealing, in the first half, with Underhill's New England upbringing, and in the second, with his capture by the Algerian pirates (reflecting Tyler's continuing interest in contemporary national problems), his being sold into slavery, and his exciting escape from a forced conversion to Mohammedanism. In the first part the author's promise to edify the reader with an account of the customs and manners of his native land is fulfilled by Dr. Underhill's amusing account of his schooling, his brief teaching career, and his medical practice. Tyler satirizes the clergy, academic practices in the public schools and the universities (Tyler draws upon his own experience at Harvard for the controversy between ancient and modern authors), the medical profession, and in general the provincialism, gullibility, ignorance, and folly of Americans, which made them easy victims for such charlatans as the quack medicos Underhill encounters. In the tradition of Swift's *Gulliver's Travels* and Voltaire's *Candide*, Tyler satirizes through the ironic mask of a naïve hero. The second half of the novel is more in the picaresque tradition of Defoe's *Robinson Crusoe* or *Moll Flanders*, replete with romantic adventure, and narrated, as is the whole work, in a plain Yankee style, rich in colloquialisms, conventional moral digressions, and a competent (if bookish) geographical verisimilitude. Even while he aspires toward the moral and patriotic ends he had announced in the preface, Tyler works ironically, satisfying a public's taste for the kind of romance which, in English novels, was supposedly inculcating vice and exciting a "fondness for false splendor." [25]

Early in 1791, Tyler traveled to Vermont to practice law around Windsor, eventually settling in Guilford in 1794, when he married Mary Palmer. Over the years he became state's attorney for Windham County, a justice on the bench of the Vermont Supreme Court — eventually chief justice from 1807 to 1813 — and he served for three years, 1811–14, as professor of jurisprudence at the University of Vermont, of which institution he had been a trustee since 1802. These legal activities, however, did not curtail his interests, for Tyler continued to write essays, reviews, and some light verse, anonymously as usual, and two more plays, both produced. In the last decade of the eighteenth century Tyler traveled the circuit up and down the Connecticut River from Greenfield, Massachusetts, to Windsor, Vermont, and he was one of an informal group of circuit lawyers and others who would meet in various river taverns of an evening for late suppers, drinking, and cards — but also exchanges of wit and readings of prose and poetry.[26] It was among this coterie of wits and scribblers that Tyler befriended a younger Harvard alumnus, Joseph Dennie, also a man of law and letters, but who gave up his legal profession eventually to write full time. From 1796 to 1798 Dennie was editor of the *Farmer's Museum*, a weekly newspaper published at Walpole, New Hampshire. Before attaining this position, however, he had collaborated with Tyler in contributing light, satirical prose and verse to the Hanover *Eagle*.

Tyler and Dennie, under the pseudonym of Colon and Spondee, posed as wholesale dealers in verse, prose, and music. Their advertisement in the Hanover *Eagle* (July 28, 1794) reads:

> Parnassian wares, classic compliments, monologues, dialogues, tria-logues, tetralogues, and so on from one to twenty logues, anagrams, hudibrastics and panegyrics, by the gross or single dozen — sonnets, ele-gies, epithalamiums, epic poems — a quantity of brown horror and blue fear — a pleasing variety of high-colored compound epithets — love let-ters by the ream — sermons for texts and texts for sermons — old orations scoured, forensics furbished, with extemporaneous prayers corrected and amended — alliterations artfully allied and periods polished to perfection — canons, catches and cantatas — serenades for nocturnal lovers — amens and hallelujahs, trilled, quavered and slurred. On hand a few tierces of Attic salt.[27]

Once Dennie assumed editorship of the *Museum* in 1796, he renewed their partnership as Colon and Spondee, and they contributed verse, essays, and reviews of books and plays to that newspaper, all with a slight Federalist bias.

The last significant work from Tyler's pen was *The Yankey in London* (1809),[28] a fictitious series of letters from an American abroad, thus showing Tyler to have come full circle in reviving the international contrast theme. His very last work was "The Chestnut Tree," [29] a long poem rooted in the conven-tional eighteenth-century romantic pastoralism. Through the course of 186 quatrains, Tyler projects future scenes, reaching into the twentieth century: portraits of social types, satirical and sentimental. An interesting realistic inclusion is the ominous forecast of industrialism in a portrait of the inhumane effects of the factory system. Even to the end, Tyler's work reveals an insistent concern of the moralist and patriot for the contemporary problems of his young nation. By no means a great literary figure, Tyler is nevertheless a colorful and fairly diverse early American writer, whose work shows a pro-found involvement with the affairs — social, political and moral — of his country. His most outstanding contribution is, of course, the creation of Jona-than in *The Contrast*.

An analysis of *The Contrast* in search for the genesis of a native tradition in American comedy logically and conveniently begins with Tyler's "identifi-cation" of Sheridan's *The School for Scandal* as his model. Historians have all made note of this, but many are almost condescending in their criticism, giving one the impression — more by implication than flat statement — that Tyler had made a good try at imitation but had really failed. For example, Moses says that the play is "not so great a 'contrast' . . . that the literary student would fail to recognize *The School for Scandal* as its chief source of inspiration," imputing a lack of originality to Tyler.[30] Or Odell, who is seldom snide, says "assuredly, one feels in reading it, that Sheridan is at least twenty miles away." [31] Such criticism implies that Tyler had all but bungled his imitation, but that the critics have forgiven him the weaknesses of his juvenilia. Such an implication, however, is a logical contradiction to the assertion by these same critics that *The Contrast* is a *native* play, that is, a comedy with native characters and dealing with native themes.

William Dunlap, America's first playwright-manager, makes the following assessment of Tyler's comedy:

> It is extremely deficient in plot, dialogue, or incident, but has some marking in the characters, and in that of Jonathan, played by Wignell, a degree of humour, and a knowledge of what is termed Yankee dialect, which, in the hands of a favorite performer, was relished by an audience gratified by the appearance of home manufacture — a feeling which was soon exchanged for a most discouraging predilection for foreign articles, and a contempt for every literary home-made effort. This comedy was given by the author to Wignell; who published it in 1790 by subscription. It was coldly received in the closet: yet Jonathan the First has, perhaps, not been surpassed by any of his successors. He was the principal character, perhaps, strictly speaking, the only character.[32]

Dunlap may have been a little jealous of Tyler's success. Even so, he is less severe than Seilhamer, who concludes that "every law of dramatic construction was violated, the piece betraying in every scene the author's want of familiarity with theatrical methods." [33] On the whole, Dunlap's is a reasonably accurate assessment of the play's major strength — Jonathan — and its weaknesses. Even an unskilled reader finds it, as Odell says, a "talky" play without much connected action until the final act.[34] Ironically, what readers today enjoy most is that talkiness, particularly the speeches of Charlotte and Jonathan. Tyler had a sensitive ear for the rhythms of his native speech, as well as an artist's ability to reproduce them cleverly in dialogue.[35] The realism of character in Jonathan, Charlotte, Van Rough, and even Dimple is achieved largely through their speech, and it may well be, as Quinn says, that "in the hands of a competent company, the old comedy actually comes to life upon the stage." [36]

Although we are interested more in any significant differences between *The Contrast* and *The School for Scandal*, the similarities must be identified first as a point of departure. These may be found in the structure or form of the plays, in certain stage devices and scenes, in plotting, and in some character types. This is a general overview, but certain parallels are perceived immediately when the two plays are examined side by side.

The School for Scandal is a five-act comedy, which uses as the basis for its main plot the good and bad brother theme. This involves the triangle with Joseph Surface, his brother Charles, and Maria, the young lady of fortune both pursue. In its second plot the play uses the theme of the old husband and young wife, a favorite cuckolding situation in Restoration comedy, but treated morally because Sheridan operates within the conventions of the sentimental period. One critic, arguing that the play is intrinsically innocent in spite of the apparent wickedness of the scandalmongering, asserts that Sheridan's real brilliance is not so much the dialogue but in the plot's illusion of wickedness.[37] Although Lady Teazle goes as far as to consider adultery with Joseph Surface, she remains virtuous and true to Sir Peter, and the culmination of the second plot is a conventional, sentimental affirmation of marital love. Natural goodness and the good sense of both Teazles surmount the temptations of scandal and fashionable folly. Both plots are unified by the motif of the recurring scandal scenes, which illustrate contemporary manners as well as provide satirical commentary on fashionable society.

Like Sheridan, Tyler uses a five-act structure, although this in itself is not indicative of any particular debt. The form was standard in contemporary drama. But it was an ambitious undertaking for a first play. Many early native playwrights confined their farces and comedies to three acts or less.[38] The five-act structure generally permits a fuller development of character and plot, but in comedy primarily plot. In *The School for Scandal* Sheridan so develops both the main (Surface) and the subplot (Teazle) that there is almost equal emphasis of each. Moreover, the expanded length of a five-act structure normally means a larger number of scenes, and thus more opportunity for building climaxes. Perhaps the enumeration is arbitrary, but there seem to be seven climactic moments in Sheridan's comedy.[39]

Where Sheridan, with experience at his craft and a superior dramatic genius, succeeds with the problems of manipulating his plot lines into a unified whole, with sustaining almost throughout the play that level of witty dialogue which is the essence of manners comedy, and with pacing the action, even in the purely conversational scenes, so as to maintain a sense of forward plot motion, Tyler fails. By and large *The Contrast* is spotty in these respects and deserves the sharp criticism of Dunlap and others. Its unevenness is partly a matter of the abrupt distinction between the comic scenes, dominated by the wit of Charlotte, the bucolic humor of Jonathan, or the foppish airs of Dimple, and the serious or sentimental scenes with Maria and Manly, in which Tyler expresses his prolix moral and Columbian sentiments.

Sheridan's Rowley and Maria are noncomic characters; that is, neither is either witty, humorous, or farcical. But their sentimentalism is sufficiently restrained so as not to conflict seriously with the play's overall comic mood. Both deliver conventionally moral speeches, but never to the length or with the inflated, stylized diction of either Manly or Maria Van Rough in *The Contrast*. Skillfully, Sheridan never lets the seriousness interrupt the comic momentum of the whole play, and just as skillfully he weaves his two plot lines into a unified whole, as it has been shown. Tyler is least successful in plotting, for while the Jonathan-Jessamy plot is a rough thematic variation of the Manly plot — in both, Yankee honesty and ingenuity rise above the sophisticated guile of New York — there is otherwise no connection, and certainly not in the action. In justice to Tyler, however, it should be noted that the Jonathan scenes are scarcely definable as a plot, and do not constitute the second plot, which involves Dimple, Charlotte, and Letitia. But Tyler's main plot is essentially comic, owing to the presence of Charlotte and Dimple. Thus, in spite of the exceptions noted the play is in the tradition of manners comedy. Some British playwrights in the late sentimental period included almost no comedy in their main plots, which were really domestic dramas. They limited the comic business, usually low farce or even bawdy, to a subplot with little if any connection to the main one. Structurally *The Contrast* does not belong to this genre. But while it is imitative of *The School for Scandal* in many respects, it does reflect the influence of the drama of sensibility, and thus is not very far out of the mainstream of British and European drama of its period. The refreshing departure from this mainstream in the antisentimental laughing comedies was, unfortunately for comedy, only momentary.

Another weakness of *The Contrast* attributable to Tyler's inexperience as a playwright is its basic lack of action, posing a serious dramatic problem.[40] There are insufficient climactic moments in the play to enliven it, to maintain the variety and pace essential to manners comedy. First, in the matter of structure the play plods along, two scenes per act, even though beginning with Act 2 Tyler alternates the scenes between the main plots and the Jonathan plot. Since there is no connected action between these plots, there are less opportunities for climaxes, which in comedy depend on action. To illustrate, in 3.1, the first turning point in the action of the main plot, Dimple is pressed by his creditors for payment of his debt, facing legal action if he cannot meet their demands. But he learns of this through a letter, and in the presence of no other characters. There is no action in the scene, and thus no real climax. Up to this point, which is midway in the play, there has been no conflict; this scene is in fact the inciting incident and belongs properly in the first act, as a similar incident is placed in Congreve's *Love for Love*, when Valentine, the hero, is dunned. In the following scene (3.2) Tyler fails to capitalize on a fine opportunity for climactic effect. Dimple, who is on the verge of boasting to Manly about his intrigue with Charlotte, suddenly discovers that the man is her brother. The scene is cut off at this very moment, because Tyler has Manly leave for another appointment, ignoring the comic possibilities of, say, Dimple having slipped and then having to retract hastily, or of Manly's mounting suspicion. Reliance on summary instead of scene, as we have noted in 3.1 above, similarly destroys the climactic effect possible in 4.2 when Van Rough, in soliloquy, reveals that he has just learned of Dimple's debt. The audience is not permitted to witness his initial reaction to this discovery. It is surprising that Tyler, who seldom misses a chance to point the moral, did so here, for Van Rough's choice of Dimple for Maria is motivated largely by his belief that the young man has a sizable inheritance. Not only would Van Rough's discovery of his error be amusing, but the old man could moralize about the "main chance."

Finally, Tyler does not fully develop the comedy in the last climax, 5.2, in which Dimple's hypocrisy is revealed, for he is too intent on stressing the moral through Manly's judgment. Manly's fervent patriotism and Puritan ethics are in fact rather evident in each of his five scenes. Early in the play Charlotte teases him with "My brother is so sentimental and so grave, that I protest he'll give us the vapours" (2.1). Although Manly's presence has a sobering effect on the comic mood throughout, it is not until the final scene that Tyler indicates the fun is over, that the issues of the play must be resolved with the seriousness they deserve. The man of wit steps aside to give the moralist the final say. Sheridan, on the other hand, knew not to interfere with the comedy, knew that the moral would emerge from the action without underlining it as Tyler did. Here, strongly in the tradition of sentimental comedy, Tyler's major concern is achieving the proper emotional response from his audience. He openly solicits admiration for Maria's virtue, as he had earlier solicited pity for her suffering, with Manly's, as a victim of Van Rough's heartless wishes.

The speeches of repentance that conclude both plays point up the difference in comic attitude between Sheridan and Tyler. Perhaps as tired of banal moral sentiments as both Sir Peter and Sir Oliver have become, Sheridan is satisfied to let Charles say only:

> Why, as to reforming, Sir Peter, I'll make no promises, and that I take to be proof that I intend to set about it. — But here shall be my monitor — my gentle guide. — Ah! can I leave the virtuous path those eyes illumine?

> Though thou, dear maid, shouldst wa[i]ve thy *beauty's* sway,
> Thou still must rule, because I *will* obey:
> An humbled fugitive from Folly view,
> No sanctuary near but Love and — You;

[*To the audience*]
You can, indeed, each anxious fear remove,
For even *Scandal* dies, if you *approve*.   [5.3]

On the other hand, Tyler gives Charlotte a speech laden with sentimental contrition.

> If repentance can entitle me to forgiveness, I have already much merit: for I despise the littleness of my past conduct. I now find that the heart of any worthy man cannot be gained by invidious attacks upon the rights and characters of others; — or that the finest assemblage of features, the greatest in dress, the genteelest address, or the most brilliant wit, cannot eventually secure a coquette from contempt and ridicule.   [5.2]

Only Dimple's preposterous ego, maintained to the end, lends a touch of comedy in these final moments. Even Jonathan's presence, normally a signal for hilarity, is barely felt, for he is given only two speeches in the scene.

Prior to the sentimental period the ethical basis of comedy was a belief in human imperfection, and comic playwrights showed the contrast between the affectation of man's respectability and the reality of his folly and vice.[41] Such comedy was implicitly moral insofar as it ridiculed vice. But it was comedy, for it busied itself with the humorous and not the moral consequences of man's frailty. Inasmuch as Tyler treats Dimple, Jessamy, and, at first, Charlotte and Letitia satirically, he stands in this classical tradition of comedy. But his choice of noncomic, virtuous persons as hero and heroine, reflects the influence of the drama of sensibility. Tyler's sentimentalism may also be seen in his prolonging the sentimental situation between Maria and her father in 1.2, inviting our sympathy if not our tears for the heroine's undeserved suffering. If we were concerned only with the aesthetics of *The Contrast*, then Tyler's mingling of two basically antithetical traditions represents an ambiguity. Yet the conflict is closely related to that between his bright comic perception and satiric wit on the one hand, and his didacticism with its moral, sentimental, and patriotic roots on the other. Not all the blame for this aesthetic ambivalence can be laid to his literary inexperience.

There are certainly instances in which Tyler imitates Sheridan without success because of the young playwright's lack of dramatic craftsmanship. Still there are instances of deviation from his model which can only be deliberate, and whether successful dramatically or not, are in no sense clumsy imitation. To cite the obvious one, the serious turn at the end of *The Contrast*, quite unlike the almost tongue-in-cheek tone of Charles's repentance speech, is very deliberate. As stiff and sententious as Manly is, Tyler never once questions satirically what Manly represents, although he permits Charlotte to make some witty remarks about her grave brother. Tyler's first responsibility was to edify. Entertaining was secondary, although he did it very well at times. He was concerned not with aesthetics, not with form, but with ideas: with the end and not the means.[42] There is no inconsistency in his unswerving thematic end.

Within the broader scope of total structure there is the matter of scene parallels. Two of Tyler's scenes, the first and last, seem consciously patterned after Sheridan's. *The Contrast* opens smartly with a scandal scene which in manner and structural position resembles Sheridan's first scene. These scenes both set a tone, reveal character, and provide exposition. Notwithstanding the more limited scope of manners Tyler had to ridicule, for New York society of the 1780s was provincial in comparison to Sheridan's London of the preceding decade, the quality of wit and humor in the dialogue between Charlotte and Letitia is rather high. There are, however, significant differences between the two scandal scenes. Sheridan's opening scandal scene is the overture to the entire play, which maintains the scandal motif throughout. Scandal links the two plots together, and although there are only three scandal scenes (1.1; 2.2; and 5.2), every character is in some way affected by the scandalmongering. Thus scandal is present in every scene as the central motivating force of the play.

Such is not the case in *The Contrast*, however, for there are only two scandal scenes (1.1 and a part of 2.1). More important, scandal is not a unifying motif in the comedy. Scandal, which has everything to do with the action of Sheridan's two plots, has nothing to do with Tyler's. At most it reveals the character of Charlotte (and Letitia), who, like Lady Teazle, has a basically moral nature, and who eventually reforms. Tyler attempts to capture the flavor of contemporary manners through the bantering gossip of Charlotte and Letitia, but they lack the malicious wickedness of Lady Sneerwell and her clique. Their scandal is more good-natured and far less effective dramatically.

The second parallel is between the closing scenes of both plays. It is clear that Tyler attempts to use Sheridan's screen device, but he does not bring it off well. Letitia, suspicious of Dimple's eagerness to get rid of her upon Charlotte's arrival, pretends to leave but conceals herself just outside the partly opened door in order to eavesdrop. (The door is less effective than a screen as stage business because with a screen the audience is able to see more of the concealed character — particularly his facial expressions.) Conveniently, Manly has come to call on his sister, and he is waiting in the adjoining library. Hearing the commotion when Dimple kisses Charlotte, Manly leaps out to the rescue. But before he can cross swords with Dimple, Van Rough, who has also conveniently come to Charlotte's apartment, arrives and rushes in to beat down their swords. Jonathan has also run in, and thus all the dramatis personae are assembled onstage for the denouement. As I have already pointed out, Tyler does not exploit the comedy fully, turning serious instead. In Sheridan's scene, which is not the denouement in the first place, most of the comedy arises from Joseph's acute discomfort, having hidden Lady Teazle and Sir Peter separately. The climax, moreover, is what the audience has expected all along: the forced discovery by Charles. The eavesdropping business of Tyler is less exciting, and in modifying Sheridan's scene he has precluded a successful comic effect. There is no suspense because Dimple is unaware of Letitia's eavesdropping and because his attack upon Charlotte, at least in Tyler's view, is serious, not comic.

A plot device common to both plays is the familiar love triangle. This does not mean that Tyler borrowed it from Sheridan, because in some form or other the triangle is basic to most comic plots. Sheridan's triangle in the main plot involves Joseph, Charles, and Maria. But Joseph has been paying polite attention to Lady Teazle by flattering her and presenting a favorable impression, in an effort to ingratiate himself with her husband, Sir Peter. However, Lady Teazle begins to mistake Joseph's attention. Suddenly, in 2.2, he finds himself in the awkward position of having to pretend affection for Lady Teazle and to deny his real interest in Maria. Thus Joseph becomes a member of the second plot triangle with the Teazles, linking together the two plots.

Tyler modifies his first triangle to a situation in which Dimple, counterpart to Sheridan's Joseph Surface, is already engaged to Maria Van Rough, but must scheme to break it off. Colonel Manly, the third member of this triangle, loves Maria but refuses to court her while she is still engaged to another. Whether there had ever been any real affection between Maria and Dimple — at least on Dimple's part — is doubtful. Theirs had been a betrothal arranged by parents. Even so, Letitia says Maria once thought she had loved Dimple (we suspect mostly from a sense of filial obedience), and that "they might have jogged on, to the end of the chapter, a good kind of sing-song lack-a-daysaical life, as other honest married folks do" (1.1). But the grand tour has changed Dimple from a "good natured . . . coxcomb" to

> a flippant, palid, polite beau, who devotes the morning to his toilet, reads a few pages of Chesterfield's letters, and then minces out, to put his infamous principles in practice upon every woman he meets.   [1.1]

Now the fop can stomach Maria's grave and sentimental manner no longer. But more important, Dimple has gambled himself into a seventeen-thousand-pound debt. And so, while he continues to be attracted sexually to Charlotte Manly, Letitia's fortune has the larger claim. Dimple, like Joseph Surface, becomes a member of a second triangle (i.e., Dimple, Charlotte, Letitia), thus linking together the two plots. Here, however, it is the two women vying for Dimple, both suspicious yet neither positive that the other cares for him.

Comic suspense is heightened by Charlotte and Letitia, hitherto close friends, striving to pretend that nothing has happened to their relationship. Tyler's handling of intrigue and complication is skillful.

Governed by the ultimate needs of his theme of native worth, Tyler makes an important modification to the good and bad brother theme of his model, for Manly and Dimple are brothers only in citizenship. They are, however, continents apart in their cultural allegiance, for Dimple has pledged himself to follow the "infamous principles" of Lord Chesterfield, as well as to maintain himself in the high fashion of a London fop. These foibles, as well as Charlotte's infatuation with scandal and the "extremes of fashion, dress, flirting, and coquetry," are very distasteful to Manly. Foreign affectation was to Manly (and no doubt Tyler, a veteran officer of the Revolution like his hero) more than just a butt for social satire. It was an unsevered tie with England, and to a patriot such a bond was an affront to the spirit of the Revolution itself. It was not simply a vice to be ridiculed, it was an immoral, even treasonous corrosion that, if unchecked, might well eat away the very foundations of the new republic. Therefore, it is not hard to see why the classic good- and bad-brother theme in a simple love triangle was unsatisfactory for Tyler. There was more at stake for Manly than just winning Maria.

In the tradition of all manners comedy, *The School for Scandal* pleads for conformity to standards of behavior deemed acceptable by society's common sense. Sheridan's satire is directed toward affectation: behavior unacceptable within the social limits. To be sure, these affectations are contemporary, as the comedy of manners demands, for they reflect London manners of the 1770s. In particular, he singles out scandal, adulterous flirtation, libertinism, and extremes of fashionable dress for satirical attack. But upon closer examination, one finds these to be only particular manifestations of timeless, universal frailties.[43] Yet these follies are seldom a serious threat to the stability of society's good sense, for society maintains its equilibrium as it always has. It rewards the good and punishes the bad, and usually it is sufficiently tolerant to show its wayward Charles Surfaces the right way home. In spite of spoofing sentimentalism in the excesses of Lydia Languish, Sheridan is a sentimentalist, for both *The Rivals* and *The School for Scandal* reflect his faith in the basic doctrine underlying sentimentalism: the perfectibility of man. Therefore, the good- and bad-brother theme, in which the nature of each brother is seemingly reversed in the beginning, is ideally suited to Sheridan's broad thematic need.

If Tyler's native theme demanded certain modifications of the plot structure of *The School for Scandal*, it also led to some striking changes in character types. These changes are not merely differences from Sheridan's characters, but from stock comic characters in the tradition of British drama. The difference between Sheridan's and Tyler's societies in economic, political, and social structure accounts for some but not all of these modifications. More responsible is the American comic attitude deriving from a national self-consciousness, a sense of uniqueness, a patriotic commitment, a Puritan moral earnestness, and a romantic idealism about the future of the new republic.[44] These currents flowed through early American drama, making it, if romantic and sentimental in that it reflected widespread impulses in Western thought and literature, above all else didactic and nationalistic. William Dunlap makes this clear in the *History*: "If the wise and the good frequent the theatre, its exhibitions must become schools of wisdom. The lessons taught must be those of patriotism, virtue, morality, religion." [45]

A partial list of characters from both plays, paired off by type, would indicate a greater degree of correspondence than there actually is:

Character type	*The School for Scandal*	*The Contrast*
Hero	Charles Surface	Colonel Manly
Heroine	Maria	Maria Van Rough
Antagonist	Joseph Surface	Dimple
Coquette, lady of fashion	Lady Teazle	Charlotte
Father, guardian	Sir Peter	Van Rough
Servant	Trip	Jessamy

When these pairs are closely compared one finds a real parallel in only three: Maria and Maria, Charlotte and Lady Teazle, and Jessamy and Trip.

The parallel between the two Marias is the closest. Both are stock heroines of sentimental drama: suffering because of some injustice, in their case pressure by their elders to marry men neither can love. Both are fond of moral sentiments and neither is at all witty. Maria Van Rough, who is the epitome of painful though unwavering filial obedience, is the more vapid of the two, although not by much. Sheridan's Maria at least offers some resistance to her guardian's dictates, but Maria Van Rough never questions the authority of her father. Yet, Tyler stands resolutely behind those qualities of romantic love and filial obedience embodied in his heroine, for her virtue survives the temporary anguish of fearing she must marry Dimple, to triumph happily in the denouement when she and Manly are united with her father's blessing. It is true, however, that as a wit Tyler cannot resist lightly satirizing the "grave Maria and her sentimental circle" through the amusing dialogue of Charlotte and Letitia. Their breezy gossip almost creates the same illusion of wickedness conveyed in Sheridan's scandal scenes, but when closely examined it is found to be mostly in fun — no one's character is assassinated, no one's reputation is more than midly impugned. (Both Charlotte and Letitia are independently encouraging the breakup of Maria and Dimple, but not through scandal.)

Tyler the moralist entertains no serious desire to spoof sentimentality, whether in Maria or Manly.

To the contrary, through Maria's song about the death of the son of Alknomook,[46] a Cherokee chief, Tyler expresses a serious, popular native sentiment: the romantic glorification of the noble, persecuted savage.[47] The American Indian himself had initiated this mythical self-image in the early treaties of the seventeenth and eighteenth centuries, and colonial Americans had accepted it as a symbol of native worth, even during the bloodiest Indians wars.[48] After her song, Maria soliloquizes:

> There is something in this song which ever calls forth my affections. The manly virtue of courage, that fortitude which steels the heart against the keenest misfortunes, which interweaves the laurel of glory amidst the instruments of torture and death, display something so noble, so exalted, that in despite of the prejudices of education I cannot but admire it, even in a savage. [1.2]

These sentiments reflect the early American attachment to their new myths, which provided the stage with such heroes as the revolutionary soldier (Manly is drawn after the mythical ideal of George Washington), the savage yet noble Indian chief (Rogers, *Ponteach* [1766]), the farmer (Woodworth, *The Forest Rose* [1825]), and the Yankee and his descendant, the frontiersman (Murdoch, *Davy Crockett* [1872]). Two of these mythical types appear in *The Contrast* in Manly and Jonathan, and a third, the noble Indian, is obliquely present in Maria's song.

A second character parallel is between Lady Teazle and Charlotte Manly, for both are independent young women caught in the dizzy world of fashion, flirtation, and gossip. Lady Teazle is a familiar type in Restoration comedy: the young country girl, wed to a wealthy elderly man, and in extravagant pursuit of those fashionable pleasures she had been denied in her maiden state, whether by the cost in money or reputation. A memorable example is Mrs. Pinchwife in Wycherly's *The Country Wife*. But Sheridan has toned down Marjery's lusty appetite in creating Lady Teazle, who is never wholly serious about cuckolding her husband. She admits Joseph Surface as her lover "no further than fashion requires," and frankly confesses her basically prudish nature to him, saying "I have so many of my country prejudices left, that, though Sir Peter's ill humor may vex me ever so, it never shall provoke me to — " (2.2). Another indication of the virtuous nature beneath her fashionable facade is Lady Teazle's motivation for attending the Scandal Club. Unlike the vengeful Lady Sneerwell, Lady Teazle vows, "I have no malice against the people I abuse: when I say an ill-natured thing, 'tis out of pure good humor — and I take it for granted they deal in exactly the same manner with me"

(2.1). Finally, differing from many virtuous ladies of sentimental comedy, in which stage convention often linked a pretense of wit to a lack of virtue, Lady Teazle shows some wit, particularly in the sex-antagonism scenes [49] with the aging Sir Peter.

> *Sir P.* 'Slife, madam, I say, had you any of these elegant expenses when you married me?
> *Lady T.* Lud, Sir Peter! would you have me be out of the fashion?
> *Sir P.* The fashion, indeed! what had you to do with the fashion before you married me?
> *Lady T.* For my part, I should think you would like to have your wife thought a woman of taste.
> *Sir P.* Aye — there again — taste! Zounds! madam, you had no taste when you married *me*!
> *Lady T.* That's very true, indeed, Sir Peter! and, after having married you, I am sure I should never pretend to taste again.   [2.2]

Beneath the repartee, the conflict reduced to its most basic terms is between crabbed age and youth.[50]

Such a quality of youthful rebelliousness is the very essence of Charlotte Manly's nature. Having left her parents to live in New York, where she is freed for the first time from the halter of filial obedience, Charlotte is happily following the whims of city fashion. Her sole *raison d'être*, as she archly boasts, is coquetry, to flirt with "Man! — my Letitia — Man! for whom we dress, walk, dance, talk, lisp, languish, and smile" (1.1). That she is unmarried is only a slight modification by Tyler of Lady Teazle, for Charlotte is in rebellion against crabbed age — her parents. This is conveyed very subtly by Tyler, mostly by a stage direction. When her brother arrives, almost his whole initial greeting is to convey their parents' blessing to Charlotte.

> *Manly.* My dear Charlotte, I am happy that I once more enfold you within the arms of fraternal affection. I know you are going to ask (amiable impatience!) how our parents do, — the venerable pair transmit you their blessing by me. They totter on the verge of a well-spent life, and wish only to see their children settle in the world, to depart in peace.
> *Charlotte.* I am very happy to hear they are well. [*Coolly*] Brother, will you give me leave to introduce you to our uncle's ward, one of my most intimate friends?   [2.1]

The cool response to Manly's message, the quick change of subject, is indicative of Charlotte's attitude, which contrasts effectively with Maria's unwavering obedience to dramatize one of the play's important themes.

We are to assume that Charlotte's affectation is, like Dimple's, foreign, and foreign affectation is Tyler's prime target in *The Contrast*. But Charlotte's wickedness is, like Lady Teazle's, a kind of fashionable facade, beneath which are hidden her more natural, virtuous inclinations. For example, in the last scene, although she has played the coquette with Dimple, when he makes his dishonorable intentions apparent, Charlotte immediately balks. The suddenness of her change — it is an instinctive reaction — is evidence of Tyler's sentimental faith in natural goodness: Charlotte's maidenly virtue ultimately triumphs over intemperate affectation. As to scandal and gossip, she is more intently engaged in it than Lady Teazle perhaps, but not with any real malice. She delights in rattling the skeletons in the closets of others, but with Yankee doggedness checks her facts beforehand: "I take care never to report any thing of my acquaintance, especially if it is to their credit, — discredit, I mean, — until I have searched to the bottom of it" (2.1). Her defense of scandal very nearly echoes Lady Teazle's: "Scandal, you know, is but amusing ourselves with the faults, foibles, follies, and reputations of our friends; indeed, I don't know why we should have friends, if we are not at liberty to make use of them" (2.1). Last, it is unnecessary to demonstrate Charlotte's wit and humor by specific example here, except to say that she is a little wittier than Lady Teazle, although her wit often tends toward humor. With some assistance from Letitia, Charlotte bears the burden of the play's wit. No other character can hold his own against this charming coquette, who has the distinction of being the first Witty Woman in American drama. It is Charlotte's sparkling dialogue in acts 1, 2, and 4 that gives to *The Contrast* the tone of manners comedy.

The third character parallel is between Sheridan's Trip and Tyler's Jessamy; both are stock comic servants, aping the manners of their masters. Like Charles Surface, Trip is trying to relieve his debts, and like Dimple, Jessamy is affecting those "infamous principles" of Lord Chesterfield. But Jessamy's comic potential is developed more thoroughly than Trip's, for Sheridan gives his character only fourteen speeches in all — thirteen in 3.2, none in 3.3, in which he appears momentarily, and one in 4.2. On the other hand, Tyler treats Jessamy (along with Jonathan) as an important minor character, giving him a large share of three scenes: 2.2, 2.1, and 5.1. In 2.2, for example, his inflated diction and syntax provide a perfect comic foil to Jonathan's Yankee dialect.

> *Jes.* Come, come, my dear friend, I see that I must assume the honour of being the director of your amusements. Nature has given us passions, and youth and opportunity stimulate to gratify them. It is no shame, my dear Blueskin, for a man to amuse himself with a little gallantry.
>
> *Jon.* Girl huntry! I don't altogether undersand. I never played at that game. I know how to play hunt the squirrel, but I can't play anything with the girls; I am as good as married.

Even as Jonathan's foil, Jessamy is comic in his own right. Tyler is as effective in satirizing libertine naturalism in Jessamy as in Dimple. The relationship between Jessamy and Jonathan is roughly the same as that between Dimple and Manly: Jessamy takes it upon himself to introduce his new acquaintance to the pleasures of the city. Thus, while Tyler found it unnecessary to modify the stock comic character of the imitative servant from the British tradition, he did expand Jessamy's role compared to that of Trip in *The School for Scandal.* There are, however, four stock characters that Tyler has modified into native types: namely, Van Rough, Jonathan, Dimple, and Manly.

Although Van Rough appears only briefly in three scenes (1.2, 4.2, and 5.2, he is an important figure in *The Contrast* because he represents parental authority and Yankee materialism, both positive values for Tyler. The aged character as a stock type had undergone some changes from the Restoration to the late eighteenth century. In Restoration comedies crabbed age versus youth furnishes many of the plot conflicts. Aged men and women

> are loathsome to the gay young blades and precocious heroines who bewilder and victimize them. For it is the young who rule with arrogant ease the *beau monde* of these plays. It is the old who are the intruders. To their sophisticated juniors, they are merely old harridans and fossils.[51]

Thus, Old Bellair in Etherege's *The Man of Mode* and Sir Sampson Legend in Congreve's *Love for Love* are ridiculed and victimized by gay, rebellious youth. But the sentimental playwrights drastically altered their treatment of this comic type. In the first place they were not challenging such traditional values as filial obedience and respect for age, like the Restoration playwrights. They were in fact reasserting these values, as Steele does with the relationship between the Bevils, junior and senior, in *The Conscious Lovers,* or for that matter as Sheridan does with the relationship between Charles and his uncle in *The School for Scandal.* Often, as the eighteenth century drew on, the parental figure was of the wealthy middle class — a merchant or man of affairs — and plays began to idealize the new middle-class virtues of thrift, industriousness, and aggressiveness in accumulating fortunes. In *The Conscious Lovers,* 4.2, for example, the merchant Sealand makes an eloquent rebuttal to Sir Bevil's snobbish attitude toward his class. By fifty years later, Stockwell, the wealthy merchant in Cumberland's *The West Indian,* had assumed genteel tastes and a refined sensibility — previously qualities of gentlemen only. Conflict between age and youth remained a favorite situation in sentimental comedy, as it has always been in all comedy, but the resolution of that conflict did not result in a decisive victory for youth. Rather, there was a happy reconciliation in which, typically, age bent sufficiently toward a moderate view to retain the respect of youth for its wisdom and experience. Age might be portrayed as stodgy, but rarely wholly anachronistic or tyrannical. Such is Tyler's treatment of Van Rough, whose exterior belies the sentimental heart beneath.

Old Van Rough is much like his name — a man of almost no genteel refinement. Yet Tyler, who lightly satirizes his humors like obsession for keeping his eye on the "main chance," is obviously sympathetic toward Van Rough's materialistic ethic. Considering that Tyler's own father had been a successful Boston merchant, his approval of the Puritan-initiated work-hard-and-do-good ethic is understandable. There is some comedy in Van Rough's old fashioned anti-intellectualism, particularly in his suspicious attitude toward the education of women:

> They us'd to say, when I was a young man, that if a woman knew how to make a pudding, and to keep herself out of fire and water, she knew enough for a wife. Now, what good have these books done you? have they not made you melancholy? as you call it. Pray, what right has a girl of your age to be in the dumps? Haven't you everything your heart can wish; an't you going to be married to a young man of great fortune; an't you going to have the quit-rent of twenty miles square? [1.2]

It is clear that Maria's reply seems utterly nonsensical to him: "One-hundredth part of the land, and a lease for life of the heart of a man I could love, would satisfy me" (1.2), for Van Rough lives in a man's world of hard cash gained by equally hard Yankee practicality: "it is money makes the mare go; keep your eye upon the main chance, Mary" (1.2). In his mind, love is "nonsense, downright nonsense, child. This comes of your reading your story-books; your Charles Grandisons, your Sentimental Journals, and your Robinson Crusoes, and other such trumpery" (1.2). It is through his dialogue, rich in colloquialisms like "in the dumps," "popp'd the question," and through his fondness for earthy saws like "money makes the mare go," and "keep your eye on the main chance" — reminiscent of Franklin's Poor Richard — that Tyler satirizes Van Rough, but more significant, that he makes the merchant completely American.

His Yankee stubbornness in holding his daughter to what he believes is an economically sound match causes Maria and Manly some momentary suffering, but Van Rough has a quick change of mind in the fifth act as soon as he has learned of Dimple's indebtedness. Yet he professes to have undergone the change partly because he had, in 4.2, overheard Maria tell Manly that, in spite of her heart's desire, she could not allow herself to receive his attentions against her father's wishes. But Tyler does not permit too sentimental a reversal in the old man, who tells Manly

and you talked very prudently, young man. I have inquired into your
character, and find you to be a man of punctuality and mind the main
chance. And so, as you love Mary, and Mary loves you, you shall have
my consent immediately to be married. I'll settle my fortune on you, and
go and live with you the remainder of my life.   [5.2]

To the end, Van Rough remains the same shrewd, practical, no-nonsense
Yankee businessman. Adapting a stock type from British drama to his American themes, Tyler has created a fresh native comic type.

The outstanding comic character in *The Contrast* is Yankee Jonathan,
whose figure is probably the most unique stage type in American drama. For
Jessamy, Tyler simply used the stock comic servant from the British tradition,
but for Jonathan there is no such clear-cut model. There are numerous variations of this comic servant type: he may be the imitative Trip in *The School
for Scandal*, the witty, manipulating Jeremy in *Love for Love*, the polished,
gentleman's companion like Waitwell in *The Way of the World*, or the trusted,
devoted, and wise old Humphrey in *The Conscious Lovers*. Yet while Jonathan
assumes some of these traits, he is not really the true descendant of any of
these variations of the type. The ancient device of tricking — practical joking
— which does not figure in Jonathan's character, for Jessamy tricks *him*, became a stock device in the Yankee plays to follow *The Contrast*. But tricking and
in general many of the farce situations commonly used with clowns in comedy
(i.e., gulling, goading, drubbing, etc.) remained stock in trade in the Yankee
plays following Tyler's Nevertheless, Jonathan per se seems to be Tyler's own.

But the origin of the stage Yankee is a question that has generated much
speculation among critics. One theory holds that the Yankee is an American
adaptation of the Yorkshire clown in English comedy, but there is no evidence
to support this contention beyond some superficial (and perhaps coincidental)
similarities in behavior.[52] If Dunlap's frontispiece to *The Contrast* is accurate,
Wignell played Jonathan dressed as the coventional English rustic: long coat,
knee breeches, black stockings, plain linen (in contrast to the more elegant
linen of the "city" characters), and what appears to be an uncombed, dark
(unpowdered) wig. But Wignell's garb did not set a pattern for later stage
Yankees, whose costumes were much brighter and more eccentric. The Englishman Wignell, who was, according to Dunlap, a comic actor rather than
a buffoon, probably played Jonathan's role with more restraint than later
Yankee actors, whose portrayals depended on "vulgarity and broad humor."[53]
It is doubtful, too, that Wignell spoke Jonathan's lines with the Yankee twang
so characteristic of nineteenth-century depictions, but rather with the rustic
dialect he would have used in portraying a conventional English clown.

Even so, as we read the play today, Jonathan comes across as distinctly
American — distinctly New England. His native "down east-ness" is largely

a matter of his attitudes, something Wignell's British delivery — if it was that — could not obscure. There is no doubt that Wignell's personal popularity helped Tyler's play, but the actor was only interpreting what the young playwright had written for him; and while Jonathan was a popular role, the play's overall Columbian sentiments caught the popular fancy then. It was, in any event popular enough to have become the first American play to be a commercial success.[54]

But Tyler did not introduce the first stage Yankee, an honor that belongs to the Irish playwright Captain Joseph Atkinson. Atkinson, who may have served in America (and would thus have some firthand knowledge of Yankees), wrote a three-act comic opera, *A Match for a Widow*, performed in Dublin on April 17, 1786. In this play, a year earlier than Tyler's, Atkinson introduced Jonathan, a Yankee servant of the hero, Captain Belmor (who, like Manly, is a veteran of the revolutionary war). Atkinson's Jonathan had "all the traits of our traditional Yankee" — he even sings "Yankee Doodle." [55] There is, however, only a remote possibility that Atkinson may have influenced Tyler, who could have heard about the comic opera from an actor. But *A Match for A Widow* was not published until 1788, a year after *The Contrast*. More accessible as a source for Yankee Jonathan was Tyler's firsthand knowledge of the real thing in his native Massachusetts.

It is true that the ballad "Yankee Doodle" was current in Tyler's day (although it was not printed until 1815),[56] and it may have suggested Yankee traits to him (and to Atkinson), although his own New England background seems a more probably source. The melody, which goes back to the early seventeenth century in England, had appeared in native American drama twenty years before *The Contrast*, in Forrest's *The Disappointment* (1767). The ballad, from which Tyler adapts the four stanzas Jonathan sings, is a version written in 1775 by Thomas Bangs, a Harvard classmate of Tyler's.[57]

Scholarship exists to prove, beyond a doubt, that Tyler's *The Contrast* is not "the ultimate source of the Jonathan character." [58] Even if Atkinson's play did not exist, American literature — including drama, of course — had been experimenting with native types prior to Tyler,[59] and the Yankee in particular is clearly a reflection of nationalistic sentiments of the day. The symbolic image of the Yankee was no chance occurrence; it was, rather, inevitable as the product of cultural evolution that shaped his character and his very form.[60] But one should not dismiss Tyler's contribution by proving he was second, or third.

After all the proofs, all the evidence, what remains is undeniable: no Yankee as successful as his Jonathan had appeared before *The Contrast*, and the success of later Yankees owed something to the magic that Tyler performed in his creation. If Tyler only mirrored what was, something of the new American ethos, he mirrored it true. It is to Tyler's Jonathan we turn today, correctly or not, when seeking the prototype. Introduced by Tyler as a kind of comic relief, a minor farce figure, Jonathan's unique personality transcended his creator's initial design to draw the breath of life.[61] He dominates not only his own three scenes but, in spirit, the whole play. Jonathan, even in 1787, was already a myth.

Tyler's Jonathan was the first successful stage Yankee in a long line, that included such names as Humphry Cubb (Samuel Low, *The Politician Outwitted*, 1789, never acted), Jonathan Norrard (J. Robinson, *The Yorker's Stratagem*, 1792), Nathan Yank (James N. Barker, *Tears and Smiles*, 1807), Jonathan Postfree (Lazarus Beach, *Jonathan Postfree*, 1807, never acted), Brother Jonathan (A. B. Lindsley, *Love and Friendship*, 1809), and Doolittle (David Humphreys, *The Yankey in England*, published 1815, produced by amateurs 1814). But the first Yankee to gain any real public acceptance in terms of a long life on the boards was Woodworth's Jonathan Ploughboy in *The Forest Rose*, 1825 — and the date is significant. A chauvinism that amounted to a kind of Anglophobia had motivated Tyler, as it had a great many Whig writers of the revolutionary period, and it had reemerged during and after the War of 1812, goaded in the 1820s and 1830s by the criticism of British travelers like Mrs. Frances Trollope (*Domestic Manners of the Americans*, 1832), who saw Americans as boorish, provincial, and Philistine. And abetting what was much in the air in this period was the success and inspiration of English actor Charles Matthews, whose *Trip to America* and *Jonathan in England*, both produced first in 1824 in England, showed American comedians that they could challenge the accepted (predominantly British) repertoire by using native materials.[62]

Ironically, the stage Yankee, whose dominant characteristics — ignorance, gullibility, uncouthness — were the traits singled out as most abhorrent in Americans, catapulted to popularity on the American stage during the period of severest British criticism. Whatever shame Americans may have felt for their lack of polish, judged by European standards, was sublimated to emerge as the shameless caricature of the stage Yankee.

> He was always the symbolic American. Unless he appeared as a tar his costume hardly varied: he wore a white bell-crowned hat, a coat with long tails that was usually blue, eccentric red and white trousers, and long boot straps. Brother Jonathan had in fact turned into Uncle Sam. Half bravado, half cockalorum . . . he was indefatigably rural, sharp, uncouth, witty. Here were the manners of the Americans! Peddling, swapping, practical joking.[63]

Thus, Jonathan did not develop slowly over centuries, as is usual with a national type, but had stepped, if not full-grown from Tyler's pen into the yellow candlelight of the theatre, at least nearly so, to mirror in caricature the national ethos. And in the nineteenth century the Yankee image grew rapidly to encompass the frontiersman or backwoodsman, famous for his tall tales and fantastic feats. The Yankee peddler was

> forever pushing into new regions, and could be descried down the years, walking to Oregon at the heels of the settlers or on the march across the plains to the gold of California. The further he receded from the view the more completely he changed into a sly thin ogre, something greater than human size. He was myth, a fantasy. Many hands had joined to fashion his figure, from the South, from the West, even from New England.[64]

After his genesis in drama, the Yankee appeared with increasing frequency in other forms of nineteenth-century American literature. He can be found in the sketches of Washington Irving; in the fiction of James Fenimore Cooper, John Neal, William Gilmore Simms, Robert M. Bird, Nathaniel Hawthorne, Herman Melville, and Henry James; and in the writings of humorists such as Asa Greene, James Russell Lowell, and Seba Smith.[65]

The popular success of the stage Yankee may have been due as much to the talented acting of comedians like Henry Placide, James H. Hackett, George Handel Hill, Danforth Marble, and J. S. Silsbee as to the skill of playwrights.[66] "Yankee" Hill, who first acted Woodworth's Jonathan Ploughboy, eventually went on to specialize exclusively in Yankee characters, both in America and abroad, until his death in 1840. Like Marble and Silsbee, Hill was a Yankee himself, and took pains to study the type in his native New England. Toward the end of his career he performed monologues and "lectures" in one man shows. One of his own amusing anecdotes illustrates the realism of his portrayal. He had been playing in a small rural town as a member of the first theatrical company ever to appear there. Although he worked hard to amuse his audience, he received a cold, polite silence. But after the performance a countryman came back to his dressing room to tell him:

> "Say, mister, I was in to the play tonight."

> "Were you? You must have been greatly entertained."

> "Well, I was! I tell you what it is now, my mouth is all sore a-straining to keep my face straight. And if it hadn't been for the women, I'd 'a laughed right out in meetin'." [67]

Once comedians realized the popularity of Yankee plays there was a greater demand for new material; many plays were written esp or another. In 1830, for example, Hackett paid three hundred dollars to James K. Paulding for *The Lion of the West*.[68]

The majority of these Yankee plays of the early nineteenth century — particularly those written to order for the comedians who specialized in Yankee parts — are conventional comedies or melodramas, or a mixture of the two, but containing in the subplot the Yankee character. Often such characters were not involved in the plot, at best aiding the hero to save the heroine in a fumbling manner. Still, their vigor gave the plays a native realism otherwise missing in the conventional comic and sentimental dramatis personae. Containing a realistic native character as they did, these plays reflect the dramatic impulse toward greater realism in character and occasionally plot, to reach fulfillment toward the end of the nineteenth and beginning of the twentieth centuries in mature social comedies like Bronson Howard's *Saratoga* (1898), Clyde Fitch's *The Climbers* (1901), and Langdon Mitchell's *The New York Idea* (1908).

As to the matter of an actor influencing a playwright, there is no doubt that Tyler created Jonathan expressly for Thomas Wignell, low comedian of the American Company. The clearest evidence of some indirect influence is internal, for in the third act Jonathan relates his visit to the playhouse and describes a character in O'Keefe's *The Poor Soldier*, Darby Wag-all, who had in fact been played by Wignell: "Why, he had red hair, and a little round plump face like mine, only not altogether so handsome. His name was — Darby; — that was his baptizing name; his other name I forgot. Oh! it was Wig — Wag — Wag-all, Darby Wag-all" (3.1). The "Wig — Wag . . . etc." is obviously doubly insured for a laugh, since Wignell, who was playing Jonathan, was describing himself in another role, (quite likely with some appropriate business such as a broad stage wink). The production Jonathan describes for Jessamy and Jenny is accurate historically. Hallam's company often paired *The School for Scandal* with O'Keefe's afterpiece and had done so on March 21, 1787, which was the only time Tyler could have seen them together between his arrival in New York on March 12 and the premier of *The Contrast* on April 16.[69]

The Contrast was published by Wignell in 1790. Tyler had given him the manuscript with the copyright, requesting that he publish it as by an anonymous author. It is unlikely that the actor had much if any direct influence on the writing of the play for he never wrote one himself. It is possible that he emended or otherwise edited the manuscript before having it published, perhaps making changes that had taken place as the play was acted over the three years. But there is no proof of this, nor can there be any. It seems likely that Wignell, who was a sharing partner in the company, was influential in convincing Hallam and Henry to accept the play and then to produce it. *The Contrast* offered neither of them an attractive part, although it did so for Wignell, of whose rising popularity they were apparently already jealous.[70] Seilhamer speculates that publication may have been delayed for three years until 1790 because of the pressure of jealously from Hallam and Henry, who refused to let Wignell use the theatre in Philadelphia for a production of the play. Wignell was forced to give only a reading at the City Tavern in Philadelphia on December 10, 1787.[71] Notwithstanding Wignell's problems with his senior partners, his brief association with Tyler was happily advantageous, considering his success in the role of Jonathan. It is interesting that for its second performance on April 18, 1787, *The Contrast* was followed by *The Poor Soldier* as the afterpiece. A good night for Wignell, better than May 19, when he used the unsuccessful *May-Day in Town* for his benefit — its first and last performance.

Perhaps the most significant question a study of Jonathan raises is to what extent he is emblematic, or as Constance Rourke says, *the* symbolic American. Allan G. Halline describes him as a clown, "as ridiculous as Dimple is odious," and to a degree Jonathan is ridiculous of course.[72] Tyler did, after all, conceive of him as a minor comic figure in the farcical subplot. A study of realistic native characters in drama of this period, notes that from 1815 to 1870 the stage Yankee was "not infrequently little more than a native stage-clown," but that "the living type is always clearly suggested by the dramatic and . . . with sufficient verity." [73]

While Jonathan's Yankee traits are satirized through contrast and exaggeration, Tyler's best comic techniques, many of these identical traits are portrayed as admirable in other characters: Yankee materialism and commonsense practicality in Van Rough, filial obedience and parental respect in Maria and Manly, and moral earnestness, patriotism, Columbian idealism, equalitarianism, and self-reliance in Manly.[74] Indeed, every one of the hero's shining qualities is present to some degree, however small, in his "waiter."

Furthermore, Jonathan's Yankee provincialism, while certainly comic, is presented as more worthwhile than the affectation, the pseudo-Chesterfieldian manners of his foil, Jessamy, who unlike Jonathan has not a scrap of conscience or inner moral worth. But the contrast between morality and vice in the two is kept at a comic level. To illustrate, in the second act Jessamy encourages Jonathan to attempt to seduce Jenny, confident that "this blundering dog [will] sicken Jenny with his nauseous pawings, until she flies into my arms for very ease" (2.2). And in the third act, fly Jenny does, but whether from Jonathan into Jessamy's arms is never revealed. There is much broad farce in Jonathan's clumsy efforts to woo Jenny, especially when he garbles the courting speeches Jessamy has taught him. Jonathan asks what he should do if Jenny becomes angry, to which Jessamy replies:

> *Jes.* Why, if she should pretend — please to observe, Mr. Jonathan — if she should pretend to be offended, you must — But I'll tell you how

my master acted in such a case: He was seated by a young lady of eighteen upon a sofa, plucking with a wanton hand the blooming sweets of youth and beauty. When the lady thought it necessary to check his ardour, . . . my master instantly dropped upon his knees, with eyes swimming with love, cheeks glowing with desire, and in the gentlest modulation of voice he said: My dear Caroline, in a few months our hands will be indissolubly united at the altar; our hearts I feel are already so; the favours you now grant as evidence of your affection are favours indeed; yet, when the ceremony is once past, what will now be received with rapture will then be attributed to duty.

> *Jon.* Well, and what was the consequence?
> *Jes.* The consequence! — Ah! forgive me, my dear friend, but you New England gentlemen have such a laudable curiosity of seeing the bottom of everything — why, to be honest, I confess I saw the blooming cherub of a consequence smiling in its angelic mother's arms, about ten months afterwards.   [2.2]

But when Jonathan tries this approach on poor Jenny, the following ensues:

> *Jon.* I believe I'll begin to do a little, as Jessamy says we must when we go a-courting — [*Runs and kisses her.*] Burning rivers! cooling flames! red-hot roses! pig-nuts! hasty-pudding and ambrosia!
> *Jen.* What means this freedom? you insulting wretch. [*Strikes him.*]
> *Jon.* Are you affronted?
> *Jen.* Affronted! with what looks shall I express my anger?
> *Jon.* Looks! why as to the matter of looks, you look as cross as a witch.
> *Jen.* Have you no feeling for the delicacy of my sex?
> *Jon.* Feeling! Gor, I — I feel the delicacy of your sex pretty smartly. [*Rubbing his cheek.*], though, I vow, I thought when you city ladies courted and married, and all that, you put feeling out of the question.   [3.1]

Jonathan may be baffled by the sophistication of the city, represented by the airs of Jenny, and the comedy arises mainly from his naïveté, but he is not defeated by it. His final speech in the scene above, while comic, is a reaffirmation of the simpler Yankee values — of native worth: "If this is the way with your city ladies, give me the twenty acres of rock, the bible, the cow, and Tabitha, and a little peaceable bundling" (3.1). Likewise comic is Jonathan's fierce independence, seen in his insistence that he is Manly's waiter, not his servant, for "no man shall master me: my father has as good a farm as the Colonel" (2.2). But in contrast to Jessamy's slavish imitation of Dimple's foppishness it is also admirable.

Tyler develops much of Jonathan's comedy through his Yankee dialect, his earthy New England idiom, and as every historian of the American theatre points out, this is a significant contribution toward native realism during a period when dialogue was often artificial by stage convention. Manly and Maria, for example, never breach this artificial pattern of dialogue. Jonathan's idiomatic speech, which set the pattern for every stage Yankee to follow, is filled with expressions like "what the dogs," "by the living jingo," "I vow," "swamp it," "dang it," "Gor," "tarnal," "tarnation," "mercy on my soul," and the frequent "I'm a true blue son of liberty." [75] His description of the playhouse is a classic example:

> *Jon.* So I went right in, and they shewed me away, clean up to the garret, just like the meeting-house gallery. And so I saw a power of topping folks, all sitting round in little cabins, "just like father's corn-cribs": and then there was such a squeaking with the fiddles, and such a tarnal blaze with the lights, my head was near turned. At last the people that sat near me set up such a hissing — hiss — like so many mad cats; and then they went thump, thump, thump, just like our Peleg threshing wheat, and stampt away, just like the nation; and called out for one Mr. Langolee, — I suppose he helps act the tricks.
>
> . . . .
>
> *Jes.* . . . And did you see the man with his tricks?
>
> *Jon.* Why, I vow, as I was looking out for him, they lifted up a great green cloth and let us look right into the next neighbour's house. Have you a good many houses in New-York made so in that 'ere way?
>
> *Jen.* Not many; but did you see the family?
>
> *Jon.* Yes, swamp it; I see'd the family.
>
> . . . .
>
> *Jen.* Well, Mr. Jonathan, you were certainly at the play-house.
>
> *Jon.* I at the play-house! — Why didn't I see the play then?
>
> *Jen.* Why, the people you saw were players.
>
> *Jon.* Mercy on my soul! did I see the wicked players? — Mayhap that 'ere Darby that I liked so was the old serpent himself, and had his cloven foot in his pocket. Why, I vow, now I come to think on't, the candles seemed to burn blue, and I am sure where I sat it smelled tarnally of brimstone.   [3.1]

In addition to the comedy of dialect in this passage, one is amused by the satire of contemporary manners in the description of behavior at the theatre (echoing Charlotte's account in 2.1) and his satire of the Puritan horror at the stage.

Jonathan and Jessamy function to parallel the theme of international contrast and native worth in Manly and Dimple. At all times onstage, Jonathan's earthy honesty is reflected in the foil of Jessamy's affectation. Both are risible, yet the audience is invited to laugh good-naturedly, if not sympathetically, at the Yankee's antics, while being more critical of Jessamy's preoccupation with Chesterfield's precepts. As the prologue clearly states,

> Our author pictures not from foreign climes
> The fashions or follies of the times;
> But has confin'd the subject of his work
> To the gay scenes — the circles of New-York.
> On native themes his Muse displays her pow'rs;
> If ours the faults, the virtues too are ours.
> Why should our thoughts to distant countries roam,
> When each refinement may be found at home?
> Who travels now to ape the rich or great,
> To deck an equippage and roll in state;
> To court the graces, or to dance with ease,
> Or by hypocrisy to strive to please?
> Our free-born ancestors such arts despised:
> Genuine sincerity alone they priz'd;
> Their minds, with honest emulation fir'd,
> To solid good — nor ornament — aspir'd.

In addition to the romantic idealism of returning to the simple virtues of the past, we also notice the Puritan-like distaste for refinements, with the grudging concession (implied) that if they *must* be sought, let it be at home, not abroad. Native worth, as suggested by Manly's name, is virile and forthright, while foreign affectation, as suggested by Dimple's, is emphemeral, even effeminate. This same distinction is carried out in the contrast between Jonathan's and Jessamy's diction, as for example their quibble over "kiss" and "buss," the latter having a more virile, rougher, more playful connotation.

> *Jon.* Stay, Mr. Jessamy — must I buss her [Jenny] when I am introduced to her?
> *Jes.* I told you, you must kiss her.
> *Jon.* Well, but must I buss her?
> *Jes.* Why kiss and buss, and buss and kiss, is all one.
> *Jon.* Oh! my dear friend, though you have a profound knowledge of all, . . . you don't know everything.   [2.2]

It should be noticed that here as in other scenes, Jonathan exhibits a kind of mother wit, a shrewdness clothed in naïveté. There always seems to be a hint of irony, of tongue-in-cheek beneath the clownish surface. Whether Wignell played Jonathan this way will never be known, but the role permits this interpretation. The great Yankee actors of the nineteenth century brought much individual interpretation to their roles.[76]

A careful analysis of Jonathan's character and function in *The Contrast* reveals that he is more than just a clown, "as ridiculous as Dimple is odious." What he represents, the spirit of native worth, pervades the whole play, contributing as important a thematic statement comically as the serious declamations of Manly. Where Tyler would never make fun of a hero drawn in the mythical image of Washington, he can and does with Jonathan. The Yankee's

> slanting dialect, homely metaphor, the penetrating rhythms of his speech, gave a fillip toward the upset of old and rigid balances; creating laughter, he also created a fresh sense of unity. He ridiculed old values; the persistent contrast with the British showed part of his intention; to some extent he created new ones. He was a symbol of triumph, of adaptability, of irrepressible life — of many qualities needed to induce confidence and self-possession among a new and unamalgamated people.[77]

In Jonathan, Tyler bequeathed a rich legacy to American literature.

Billy Dimple, the beau of *The Contrast*, differs little from the stock type to be found in the contemporary British drama. Initially, the British tradition distinguished between the rake or sensualist on the one hand, and the fop on the other. Two classic examples are the rake Horner in Wycherly's *The Country Wife*, and the fop Sir Fopling Flutter in Etherege's *The Man of Mode*. In every Restoration comedy there is at least one of each type. But the rake as hero could only exist in that very special social atmosphere of the Restoration court in London, during a brief period that has become synonymous with libertine naturalism and cynicism. Once the reactionary ethics of sentimentalism had set in, supported by a middle-class morality that had never approved of the behavior of Charles's court, significant changes in the stage rake took place.[78] Morality rose up to condemn sensualism and to restore virtue, particularly sexual virtue, to its ethical throne. As a result, whereas many sentimental comedies of the eighteenth century contain the rake, he is no longer the triumphant, almost amoral, free spirit like the Horners and Mirabells of the preceding period. In fact he is seldom worthy of the title, for his sensual pleasures are rarely portrayed onstage, and if so, never with the witty aplomb of his Restoration forebears. Sensualism, once a courtier's manner, and at worst a folly, had become a sin in the new moral climate on the sentimental stage. Now in the conventional plot of the sentimental comedy, the rake underwent a moral whitewashing, moving closer to the fop. His reputation became more and more a matter of the past, and less and less a matter of the onstage present. There was little action in scene to substantiate his sensualism.

It was mostly talk. He might be incorrigible, but not usually, for this would be antithetical to the sentimental faith in man's perfectibility. Thus, more often the rake experiences a change of ways, a sudden reform as his better nature transcended his libertinism. Toward the end of the eighteenth century there were few rakes left to reform, for the type had been modified to a good-hearted but irresponsible and pleasure-loving dandy, like Belcour in Cumberland's *The West Indian.*

In early American drama, the beau of the late eighteenth century, such as Dimple, usually combines the showy traits of the fop with the sensualism of the rake.[79] Like Etherege's coxcomb, Sir Fopling Flutter, who is satirized for his Gallic affectation, Dimple is ridiculed, but because he has become an Anglophile, a pseudo Chesterfieldian.[80] Although Dimple has an interest in the art of pleasing for personal advancement, his application of the Chesterfieldian precepts is aimed almost wholly at gratifying his sexual desires. Lord Chesterfield's letters to his son were written mainly to guide the awkward young man properly into a distinguished political or diplomatic career. There are no such ambitions apparent in Dimple, who is too hedonistic and vain to be interested in any long-range goals. Financing his immediate pleasures and maintaining his dashing reputation are his day-to-day concerns.

It is evident that Tyler based the character of Dimple on Sheridan's Joseph Surface; nevertheless, a close comparison shows some significant differences between the two. Both are hypocritical rogues, energetically seeking their fortunes through marriage, and both, ultimately, are entangled in their own intrigues to be exposed for what they are. While both are presumably libertines, there is hardly any evidence onstage of their rakishness, as there would be in a Restoration comedy. At one point Joseph suggests an assignation to Lady Teazle, but he is interrupted in the act of taking her by the hand (4.3). Likewise, Dimple's attempt to force his embraces on Charlotte is thwarted at its inception by the arrival of Manly, Van Rough, and Jonathan to the rescue of abused maidenhood. There are only two allusions to Dimple's libertinism, one by Letitia, who tells Charlotte that he daily puts Chesterfield's "infamous principles in practice upon every woman he meets" (1.1), and the other by Jessamy, who describes Dimple's seduction of Caroline (2.2).

One difference between the two characters is that Joseph's pose as a man of sentiment is just that — a pose, a mask from behind which he hopes to effect his selfish ends. Lady Sneerwell is well aware that he is "a sentimental knave." When he begins a typical sentimental pronouncement, she cuts him short by reminding him that he is among friends, to which Joseph replies, "Egad, that's true! — I'll keep that sentiment till I see Sir Peter" (1.1). On the other hand, Dimple's commitment to Chesterfield's precepts, however limited or misconstrued, is sincere and not a pose to be dropped in privacy. At the beginning of act 3 he is savoring the *Letters* at toilet when he learns of his serious financial difficulty. Though shocked, he maintains the proper composure: "Now, did not my lord expressly say that it was unbecoming a well-bred man to be in a passion, I confess I should be ruffled." He must break off his engagement to Maria with proper finesse.

> I love the person of Charlotte, and it is necessary I should command the fortune of Letitia. As to Maria! — I doubt not by my *sang-froid* behavior I shall compel her to decline the match; but the blame must not fall upon me. A prudent man, as my lord says, should take all the credit of a good action to himself, and throw the discredit of a bad one upon others.
>
> [3.1]

Even in his most trying moment, when he is exposed in the fifth act, Dimple does not lose his manner.

> Ladies and gentlemen, I take my leave; and you will please to observe in the case of my deportment the contrast between a gentleman who has read Chesterfield and received the polish of Europe, and an unpolished, untravelled American. [*Exit*]   [5.2]

He remains true to his adopted ("foreign") ethical code.

The basic difference between these two hypocrites may be traced to the difference between Tyler's and Sheridan's social values, which gives rise to the different comic attitudes of each. Sheridan satirizes Joseph for failing to conform to the accepted code of behavior, while Tyler ridicules Dimple for the opposite, for conforming to a code which, if foreign in origin, was nonetheless very fashionable in New York social circles. Fashion and manners in New York's polite society closely followed those of London during the mid-to-late eighteenth century, for there was a steady flux of British visitors and army officers to bring with them the latest fads and fancies.[81] Then too, like the Virginia planters, many New York merchants sent their sons on the grand tour to finish their education. Dimple had been sent to England and Europe to "see the world and rub off a little of the patroon rust" (1.1).

A satiric sketch of some New York beaux of 1754 describes Dimple with delightful fidelity.

> Condumanus, who has not long since visited London, confined all his speculations there to Haddock's Bagnio, Vauxhall, Covent Garden, or some luxurious seats of pleasure. . . . Guglio can boast the honour of having been several times drunk in London. He . . . has heard Garrick act; been at both theatres, and can correct the errors of the stage; knows how the actors should strut; how he should startle and tremble when a

ghost appears; how he should singly kick up his heels when he makes his exit.

Little Clodis Friskabout, besides all these improvements, has many others; he has accomplished himself in all the arts that constitute a complete gentleman. He . . . has conversed with the Gentlemen of the Inner Temple; he has been present at balls and masquerades, and distinguished himself there in that most polite accomplishment, whereof he is now complete master. He . . . has been author to all the new cock'd hats and scratches in town; has learnt the art of address from the gentility of Covent Garden; which, by Jove,' he swears has ruined his constitution. Amongst the accomplished beaux, he has learned those elegant expressions, *Split me, Madam; By Gad; Dam me*; and fails not to use them on all occasions.[82]

Like the beaux above, Dimple has seen "the brilliant exhibitions of Europe," therefore learning to "despise the amusements of this country" (4.1).

Dimple's outrageously foppish manner is always comic in the play, especially his vanity and mincing fastidiousness. These qualities are always presented in contrast to the masculine image of Manly. Obviously Tyler saw the risible in his fop, but behind the caricature lies a serious concern for morality. Dimple's manners are, to Tyler, more than the social improprieties of a Joseph Surface. They are a violation of, an affront to, the noblest social ideals of the new democracy — those epitomized in Manly. Thus, while Tyler uses a stock type in Dimple, he has significantly modified it — largely though the judgment of others upon Dimple — in accordance with his comic attitude, which is different than Sheridan's. To pinpoint this matter, if we compare Dimple to Etherege's Sir Fopling Flutter, we find Dimple absurd, but also odious, while Sir Fopling is nothing more than absurd. It is the distinction between folly, on the one hand, and immorality or vice, on the other. In 1832, forecasting the direction he hoped American drama would take, Dunlap wrote: "If the wise and the good frequent the theatre, its exhibitions must become schools of wisdom. The lessons taught must be those of patriotism, virtue, morality, religion." [83] Forty-five years earlier, Tyler's comedy had given American drama its start in that direction.

Colonel Manly might well be a fictionalized portrait of Royall Tyler himself, but for one thing: he is anything but dashing and witty, as Tyler is known to have been. Like Tyler, Manly is a veteran of the revolutionary war, returned to his country's service: "The public tumults of our state have induced me to buckle on the sword in support of that government which I once fought to establish" (2.1). Manly's remark is clearly an allusion to Tyler's own activity in western Massachusetts during the Shays Rebellion. There can also be no doubt that Manly's numerous nationalistic sentiments — his reverence for Washington, his lobbying for congressional aid to disabled veterans, his admiration for Lafayette, his faith in federal currency (he will not sell his notes as some had done), and a confidence in the federal union shown in his long monologue on the division and fall of the ancient Greek states — reflect Tyler's own patriotic faith. Manly models himself after the newly established mythical image of Washington as Patriot-Hero. He wears his mantle of citizen's responsibility willingly and proudly, but with a grave, almost humorless mien, which weighs on the comic mood of the play. Perhaps this was intentional on Tyler's part. Washington, even by those who adulated him, was not known for his quick wit.[84] At any rate, Manly little resembles the conventional hero of a comedy of manners.

But *The Contrast* is not a comedy of manners in the traditional sense of the form. It is imitative in form and somewhat in characters of Sheridan's manners comedy, and there is much argument in favor of classifying it as such. Many of its characters are stock types or native modifications of them from the British comic tradition. It satirizes fashionable folly as does all manners comedy. Its triangular plot situations are traditional in the comedy of manners. It even has passages of witty dialogue, an essential feature of all manners comedy. But it is not pure manners comedy. Its primary focus on subject rather than on form, its treatment of contemporary social, economic, and even, indirectly, political problems; its movement away from the universal toward the more realistic treatment of characters; it moral and reforming spirit demanding a reassessment of certain social values — all these elements mark it as a social comedy. Tyler's comic attitude is native and it is significantly different than Sheridan's, or more broadly, than the British tradition in general. This difference accounts for numerous deviations from the British model in plot, characters, and themes that are *not* attributable to Tyler's inexperience as a playwright. Sheridan's *The School for Scandal*, in the convention of traditional manners comedy, coped with no serious or new problems, nor conveyed any startling messages thematically. (There are indeed real problems involved in manners comedy, problems such as divorce, inheritance, and arranged marriages for example, but the playwrights are not primarily concerned with abolishing these problems. Instead of reforming, they tend to maneuver around them.) Good sense has and always will prevail in the acceptable patterns of social conduct; therefore, manners comedy urges conformity to these patterns. Charles Surface comes to accept this creed, confesses, and is, like the prodigal son, forgiven his social trespasses. He is finally rewarded with the symbolic fatted calf: Maria and a comfortable inheritance. He presumably goes on to live happily ever after.

A wayward Charles Surface, however, was wholly unsuitable for Tyler's hero, because his native themes demanded a Manly who, with his Puritan-derived moral earnestness, his steadfast independence of thought, his fervent, chauvinistic patriotism, and his democratic idealism, can function as the moral center of the play. Manly's judgment upon Dimple and what he symbolizes is never a simple matter of society's good sense slapping an errant member's wrist, for Dimple's behavior conforms to acceptable social behavior in polite New York. With Yankee independence Manly has derived his ethics from his own experience, and he judges thereby. There is no taint of social conformity.

We may seriously question the propriety of the strong nationalistic emphasis in *The Contrast*, arguing perhaps that political problems do not come within the scope of social comedy, and certainly not manners comedy. Yet Ben Jonson had satirized political corruption, and the Restoration playwrights often satirized the Puritan, who had been a political force during the Interregnum. Moreover, political satire had been a dominant element in the Old Comedy of Aristophanes. Even so, it is rarely found in the British tradition of late eighteenth-century comedy beyond the inclusion of a stock character such as the corrupt politician, and only now and then. But the unique political and national situation in America during the late eighteenth century had no parallel in England then or for some centuries before. English kings had come and gone, often in bloody turmoil, but the continued existence of the English political state was not threatened. During the Restoration, when the comedy of manners flowered, although there had been an interregnum for sixteen years, England's sovereignty was not an imminent issue. In the late eighteenth century, however, the American colonies had revolted and fought against a power without, and were immediately thereafter occupied with pressing internal problems of confederation, serious political factionalism, and even rebellion. Nationalism was in the air, was the dominant spirit of the times, and with the future of the republic in everyone's mind, it was often difficult to make much distinction between "political" and "social" issues. Americans, convinced and proud of their democratic uniqueness, a little embarassed by their political newness, and constantly reminded of their cultural immaturity by their visitors, particularly the British, were naturally defensive, and in many cases belligerently so. Hence the chauvinistic nationalism, at times hardly separable from Anglophobia, in our literature, and especially the drama of the late eighteenth and early nineteenth century.

Manly, then, served as the spokesman for the dominant moral and nationalistic sentiments of Tyler. His impassioned soliloquy in 3.2, with its nationalistic overtones, is a good example of the mingling of social with political criticism in this comedy.

> Luxury! which renders a people weak at home, and accessible to bribery, corruption, and force from abroad. When the Grecian states knew no other tools than the axe and the saw, the Grecians were a great, a free,

a happy people. The kings of Greece devoted their lives to the service of their country, and her senators knew no other superiority over their fellow-citizens than a glorious pre-eminence in danger and virtue. They exhibited to the world a noble spectacle, — a number of independent states united by a similarity of language, sentiment, manners, common interest, and common consent, in one grand mutual league of protection. And, thus united, long might they have continued the cherishers of arts and sciences, the protectors of the oppressed, the scourge of tyrants, and the safe asylum of liberty. But when foreign gold, and still more pernicious, foreign luxury had crept among them, they sapped the vitals of their virture.

. . . .

Oh! that America! Oh! that my country, would, in this her day, learn the things which belong to her peace!

It is this speech, perhaps above any other in the play, that gives us direct insight to Tyler's comic attitude. Manly's fervent tone is in the tradition of the passionate patriots like Thomas Paine, the anti-Tory pamphleteer of the revolutionary period, whose republican idealism, like Tyler's, was sweepingly romantic in its vision of America as the future bastion of neo-Grecian democracy. What little native drama there was up to 1776, represented by authors like Mercy Warren (*The Group*, 1775), John Leacock (*The Fall of British Tyranny*, 1776), and Hugh Henry Brackenridge (*The Battle of Bunker's Hill*, 1776), was highly polemic in sympathy with the Whig cause. Anti-British feelings were naturally highest on the eve of the Revolution, but they continued into the early decades of the nineteenth century. During Tyler's period, before 1800 roughly, these feelings manifested themselves in a chauvinistic rejection of most things foreign and a defense of those things native.

However, the demand for "home manufacture," to which Dunlap ascribes part of the success of *The Contrast*, was short-lived. Its brief appearance during Tyler's period is a reflection of the growing romantic spirit everywhere. The American nation and its drama emerged at the dawn of that era in which man's uniqueness, among other romantic tenets, was celebrated politically and socially. Obviously the drama of the period would mirror these new attitudes.[85] Certainly Manly and his comical shadow, Jonathan, are two characters created in the image of the common man; their values are essentially new and native.

Dunlap might well have been talking about Manly when he described his eighteenth-century countrymen as a "people beginning to feel that they were called to a new state of existence." [86] Without some awareness of eighteenth-century literary conventions, it is difficult for the modern reader to take Manly seriously, for we are not conditioned to rhapsodic moralizing and effusive sentimental utterance in modern drama. Or, why Tyler permits Charlotte to satirize her brother is additionally confusing, for the playwright seems to occupy two points of view, shifting from the witty and satiric — almost purely comic — to the completely moral, serious, and patriotic. Nevertheless, Tyler's audience did take Manly seriously, recognizing that he symbolized the new virtues independently conceived and just as independently effected. He is, in short, the dramatic personification of Yankee morality, that can shield American virtue from the pernicious influence of foreign affectation.

Turning finally to the element of wit and humor in the play, we find Tyler closely allied in comic spirit to the sentimental playwrights. The comedy, other than that arising from the several farcical situations, stems from humor — a genial recognition of human frailty — rather than wit. Where there is wit, it is softened by humor. It lacks the brevity and therefore the startling effect and quick bite of wit as seen in the Restoration comedies. But this is not surprising. It was impossible for any distinctions such as Truewit, Witwoud, and Falsewit to exist in *The Contrast* as they had in Restoration comedy, because, in addition to the fact of Tyler's inexperience as a dramatist, no ideal of witty decorum dominated the upper-class society of New York as it had the courtly circles of Restoration London.[87] Congreve's ideals, for example, are primarily aesthetic and intellectual, whereas Tyler's are moral and nationalistic, and his comedy is subservient to these ends. During the Restoration period, manners were the *ne plus ultra* of social refinement, the high achievement of a social ethic dominated by the ideal of decorum. Within the limited circles of courtly society, manners were a way of life, and only within such a unique environment could what is called Restoration wit flower. But sophistication, social stability, cultural maturity — these were not yet developed in American society, and manners, as Tyler's prologue implies, were suspect. Tyler's satire of Chesterfieldian manners through Dimple is a continuation of a tradition, and a milder continuation it should be added, begun in the satiric closest dramas of Mercy Warren, namely *The Motley Assembly* (1779) and *Sans Souci* (1785).

Tyler's exposure to New York society had been only a brief month before his play was produced, and one may presume that the follies he attacked reflect his own immediate experiences, many of which were evidently at the theatre. Thus it is that behavior at the playhouse is satirized four separate times in the play. (Jonathan's account has already been quoted above.) Charlotte's account of an evening at the theatre is doubly entertaining because of her awareness of the affected behavior of herself and friends, and she particularly delights in shocking Manly.

> Everything is conducted with such decorum, — first we bow round to the company in general, then to each one in particular, and we have so many inquiries after each other's health, and we are so happy to meet each

other, and it is so many ages since we last had that pleasure, [and if a married lady is in company, we have such a sweet dissertation upon her son Bobby's chin-cough;] [88] then the curtain rises, then our sensibility is all awake, and then, by the mere force of apprehension, we torture some harmless expression into a double meaning, which the poor author never dreamt of, and then we have recourse to our fans, and then we blush, and then the gentlemen jog one another, peep under the fan, and make the prettiest remarks; and then we giggle and they simper, and they giggle and we simper, and then the curtain drops, and then for nuts and oranges. . . . Oh! the sentimental charms of a side-box conversation.[2.1]

We are also amused by the antisentimental cut here as in other speeches by Charlotte. Unlike Charlotte, however, Dimple lacks a good-natured perception of his own vanity as he belittles New York amusements:

Manly. Do you never attend the theatre, sir?
Dim. I was tortured there once.
Char. Pray, Mr. Dimple, was it a tragedy or a comedy?
Dim. Faith, madam, I cannot tell; for I sat with my back to the stage all the time, admiring a much better actress than any there — a lady who played the fine woman to perfection; though, by the laugh of the horrid creatures round me, I supposed it was a comedy. Yet, on second thoughts, it might be some hero in a tragedy, dying so comically as to set the whole house in an uproar. — Colonel, I presume you have been in Europe?
Man. Indeed, sir, I was never ten leagues from the continent.
Dim. Believe me, Colonel, you have an immense pleasure to come; and when you shall have seen the brilliant exhibitions of Europe, you will learn to despise the amusements of this country as much as I do. [4.1]

This passage is a good example of Tyler's repartee. In general, the individual speeches are a little long for good wit, and they detract from the spirit of rapid give and take of the best repartee in Restoration manners comedy. One character tends to dominate the railery, while others feed him lines like dutiful straight men. Thus, there are no true witty exchanges, no verbal duels.

The affectation of Dimple is magnified in his servant, Jessamy, whose dissertation on decorous laughter is the farcical *pièce de résistance* in the play.

Jes. Why, you know, Mr. Jonathan, that to dance, a lady to play with her fan, or a gentleman with his cane, and all other natural motions, are regulated by art. My master has composed an immensely pretty gamut, by which any lady or gentleman, with a few years' close application, may learn to laugh as gracefully as if they were born and bred to it.

Jon. Mercy on my soul! A gamut for laughing — just like fa, la, sol?

Jes. Yes, it comprises every possible display of jocularity, from an *affettuoso* smile to a *piano* titter, or full chorus *fortissimo* ha, ha, ha! My master employs his leisure hours in making out the plays, like a cathedral chanting book, that the ignorant may know where to laugh; and that the pit, box, and gallery may keep time together, and not have a snigger in one part of the house, a broad grin in the other, and a d —— d grum look in the third. How delightful to see the audience all smile together, then look on their books, then twist their mouths into an agreeable simper, then altogether shake the house with a general ha, ha, ha! loud as a full chorus of Handel's at an Abbey-commemoration.

Jon. Ha, ha, ha! that's dang'd cute, I swear.

Jes. The gentlemen, you see, will laugh the tenor; the ladies will play the counter-tenor; the beaux will squeak the treble; and our jolly friends in the gallery a thorough bass, ho, ho, ho!   [5.1]

Tyler's imagination tends toward the broadly ludicrous, toward burlesque, to provide some of the play's most hilarious moments.

Charlotte is the wittiest character. But she seldom rises to pure wit, for her comparisons, while amusing, lack the brevity, the pungent conciseness of high wit. Compare, for example, Fainall's

> Marriage is honorable, as you say; and if so, wherefore should cuckoldom be a discredit, being derived from so honorable a root?
>
> [Congreve, *The Way of the World* 3.1]

with Charlotte's

> As if a lady could not be privileged to spend a man's fortune, ride in his carriage, be called after his name, and call him her *nown dear lovee* when she wants money, without loving and respecting the great he-creature.
>
> [1.1]

Both reflect a similar cynical attitude rejecting conventional values, but while Fainall's wit is epigrammatic, climaxed by the sexual pun on "root," Charlotte's expression is a little prolix, as is her description of Manly's sentimentalism.

> His heart is like an old maiden lady's bandbox; it contains many costly things, arranged with the most scrupulous nicety, the misfortune is that they are too delicate, costly, and antiquated for common use.   [2.1]

Her similitude is a trifle forced by Restoration standards; it has the same indecorous self-consciousness of Witwoud's attempts in Congreve's *The Way of the World*. It is not worthy of a true-wit character.[89] On the other hand, Charlotte is capable of penetrating satire.

> Why, my dear Henry, you have such a lofty way of saying things, that I protest I almost tremble at the thought of introducing you to the polite circles in the city. The belles would think you were a player run mad, with your head filled with old scraps of tragedy; and, as to the beaux, they might admire, because they would not understand you.   [2.1]

This similitude is as witty as anything Sheridan wrote. For the most part, it is Tyler's lack of discipline, of decorum (the balance between fancy and judgment is tipped toward the former) that marks much of Charlotte's dialogue as humorous rather than witty.

To attempt to establish any clear-cut native tradition of wit (and humor) on the basis of evidence in a single play is more wishful than feasible. Wit is wit, and humor is humor, regardless of nationality or even period — at least, as I have defined these terms in the Introduction. Although there are many shades of interpretation as to exactly what wit is, most critics agree on one thing: wit is highly intellectual and is most likely to arise in societies that are highly sophisticated and that have well-established and defined social classes. Obviously Tyler's America meets none of these qualifications. However, since *The Contrast* is the first American comedy, it is entitled to a close examination for any tendencies in wit and humor that might eventually, that is historically, prove to be native.

Jonathan and Charlotte, as has been shown, are the two characters who reveal any kind of wit or humor. What stands out about Jonathan is a kind of self-consciousness, but not an embarrassed self-consciousness, for like the traditional picaro, he adapts quickly to new situations, and in one way or another manages to extract himself from difficulties. His self-consciousness is more an awareness of himself as a comic hero. Charlotte has this same frank quality, for as mocking as she is of Maria and her sentimental circle, she is always good naturedly aware of the comic aspects in her own affectation. By contrast, such awareness is completely lacking in either Dimple or Jessamy. Dimple especially is sensitive to any ridicule of himself, which is often true of the hypercritical person. When he is exposed at the play's end, his only defense is to retreat into even more ridiculous affectation.

Somewhat like Falstaff, Jonathan soon recognizes his own comical exterior and is unafraid to exploit it. He enjoys laughter because he is a genial soul. And while he is never adverse to being the butt of a joke, he never wholly sacrifices his dignity. Somehow, a scrap, and perhaps more, always remains.

Can Jonathan be as naïve as he seems at first? Reconsider his description of the visit to the playhouse. Is it possible that, having been initially fooled into thinking it was a show where Mr. Morrison, the hocus-pocus man, "could eat a case knife" — recall his genuine amazement when Jessamy tells him otherwise — he seizes upon the comic situation and exaggerates the experience, spins a good Yankee yarn with a straight face and tongue-in-cheek, and doubly enjoys the laughter of his audience from behind the mask of incredulity? This is impossible to prove from the text, which has very little direction to the actors, and Wignell may not have played the role this way. But we do know that as the Yankee type developed in the nineteenth century, it was in this direction of the clown with a shrewd perception beneath his bumpkin exterior. The tradition of the naïve, incredulous mask from behind which to spin the tall tale was, as we know, Mark Twain's trademark, both in person on the podium and in the various comic heroes of his writings.[90] The same tradition has in fact proved successful for a number of popular comedians in the twentieth century, such as Will Rogers, Bob Burns, and more recently Herb Shriner, Charlie Weaver, Jonathan Winters, Andy Griffith, and Bill Cosby.

There is surely a traceable native tradition of humor here. Jonathan's fondness for spinning a good yarn about folks back home, for illustrating his point with an anecdote, always enriched by novel Yankee metaphor, for talking more about people than ideas, for the fable, for comic hyperbole, for punctuating his speech with profanity — or euphemized expletives — for stoutly maintaining that the impossible is the gospel truth, and for wearing a straight face all the while — these were the dominant traits of all stage Yankees to follow. All these qualities are the very wellspring of native American humor.

In examining *The Contrast* in plot, character, dramatic structure and theme, and wit and humor, we have found evidence of conscious deviation from the British comic tradition. The search has been simplified because the so-called British tradition has, in this particular case, been limited mainly to a single play, Sheridan's *The School for Scandal*, which Tyler used as a model,[91] although there has been frequent reference to representative comedies from the Restoration and sentimental periods. Some deviations from the British model are unquestionably the result of Tyler's inexperience at playwriting. Still, the most significant changes seem to have arisen from a native comic attitude, itself motivated by Tyler's moral and patriotic sentiments, which were representative of American authors in the revolutionary period. Such modifications of the British tradition in character, plot, and theme are sufficiently marked so that we may term them native. But a tradition — and we are in search of a native tradition — is more than a single play; it is a historical pattern. If there is any emerging tradition of native wit in this play, it is in the nature of Jonathan's Yankee humor, as much a matter of form and delivery as subject matter. Finally, there is no significant deviation in dramatic structure, for early American playwrights were least concerned with the aesthetics of literary form. Subject matter was too vital, too demanding then.

In all, while imitative to a degree, *The Contrast* is also innovative, and bears in it many of the seeds of future native American social comedy.

3

Three Significant Comedies:
1789–1828

PROCEEDING in time from 1787 (*The Contrast*), we will examine three comedies written in the period extending to 1828; namely, William Dunlap's *The Father* (1789), James Nelson Barker's *Tears and Smiles* (1808), and Robert Montgomery Bird's *The City Looking Glass* (1828). These three comedies are useful here as clear indications of the developing native tradition. But each proves interesting because of its intrinsic dramatic merit, and, conveniently, they are distributed chronologically across four decades with some evenness, beginning with Tyler's day.

William Dunlap, The Father *(1787)* [1]

William Dunlap's life (1766–1839) spans the tumultuous early years of both our republic and its theatre. His achievements as a popular playwright, and also as producer and manager — in spite of some failure — have earned him the title of Father of the American Theatre. He began his career as a portrait painter at sixteen, but soon turned to the theatre, with which he was associated professionally almost continuously from 1789 until 1812, when he retired as assistant manager of the Park Theatre in New York. Even after that he continued to write plays until 1828. Dunlap, who is America's first professional playwright, wrote sixty-five plays in all — thirty original and the rest translations and adaptations, primarily from contemporary French and German theatre.[2]

From 1796 to 1797 Dunlap managed the John Street Theatre in New York as a partner in the Old American Company with Hallam and Hodgkinson. After Hallam retired from active participation in the company, Dunlap and Hodgkinson managed it, opening the new Park Street Theatre in 1798. But

Hodgkinson left shortly for Boston, to take over the Haymarket Theatre in 1798. Thus, after Dunlap had made financial arrangements with the Hallams, who still owned a large share of the company, he assumed sole ownership. Dunlap managed the Old American Company at the Park Theatre until his bankruptcy in 1805. In 1806 he returned to the Park Theatre as assistant manager for the tragedian, Thomas A. Cooper, who leased the theatre until 1812.

Following this Dunlap again took up miniature painting, as he had done in the interim from 1805 to 1806, but continued to pursue his literary interests. Among his publications are a biography, *The Life of Charles Brockden Brown* (1815); the first history of the American drama, *History of the American Theatre* (1832); and a temperance novel, *Thirty Years Ago; or, The Memoirs of a Water Drinker* (1836). Most important is the *History*, even though there are many inaccuracies and omissions. Seilhamer's damning comment, "There probably never was a book written to throw light upon a subject that succeeded so completely in confusing it," [3] was not entirely motivated by professional jealousy. Nevertheless, Dunlap's *History* is a valuable record of personalities and times. There is in it a colorful freshness and intimacy almost nonexistent in Seilhamer's more ponderous — and still inaccurate — volumes.

The Father; or, American Shandyism was Dunlap's second play and has the distinction of being the second native American comedy to be performed professionally. In 1787 Dunlap had returned to New York from three years in London, where his father had sent him to study painting under the tutelage of the American artist, Benjamin West (1738–1820), but where, according to his own account in the *History*, he had become a devotee of the theatre. Reminiscing about himself, always in the third person, he writes:

> The theatre had been his delight, and he had seen all the great performers on the English stage at that period, and as many plays as his finances permitted. The theatres of Drury Lane, Covent Garden, and the Haymarket had been visited for the sake of the performances exhibited, and not as scenes of dissipation. All Shakespeare's acting plays, and many others, especially the new pieces of the day, had been before him, represented by the immediate successors, and some of the contemporaries of Garrick.
>
> Young, and filled with these recollections, he first saw the American company on his return, performing upon the stage where, as a boy, he had witnessed the representations of Shakespeare, Home, and Cumberland by the officers of his Britannic majesty [Howe's Thespians] during the cessations of their military exertions for suppressing the rebellion. He heard of the success of the "Contrast," and although it was already put on the shelf of the prompter, or buried in his travelling chest, the praises bestowed upon it lit up the inflammable material brought from abroad, and a comedy in five acts was written in a few weeks.[4]

Unfortunately for Dunlap, that play, *The Modest Soldier; or Love in New York,* was accepted but never produced by the Old American Company; it evidently lacked suitable roles for Henry and his wife.

Nothing is known of the play, which has not survived, except that it seems to have been inspired by if not imitative of *The Contrast,* for Dunlap gives the dramatis personae in his *History* as a "Yankee servant, a travelled American, an officer in the late revolutionary army, a fop, such as fops then were in New-York, an old gentleman and his two daughters, one of course lively and the other serious." [5] The inclusion of two daughters, one lively and one serious, suggests that Dunlap, while a novice at his craft, was nevertheless aware of the need for a conventional balance or contrast of types in a well-made comedy. His experience at the London theatres could have taught Dunlap this.

And yet Dunlap was innocent of the jealousies over parts in an acting company, or at least claims to have been innocent of these petty feuds among leading actors and actresses that obviously sabotaged his first effort. He must have his tongue in his cheek when he writes that he

> proceeded to write a second, in which, without design, one part was suited to Henry, another did not displease his wife, and the lively lady was evidently inferior to the character assigned to the manager's lady [Mrs. Henry]. This second comedy was seized with avidity by Henry. The author was easily persuaded to let the second come out first; and the first was ultimately consigned to oblivion. No doubt a merited oblivion. [6]

Success for native playwrights in this early period, and even more so in the following century, when great stars like Edwin Forrest, Edmund and Charles Kean, Junius Brutus Booth, and William Charles Macready ruled their companies with despotic sway, was more than a matter of skill at their craft.

In its simplest form the plot of *The Father* is this: New York, 1789. The heroine, Miss Felton, is living with her sister and brother-in-law, Mr. and Mrs. Racket. Mrs. Racket, hoping to make her inattentive husband jealous to stimulate his lagging affection for her, is openly encouraging an affair between herself and his friend Marsh, who is an imposter posing as Captain Ranter of the British army. Seizing his advantage under these circumstances, Ranter hopes to seduce Mrs. Racket, but his major plan is to marry Miss Felton for her fortune, before making his escape. To the Racket household come Colonel Duncan and Cartridge, the former wishing to visit his wards, the two sisters. Upon his arrival he learns of Mrs. Racket's flirtation from Miss Felton, who also confides that she was secretly betrothed to a Captain Haller of the British army while recently visiting Halifax. She is now awaiting his arrival for the marriage, subject of course to her guardian's approval, but she was not heard from Haller in many weeks, and fears for his safety. To add to her anxiety, she has noticed in Captain Ranter's possession a ring that Haller had shown her, telling her his dying father had given it to him on the battlefield, crying only "the ring — your father." From this information Colonel Duncan is positive that Haller is his son, whom he had supposed was killed at Bunker's Hill. Colonel Duncan and Miss Felton question Ranter about the ring, and he tells them that Haller had been a close friend, and that he had given him the ring as a token of remembrance and gratitude for favors rendered. Haller, Ranter informs them, was dying at the time.

However, Haller and his friend, Lieutenant Campley, turn up at the Racket house, the former disguised as a blinded veteran of the British army. They are seeking Marsh (Captain Ranter), who had been Haller's servant and who had stolen his officer's uniform. The disguised Haller tells Colonel Duncan that he knew Captain Haller, and that the man is still alive. Ranter, growing more and more fearful of discovery, although he does not recognize his master beneath the disguise, decides to move swiftly. He first attempts to borrow money from Racket, but without success. Next he meets Mrs. Racket at a party, and then returns with her to her house, planning to seduce her.

In the darkened room Racket has been forcing his attentions on the maid, Susannah, but her screams summon the widow Grenade and Dr. Quiescent, who inadvertently stumble into each other's arms in the dark. Shortly afterward Ranter arrives with Mrs. Racket and attempts to force his embraces upon her, but her screams bring Colonel Duncan and Cartridge with a light. In the scramble, the widow ends up in Ranter's arms, and Mrs. Racket in her husband's. Racket, who is shamed, begs his wife's forgiveness, and exonerates Susannah from any blame. He then orders Ranter out of his house, but before the imposter can escape, Captain Haller and Lieutenant Campley arrive to seize him and reveal his true identity as Marsh. He repents, and receives their forgiveness, the company certain that his reform is genuine. At the end Colonel Duncan is united with his long-lost son, Haller, who in turn is united with his betrothed, Miss Felton; and the Rackets are reconciled.

It is clear from the plot summary that *The Father* follows the lines of the conventional late eighteenth-century comedy. The themes of marital unhappiness, separated lovers, and the long-lost son are conventional in many sentimental comedies, for the situations involved are openly designed to elicit an audience's sympathy and tears. Miss Felton must endure the courtship of Ranter and Quiescent, while secretly engaged to the absent Haller, and to make matters worse, she fears he has come to some harm. Colonel Duncan is overwhelmed with joy upon learning that his long-lost son is not dead, only to fear almost immediately that something terrible may have happened to the boy. Both Miss Felton and Colonel Duncan are presented as sentimental characters, but with some restraint. We witness Miss Felton's tearful concern for her lover onstage, but the evidence of her tender charitability toward the needy — she spends most of her allowance aiding the poor — is reported in summary by the widow Grenade and is not drawn out in scene. The colonel's sentimental reminiscences over dead army comrades, his tearful response to the widow's description of Miss Felton's charity, and his own generous attitude toward the blinded war veteran are counterbalanced by Cartridge's direct reference to their similarity to Sterne's Uncle Toby and Corporal Trim. The farcical nature of his Sternean pair is barely developed by Dunlap, who modestly omits the old man's embarrassing groin wound, and who does not burlesque Duncan's interest in the widow. But it is there nevertheless, serving to offset their sentimentalism. Unlike Sterne, however, Dunlap does not particularly mock that sentimentalism.

The straight sentimental "scenes" (although the first edition of this play is not divided into scenes per se, the acts break naturally into scenelike divisions by virtue of the grouping of characters in action) number only three, are not overly long, and are all followed by or follow scenes generating a comic mood. For example, at the beginning of act 2 Colonel Duncan, in telling the widow Grenade and Miss Felton of his war experiences, moves himself and Miss Felton to sentimental tears. Following Miss Felton's exit, the widow then sustains the sentimental mood by telling him of a recent case of the young woman's charity. Altogether the scene extends for five out of the twelve pages in the act, but it is terminated by the entrance of the farcical Dr. Quiescent, babbling on about medical science. Thus the mood quickly reverts back to the comic for the remainder of the act. By such rapid changes Dunlap is able to sustain the overall comic mood of his play. In the fifth act, the denouement, which involves the conventionally sentimental reuniting of father and son, and of lovers, is kept brief. But more important, it follows the hilarious mix-up of characters on the darkened stage in the preceding farcical scene. Exercising restraint, Dunlap does not carry to excess the repentance and reform theme in the case of Mr. Racket and Captain Ranter. Following the confession of his villainy, Ranter is quickly forgiven by all, to end the play.

Dunlap's lighter, more tolerant approach to folly, in contrast with Tyler's almost Puritanical judgment, is no indication that he was unconcerned about his country's moral life. To the contrary, as previous references to his *History* have shown, he was indeed a serious moralist. What is absent in this play, however, is the chauvinism, the militant Columbianism found in *The Contrast.* Dunlap's own description of *The Father* clearly identifies his intentions: "The author made an attempt to soften the asperities which war had created, and to reconcile his countrymen to their British brethren." [7] First of all, Captain Ranter is in no way the foppish beau that Tyler's Dimple is; he is rogue, yes, and has dishonorable intentions as regards Mrs. Racket, but he is hardly a rake. Nowhere does he expose the boastful facade, the sexual vanity of Dimple. Secondly, that Colonel Duncan was born in the British Isles is another indication of Dunlap's new approach to the broad theme of international contrast. Duncan is proud of his American citizenship and his service in the revolutionary army: "This glorious badge [the Order of Cincinnati] marks me out to my countrymen as their friend, the soldier of liberty, and companion of Washington" (2). Yet he is at once sympathetic toward the wounded British veteran (Haller in disguise), whom Jacob has refused entrance.

> *Col. D.* Very well, Cartridge, see who is at the door. [*Exit Cartridge.*]
>
> *Jac.* Ah, sir, I never was soldier for my own liking: I never like any pody petter for being a soldier; 'twas soldier took me away from my old moder to make me come here, and dat kilt her, and I don't know vaut I should like um for. [*Exit Jacob.*]
>
> *Col. D.* [*Alone.*] The softening influence of liberty has not yet melted from his heart the scaly crust with which tyranny and oppression has surrounded it. Who is it, Cartridge?
>
> *Cart.* An old soldier, sir; he says an English soldier, Your honour.
>
> *Col. D.* Not the worse for that, Cartridge.
>
> *Cart.* No, your honour. I think not the worse of a soldier or a man for being English; we are no longer enemies, your honour, and if we were, he is in distress, and blind. [4]

Finally, it is clear that the marriage of Haller to Miss Felton symbolizes the new harmony between England and America. Dunlap's moderate attitude probably can be attributed to his father's loyalist sympathies, and in fact service as an officer in Wolfe's regiment at Quebec.[8] We know from the *History* that Dunlap had lived in New York during the British occupation.[9]

Like many of the early native playwrights, Dunlap is better at writing farce comedy than wit. This is not to judge him in any way, for one of the play's strengths is its bustling, good-natured pace, which in large measure stems from the amusing farce situations and characters. We have noted the successful farce mix-up scene just preceding the denouement. Earlier there are those amusing moments with the babbling humors character, Dr. Quiescent, wandering in and out of scenes. There are also the fortification games of Colonel Duncan and Cartridge. In farce it is chiefly what characters *do* that is risible, whereas in wit the comedy arises from dialogue, from the word more than the deed. Therefore, the environment for wit is normally repartee and raillery, which appear in only three scenes of *The Father*—far overweighed by the farce. An example of the quality of Dunlap's wit is found in the following passage, from a scene between Mrs. Racket and Captain Ranter:

> *Rant.* By all that's pretty and amiable, you look so divinely. Let me die, but that I see the roses come and go, I should think you had been

putting on rouge this morning. I should swear nature could not shew so charming, so delicate a tint.

Mrs. Rack. [*Aside.*] Well, there is nothing like a British officer, after all. [*Aloud.*] Oh, this is too gross; I am angry; you make me blush.

Rant.   [*Aside.*] I am much mistaken if you do not blush the same tint all day, for all that. [*Aloud.*] I never was convinced of the reality of witches til I saw you.

Mrs. Rack. How so?

Rant. Why, besides that bewitching power you have over every heart — [*Takes her hand. She draws it away and frowns.*] You — you — you must deal with the devil to get these English fashions so soon; for, as I live, you exhibit the modes of Westminster at New-York, before they have got t'other side of Temple Bar.

Mrs. Rack. I never wore it but once before to-day, and then there were so many ill-natur'd observations made that it was delightful. Meekly always makes it her business to come and tell me all the remarks that are made upon me that she thinks will mortify, with a pretended friendly officiousness, but she quite mistakes my feelings. "Law," says one, "what an out-of-the-way thing Mrs. Racket has got on! that woman tries to deform herself, tho' there's little need." Says another: "Why the thing would look well enough if it was on a person of tolerable shape, and put on with any taste." "Aye," cries the third, "she has always some extravagant new dress or other; we shall have her husband calling his creditors together for a shilling in the pound."

Rant. Ha! ha! ha! envy is the shadow, madam, that always attends superior elegance or taste of any kind; but apropos, the ball last night.

Mrs. Rack. Oh! ah! Don't you think we have a very curious set of originals in our city? We are a match for the most polish'd people in Europe; we can shew you lawyers without common sense, soldiers without courage, gentlemen without politeness, and virtuous ladies without modesty.   [1]

Even a quick reading shows that the repartee is almost barren of witty similitudes, yet Mrs. Racket's satiric mimicry is amusing. What is funny for the most part are the people being described; the manner of description itself is not especially clever or amusing. This is then largely humor, not wit.

Missing, therefore, is the sharper edge we find in Tyler's satire: Ranter's clever flattery of Mrs. Racket, and her raillery at the boorishness of her society are more good-natured than sharp. Dunlap's best comic efforts are of this sort — for example, Racket's account, in scene 1, of how he rode a bucking cow while he was drunk, and how it threw him into the mud. The situation is funny;

this is humor and would be farce if presented in scene instead of summary. High wit, as epitomized by the dialogue of the clever rakes and belles of Restoration comedy, was really a matter of sophistication and decorum, including an acute consciousness of language, that was a way of life in the fashionable society of Charles II's court. It was unlikely to be found in the admittedly provincial society of late eighteenth-century America. For here there was yet no ideal of elegant, aristocratic sophistication, no established tradition of culture out of which, according to Meredith, wit invariably emerges.[10]

Thus, in early American comedies wit appears fragmentarily, in moments of raillery and satiric diatribe against manners, or whatever, as in both Tyler and Dunlap, although more frequently in the former. Tyler's wit, seen in Charlotte and Dimple, lacked sufficient brevity, was too often strained or drawn out. Certainly the same may be said of Dunlap's, as we have seen in the passage quoted above. But Tyler, with his hilarious Jonathan scenes, introduced a pattern of farce humor that can be traced in most of the comedies covered by this study. Such broad humor seems to have been palatable to the native taste, and its good-natured, rough spontaneity congenial to the democratic ideals of the emerging American ethos. Restoration wit grew out of an aristocratic sophistication and a social leisure foreign to the bustling young America of the eighteenth century.

Dunlap also followed in Tyler's footsteps with the Yankee character of Susannah, although neither the importance of her role nor the depth of her characterization are comparable to Yankee Jonathan's. Susannah is, very simply, a virtuous, ingenuous maiden, without the spontaneous sense of humor or the ingenuity of Jonathan. Her dialect, while realistic, is less colorful than Jonathan's, for Dunlap was not a native of New England like Tyler.

> *Susannah.* Ma'am, ma'am; Mrs. Bounce Flobby wants you to go a-hopping with her.
>
> *Mrs. Rack.* Shopping, I suppose you mean.
>
> *Sus.* I guess she did mean so; for the nation knows she doesn't look much like hopping, I guess.
>
> *Mrs. R.* Now we shall overturn every shop in William Street; *allons.* [*The Doctor and Captain officiously wait upon her out.*]
>
> *Mr. Rack.* Susy, you must not forget what you are to do for me this evening.
>
> *Sus.* Law souls! I protest I can't think, nor guess n'ither. What you want to dress yourself in madam's clothes for? Not I! But I vow you sha'n't put them on in my room, no more you sha'n't. You may frolick in mistress's room, but you sha'n't frolick in mine, no more you sha'n't.
>
> [2]

Even in her limited role, however, Susannah is a realistic native type, as are the Rackets, although in Mr. Racket the ideal of the upright, industrious Yankee businessman, or man of affairs, is absent, for he is both dissipated and lazy in the conduct of his business. Miss Felton, the ingenue, is a stock sentimental heroine, who shows little native character. But Colonel Duncan, notwithstanding his creation in the image of Sterne's Uncle Toby, carries on the ideal of the revolutionary war hero, or the mythical image of Washington.

The most interesting developments in character are Dunlap's fresh concept of the villain, and his success, however minor, with a German dialect character, namely Jacob. Captain Ranter, or Marsh, is not the vain, effeminate dandy that Tyler's Dimple is. Dunlap makes nothing of his British nationality, nor does he portray him as the product of foreign decadence. He is treated, perhaps in a conventionally sentimental manner, as a basically decent fellow gone astray but eventually repentant and returned to the fold of virtue. Ranter is a far more subtle rogue than Dimple, and until his final upending demonstrates his capability in coping with emergencies, any of which might reveal him for the imposter he is. For instance, in act 4, when Colonel Duncan challenges his assertion that Haller is dead, having heard the opposite from the old wounded soldier (really Haller in disguise), Ranter counters:

> *Capt. R.*   When was he so?
> *Col. D.*   Lately, very lately — I suppose. I do not know the time; I did not ask.
> *Capt. R.*   And am I to be abused because he was well, months, perhaps, ago? There has no vessel arrived since I came. The person from whom you received your intelligence has probably travelled from Boston by land; when he left the place Haller might have been alive, and dead before I departed. Is this usage for Captain Haller's friend? For shame, sir! age should have been more circumspect.   [4]

There is almost a touch of Iago in Ranter's cleverness here. Later, in act 5, after he has been ordered out of Racket's house, having just been exposed in his attempt to seduce Mrs. Racket, Ranter is accosted by Colonel Duncan, who tells him that Haller is his son, and that he doubts whether Ranter came by Haller's ring honestly. Once again thinking quickly, Ranter replies:

> Sir, Captain Haller did not know that he had a father living. But, sir — I — I am very sorry that I should be the messenger of ill news to a father; and, sir, as I suppose his ignorance of you occasioned his giving the ring to me, I am ready to give it to one who has undoubtedly a prior title. [*Offers the ring.*]   [5]

Ranter is likewise a charming rogue, and not without a sense of humor. While Jacob is the German (or New York burgher) dialect character, Ranter's mimicry of that dialect in a satiric description of a party is very amusing.

> I was seated between old Mrs. Mumble Crust and Mrs. Bounce Flobby, while opposite sat the elegant Miss Van-brot-wagenhauf and her pappa. "I thinks, Captain," says Mrs. Mumble, "it's mighty warm, eh? he, he, ha! don't you think so, Captain? he, he, he, ha!" "It must be expected," says I, "that I should be warm, situated between two ladies whose charms —" "I guess," cries Madam Bounce Flobby, interrupting my compliment, "I guess the Captain is pretty well squeezed between us, for we are none of the smallest." "Ha! ha! ha! madam," says I; "I swear your wit is too much this warm weather." "I thinks it is confounded hot," cries Mr. Van-brot-wagenhauf, taking off his wig and rubbing his pate; "I sweats like a tea water man's horse. Cot pless me, I am all of a muck." "Law, pappa!" cries Miss Van-brot-wagenhauf; "how can you use such wulger dispressions?" [5]

But of course the dialect character in the play is Jacob, a disgruntled servant, who had been a Hessian mercenary for the British. Although his role is very minor, his character marks the first real effort to use a foreign comic dialect in native American drama. (Tyler's "Got knows, mine friend," *The Contrast* 3.1 is the first usage, but only incidental.)

We find a significant development of structure — a matter of setting and scene manipulation — in *The Father*. Tyler, using *The School for Scandal* as his model, attempted to write a comedy of manners in the drawing-room tradition, but failed in part to convey the illusion of pace and action, at which Sheridan was eminently successful. The fault was mainly in the sparseness of witty repartee that necessarily generates such an illusion of physical action where there is in reality little. Most of the life in *The Contrast* depends upon the farcical Jonathan scenes, which have little relation to the main plot. Dunlap, obviously more familiar with professional theatre, even though a novice playwright himself, did not confine his action to the drawing room and the mall. The scene of the entire play is Mr. Racket's household, which, if in some ways is limiting because the social satire is handled in summary more than scene, permits Dunlap a greater freedom of action. Tyler tends to limit scenes in *The Contrast* to groups of two or three characters, and he all but isolates one scene from the next. In *The Father*, however, we always sense the daily hum of domestic activity, the intercourse of masters and servants. In limiting his comedy to a single setting, Dunlap deviates from the convention of his age. During the period from the Restoration to about the mid-nineteenth century, playwrights, especially comic playwrights, generally used many and rapidly shifting scenes. The convention was facilitated by the groove system of sliding scene flats out from either wing simultaneously, to meet at the center, thus terminating one scene by the simple mechanical device of cutting it off from view, and permitting another to commence almost simultaneously in front of the new set. But Dunlap compensates by using a steady flux of entrances and exits (in the farce convention), which gives the illusion of action and motion where there may be no actual change of scene. While Tyler is more in the convention of his age in his frequent shifting of scenes, they are uncomfortably abrupt because there is no continuum of brightly paced dialogue or connected action to serve as transition between them.

As the second native comedy, Dunlap's *The Father* reveals several interesting aspects. Dunlap manages to champion the conventional moral attitudes of sentimental comedy without becoming excessively sentimental. Thematically, he shows that patriotism and chauvinism are not synonymous. The satire is milder than in *The Contrast*, but on the other hand, Dunlap rises less often to wit than Tyler. As a second play by a novice playwright — Dunlap was only twenty-three — *The Father* has a sound dramatic structure as well as a good array of character types necessary in the conventional, well-made comedy of the period. But Dunlap's play is not simply imitative of British comedy in its array of characters. In almost every case he has modified a stock British type, making it realistic, and, where possible, genuinely native. His comic forte is farce, and *The Father* has about it that good-natured, bustling humor one finds in the comedies of, say, Farquhar. Thus, Dunlap furthers the native tradition of realistic comic types and his setting and plot expands the more limited conventions of British drawing-room comedy. It is perhaps more accurate to see *The Father* as a sentimental farce, at least in the theme and plot.

James Nelson Barker, Tears and Smiles *(1808)*[11]

James Nelson Barker (1784–1858) is one of the two most prominent native playwrights — the other being John Howard Payne — in the first quarter of the nineteenth century.[12] Between 1804 and 1824 he wrote ten plays (one incomplete), of which only five survive.[13] His importance stems not so much from the quantity but the quality of his plays, and also from his use of native themes in six plays, during a period when native drama was discouraged by theatre managers and actors, many of whom were British.

The stage in the nineteenth century, in both England and America, was dominated by its great actors — Edmund Kean, Edwin Forrest, John McCullough, and Edwin Booth, to cite the more lustrous. To begin with, most of these great stars were British, and brought with them their best roles from the London stage. Quite naturally they would be less than eager to attempt native American parts, and just as naturally the theatre managers, concerned first with the box office, were eager to accommodate them.[14] If certain canons of taste prevailed in the nineteenth-century American theatre, favoring, for example, the popular translations from European melodrama, and the sentimentalized comedies and romantic spectacles, and if such canons were prejudicial to native American plays as they clearly were, we must not attribute the prejudice to any inherent or deep-rooted antipathy on the part of audiences. Their tastes and demands were governed by what they saw. Even Barker, an established and respected Philadelphia playwright, allowed manager Woods and tragedian Cooper to perpetrate a hoax upon not only the public but the actors as well in pretending that Barker's *Marmion* (1816; first produced 1812) was by an English playwright, Thomas Morton. This is the more remarkable in view of Barker's own high patriotism, particularly on the eve of the War of 1812. Moreover, based as it was on Walter Scott's popular narrative poem of the same title, *Marmion* seemed — and was — a sure success. It held the boards for thirty-six years.

The son of Gen. John Barker, a revolutionary patriot, James Nelson Barker fought in the War of 1812 as a captain in the artillery, retiring from military service in 1817 with the rank of major. Like his father, Barker was a staunch member of the Democratic party, and was very active in Philadelphia politics, holding variously such positions as alderman, mayor, and Collector of the Port of Philadelphia. After 1838 he went to Washington to fill a high office in the Treasury and he remained active in federal offices until his death in 1858, having survived more than one change of administration. Unlike William Dunlap, Barker was not a professional playwright. He was, however, intimately associated with the Philadelphia theatre, earlier as a playwright and as a dramatic critic for the *Democratic Press* (1816–17), and later as a patron — he became a stockholder of the Walnut Street Theatre in 1818 — and as a generous advisor to other playwrights. Among his literary and theatrical friends were such men as William Dunlap, William B. Wood, Robert Montgomery Bird, David Paul Brown, Richard Penn Smith, and James McHenry.[15]

Barker himself, in a letter to Dunlap, records the occasion of his writing *Tears and Smiles.*

Tears and Smiles, a comedy in five acts, was written between the 1st of May and the 12th of June, 1806. The idea of writing was suggested at a dinner of the fishing company, at their ancient castle on the Schuylkill, on which august occasion you yourself were a guest. The topic happened to be Breck's *Fox Chase*, which had been first acted on the preceding night. Manager Warren, who was present, asked me to enter the lists as a dramatist, and Jefferson put in for a Yankee character. By-the-way, such a Yankee as I drew! I wonder what Hackett would say to it. The truth was, I had never even seen a Yankee at the time.[16]

Some of Barker's bright sense of humor, abundantly evident in the comedy itself, is conveyed in the letter, which goes on to recount the excitement of the first two performances.

It was first acted March 4th, 1807, to a brilliant audience, and with complete success. Notwithstanding, I must confess that one of the deities of the gallery, where I had ensconced me, did fall fast asleep (O all ye gods!) in the second act. Nay, others appeared likely to follow his example, during the sentimental dialogue, and were perhaps only kept awake by the expectation of seeing "that funny fellow, Jeff., again." Never did I hail a "funny fellow" with so much glee as on that eventful night. The prologue was kindly undertaken by Wood, who began in his most lofty manner, "With swelling port, imperious, and vain," and there he stopped, at a dead fault. After in vain endeavoring to recall what was to follow, he addressed the audience; — "Upon my soul, ladies and gentlemen, I am so unaccustomed to this kind of speaking, that I must beg, &c. &c.," in his peculiar jaunty way, and with his usual happy effect. The piece was announced for repetition on the next night, the author was "trotted out." and ambled through the lobbies and boxes, and the booksellers made proposals — what a triumph for a tyro! I gave the copyright to Blake, who transferred it to Longworth. On the second night, being in the green-room, several of the ladies complained, on coming off, that they were put out in their parts by the loud and impertinent remarks from one of the stage boxes. My course was instantly adopted. I went around to the box, and calling out one of the gentlemen, made such an expostulation as had the desired effect. The conduct of those persons had been so flagrantly indecent as to draw upon them sounds of disapprobation from several parts of the house. They were certain witlings about . . . who, induced by the reputation the piece had gained on the first night, to lay aside their habitual apathy towards American productions, were now aroused only to malignant feeling, as I was neither politically nor socially of their set.[17]

The plot pattern is this: Philadelphia, 1808. Louisa Campdon, who loves Sydney, a young naval officer, is betrothed by her father's wish to Fluttermore, a "Gallicized" fop she detests. Mr. Campdon, who made his fortune as a merchant in Europe, admires Fluttermore's polish, acquired on the grand tour. Campdon is sure he will make Louisa a fine husband. Learning that Sydney has just returned from a victorious engagement against the Mediterranean pirates, however, Campdon fears Louisa will run off with him. Thus he presses for an immediate marriage to Fluttermore. But this is against the advice of his brother, General Campdon, who, although he is Fluttermore's guardian, cannot stomach the fop and favors Sydney for Louisa. Louisa seeks advice from her friend, the Widow Freegrace, who romantically urges her to obey her heart and not her father. The widow, who is eager to remarry, is being courted by O'Connor, a dashing Irishman. But she has been rescued only recently from a runaway carriage by a charming rake named Rangely, whom she does not know, and who is seeking her identity. The widow introduces Louisa to her friend, Mrs. Clermont, a mysterious woman saddened by a tragic past. Miss Starchington, the widow's elderly sister, has been prying into Mrs. Clermont's affairs, desiring to learn her mystery.

A short time later Sydney encounters Louisa, and disregards Osbert's counsel to not interfere in Louisa's pending marriage. Heeding instead the Widow Freegrace's advice, Sydney plans to ask Louisa to elope with him before the wedding to Fluttermore can take place. Meanwhile, Rangely has finally learned the identity of the beautiful woman he rescued, but upon arriving at Mrs. Clermont's lodging, where Nathan Yank has seen the Widow Freegrace, Rangely sees her ride off in the company of O'Connor. He follows them out to General Campdon's estate and gets into a heated argument with the Irishman, who challenges him to a duel. Rangley accepts and they ride off to fight. Then Sydney arrives with his friend Osbert, and persuades Louisa to elope. Later, however, Osbert reveals to Sydney that he is his father, and orders him not to go through with the elopement, with which Sydney complies.

In the meantime, Clara, who had had a previous affair with Fluttermore, the fruits of which were a son, has returned with the child to her home, completely destitute. She is welcomed by her friend, Louisa, who immediately summons Fluttermore to face him with his shameful past. The moment he sees Clara, Fluttermore is overcome by guilt. In the garden without, Rangely returns from his duel, to find the Widow Freegrace. She accepts his proposal of marriage only when he promises her he will reform. After they retire, Miss Starchington and Galliard appear, with the supposedly prudish old spinster making none too subtle advances toward the reluctant Frenchman. Hearing others approaching, however, she forces Galliard to hide with her for reputation's sake.

Thereupon Sydney and Louisa enter, with Sydney, who has just learned of Fluttermore's dishonorable affair with his sister, threatening to do him violence. But Fluttermore appears, having just married Clara within. Satisfied, Sydney then identifies Osbert as the father of Clara and himself, and Campdon consents to a marriage between Louisa and Sydney. Rangely and the Widow Freegrace emerge from the arbor to announce their betrothal, followed by Miss Starchington and Galliard. However, the old spinster is unsuccessful in trying to accuse the Frenchman of having dishonored her. Next, O'Connor returns from the dueling ground only slightly wounded, to indicate that he bears Rangely no grudge. Finally, the Widow Freegrace brings out Mrs. Clermont, who turns out to be the wife Osbert had long believed dead. The play ends with a tableau, Mrs. Clermont falling upon her husband's neck, and the children, Sydney and Clara, kneeling at her side.

As with *The Father*, one sees that Barker's plot follows the pattern of a conventional sentimental comedy, although *Tears and Smiles* has a more complex plot than Dunlap's play, in addition to a wider range of characters. Many of the favorite sentimental situations and character types are present — the orphaned ⌐hildren (Sydney and Clara); the distressed daughter (Louisa), who loves one but is being forced into a marriage with another by a stubborn father; the long-grieving widow (Mrs. Clermont); the dishonorable seducers, whether rake or fop; and so forth. While Osbert is certainly a sentimental character, his capture by barbarian pirates and his long enslavement reveal the influence of the increasingly popular romantic melodrama on Barker. Quinn notes the similarity between this play and *The Contrast*, citing the obvious parallels between Sydney and Tyler's Manly: both are military heroes who win the heroine away from the fop, although Sydney's rashness marks him as more of a romantic type than the conservatively sentimental Manly, and Fluttermore's foreign affectation is French, not English like Dimple's. In addition, the patriotic theme of *Tears and Smiles*, as in Dunlap's comedy, is not as emphasized as in Tyler's play.

Barker is less the moralist than either Tyler or Dunlap, for whereas Fluttermore has actually dishonored Clara (recall that Dimple and Captain Ranter are licentious more by intention than deed) his eventual reform is presented briefly and without any sentimental emphasis. It is in fact overshadowed by other matters in the denouement, notably the sentimental family reunion and the comic thwarting of Miss Starchington in her effort to force Galliard into a marriage. There is hardly time for anyone to reprimand Fluttermore before he marries Clara, as events tumble on the heels of one another. This is not to deny that Barker has built his play on the sentimental formula, involving such conventional themes as filial obedience, family reunion, and the rake's reform. But he is clearly more interested in entertaining his audience than in edifying them, exhibiting less enthusiasm for moral judgment than either Dunlap or Tyler. Tyler's comic mood is uneven because he makes a rather consistent distinction between comic and serious scenes. Most of the funniest comedy takes place in the Jonathan plot, which has no real connection with the main plot. Dunlap, on the other hand, manages to sustain the overall comic mood in *The Father* by not overemphasizing his serious scenes and by presenting most of the principal characters as inherently comic, whether sentimental types (such as Colonel Duncan) or not. Dunlap is unafraid of disrupting his moral themes by the inclusion of farce-comedy, and Barker is less so, having even more of that good-natured comic viewpoint evident in Dunlap.

We recall that Dunlap had departed from the conventional drawing-room setting that Tyler had used, as well as demonstrating a more professional skill in exploiting his household setting. In *Tears and Smiles* Barker broadens his setting still more, for the action takes place "in and near Philadelphia" in a number of settings, including the lodgings of Mr. Campdon, Mrs. Clermont, Rangely, and Osbert — and very important, the streets without. There is even one pastoral setting at General Campdon's country estate. By thus enlarging his setting, Barker takes an important step in the direction of realism. He is able to create a picture of Philadelphia domestic and social life in scene, and not simply in summary, as had Tyler and Dunlap with their more limited settings.

If Dunlap could create the illusion of a busy household in *The Father*, Barker's scope approaches being city wide. One feels that there is action occurring simultaneously in different places, a feeling never present in Tyler's play. For example, in 2.3 the action takes place within Mrs. Clermont's house, involving Mrs. Clermont, Miss Starchington, the Widow Freegrace, and O'Connor (four characters plus a servant). The following scene takes place in the street before Mrs. Clermont's house, and involves Rangely and Yank, who are looking for her house, and who are shortly joined by Fluttermore and Galliard. In the next scene, still in the street (really a continuation), the four men are joined by General Campdon. At the conclusion of this scene, the action inside and outside the house is connected. As all but Yank leave with the general, the Widow Freegrace appears in the window and sees Rangely, recognizing him as the man who had rescued her runaway carriage. Then as O'Connor and the Widow Freegrace leave Mrs. Clermont's house, they meet and converse briefly with the waiting Yank. With one exception (the duel between Rangely and O'Connor), all of Barker's important action takes place in scene, giving the comedy a lively realism.

In spite of the predominance of brisk action in *Tears and Smiles*, Barker relies less on sheer farce than either Tyler or Dunlap, and the best comic moments are those scenes in which Fluttermore rails at American provincialism or boasts of his brilliant European reputation; or in which there is a brief but sharp exchange of repartee, in the tradition of sex antagonism, between the Widow Freegrace and Mr. Campdon. Like Tyler's Dimple, Fluttermore is a foppish rake in the comic tradition, although his affectation is French rather than British. The pompous egotism of each is similarly ludicrous, yet Fluttermore's character is more fully developed than Dimple's, with the result that he is more realistic. He is certainly more suave and witty. Where Dimple is sensitive to criticism, Fluttermore can shrug it off, or respond in spirit, revealing a sense of humor in his delight at the give and take of a teasing exchange. His first appearance is a comic masterpiece.

Rangely. I think I should know that face: it is Fluttermore. But his dress! What a metamorphosis! [*Enter Fluttermore and Galliard.*] Ned! My dear Ned!

Flut. Ned! [*Sees Rangely.*] ha! Jack Rangely, by gad!

Ran. Honest Ned, I'm so glad to see you — [*Shakes his hand cordially.*]

Flut. That you mean to dislocate my shoulder. Hold, for heav'n's sake! or you'll shake my whole system into *derangement*; the bones out of my body, and the powder out of my head!

Ran. [*Examining his figure.*] But what the devil!

Flut. Ay, you wonder, Jack. A little *transformé*, you see.

Ran. You are indeed.

Flut. Yes, burst from darkness into the blaze of fashion; chang'd in an instant —

Ran. From a worm to a butterfly.

Flut. Butterfly! yes, faith; good metaphor. Once a bookworm, a college chrysallis; now a butterfly, light, airy, *emerilloné*. 'Gad a *bonne similitude* — Made the grand tour.

Ran. The grand tour?

Flut. Yes, just returned.

. . . .

. . . I can't conceive what you possibly do in this corner of the globe. No opera; no masquerade, nor *fete*, nor *conversazione*; a diabolical theatre; and not even a promenade, where one might — [*Examining his figure.*] Then your women; such dowdies! No air; no manner. And your men: *O Ciel!* Such beings! — 'Gad, Jack, you must go to Europe! You see what it can do.

Ran. Why, if I could ever hope to attain that brilliancy —

Flut. Pshaw, man! Don't despair. There are very pretty degrees, you know, below the summit of excellence. I rather fancy, indeed, that the *eclat* which attended *me* is not to be repeated every day. Why, sir, I was absolutely a comet.

Ran. Indeed!

Flut. Set Paris in a blaze; shook London to its centre; dazzled most of the Italian cities; made Vienna totter; and was the gaze everywhere. Ha, monsieur?

Gal. Oh! *oui*; wherever you are, *de peuple gape at you*. Yes; dam 'tis not true.

Flut. Then for the women. I don't know what can be found so delectable about me; but in strict truth, all ranks — Hark ye, Jack: *entre nous* — [*Whispers.*]

Ran. The princess! Impossible!

Flut. True; poor Eugene! As to the wives and daughters of petty princes or electors; pretty *amusettes,* or so, for an idle hour. Show you my diary.

Ran. What, did you keep a diary?

Flut. Not a vulgar gazetteer-like thing; distance of post-towns, and all that — *Le voici*! [*Shows a small morocco book.*]

Ran. Heavens! here's a list of names might become the docket of a sheriff of the country!

Flut. A few. This side, princes, or so, my particular friends, with whom I've passed whole *days. L'autre cote,* princesses, and that kind of thing, with whom I've passed whole (*ahem*) — hey, monsieur?

Gal. Oh, *by de lor,* you have made good mode *pour passer le temps.* Yes.

Ran. Excellent pastime, I dare swear. But have you gained nothing else?

Flut. Oh! customs and manners, and all that; laws, and the like. O yes; profound too. The English can't dress, talk, nor cook so well as the French. The Italian opera is a dev'lish deal finer than anything in the world. The *elegantes* have introduced hair-powder into Paris; and the emperor, gunpowder into Germany. Then for laws; for laws. They are every where better than ours, because every where else the *bourgeois* are kept under. *En fin,* I have found that the new world is too given to please the palate of a man of *gusto;* and that Europe, like a ripe beauty, is the only object worthy a connoisseur's attention. [1.4]

It seems likely that Barker was familiar with *The Man of Mode,* for Fluttermore is reminiscent of Etherege's grand fop. Fluttermore is unmistakably American in his spontaneous good nature — no doubt even vulgar by Sir Fopling's own standards — yet there is something of the Restoration beau in his enormous vanity. His eagerness to share boudoir secrets with Rangely suggests Sir Fopling's:

Ah, Dorimant — Courtage, I would say — would thou had spent the last winter in Paris with me! . . . No stranger ever passed his time so well as I did some months before I came over. I was well received in a dozen families where all the women of quality used to visit; I have intrigues to tell thee more pleasant than ever thou read'st in a novel.

[*The Man of Mode* 4.1]

The dominant values of this play are conventionally sentimental. Even so, through Fluttermore, Barker makes some amusing thrusts at that very mode, while simultaneously satirizing the fop's affected cynicism, which is far too good-natured to be serious.

> *Flut.* But apropos! if I recollect right, gad! I believe I'm to be married tonight — didn't you say something of that kind?
> *General Campdon.* Was there ever such a lukewarm —
> *Flut.* Why, lord! would you have me to get into a passion about a bagatelle?
> *Gen.* Bagatelle, sir! have you no sensibility of your happiness, in getting the finest girl in the world:
> *Flut.* O lord! yes, a vast deal of sensi — but as to rapture and ecstacies, and that kind of thing, gad they're all out; left the fashionable world long since. Those monopolizers, the novelists, have bought up all the old-fashioned article, and if you want it now, you must apply to the only shop where 'tis to be had; *savoir,* the circulating library.   [2.3]

The same flippancy provides a buoyant humor in Fluttermore's description of Philadelphia domestic and social life.

> *Flut.* . . . Once a week or so, you'll emerge from the elegant cares of your counting-rooms, to take the benefit of the dust with spousy, to your rural cot on the high road; and once a year catch an ague, for the benefit of your health, at one of your brilliant watering places. Amiably domestic, you'll play cards for kisses with lovey; or make one of a tea-drinking circle in the American taste; staring at each other like a room full of wax-figures; and gloomy as a Presbyterian synod.
> *Ran.* Admirable!
> *Flut.* You don't dance, therefore madam's annual cotillion is nothing to you; but you'll visit your unparalleled theatre, perhaps once a winter, to see some delectable American muse, in the shape of a comedy; and end the year merrily at Christmas, by settling your books, and collecting your debts.   [4.2]

Beneath Fluttermore's breezy generalization, however, lies penetrating social satire. Tyler had made light of fashionable New York's social life, with particular reference (by Dimple) to the crudeness of the theatre and the assemblies. But one is as amused by Dimple's affected disdain as the satire itself. In Dunlap, there was only light satire of fashions and intimate parties. But here Fluttermore's cleverness is matched if not overshadowed by the realistic description of the social pattern he mocks. It is less the crudity of any given social pursuit than the determined, even dogged monotony of the whole routine. Successful satire is grounded in the truth, but cleverly dressed in wit or humor, as the case may be. Fluttermore's observations are not amusing merely because they are clever, like those of Dunlap's Captain Ranter, or silly like those of Tyler's Dimple, although Fluttermore has moments of absurdity. His satire succeeds because there is obvious truth in it.

Perhaps most damaging is the concluding thrust at materialism, on the un-Christmas-like balancing of accounts at Yuletide. The irony is caustic, the more startling in view of the sympathy for the materialistic American ethic we saw earlier in Tyler. Even Dunlap's satiric portrait of the American businessman in Racket did not question materialism; if anything it furthered Tyler's view by criticizing Racket's indolence. But in Barker's presentation of Mr. Campdon as placing monetary gain over any interest in national affairs we see the first serious challenge in American drama to that materialistic ethic.

> *Gen.* . . . You should know sir, that, as one of its members, our country is interested in everything that takes place in the great family of nations. And as I have fought, brother, I can feel for its interests.
>
> *Mr. Campdon.* Ah! the old tale — you have fought. I confess I was always of a specific disposition, and preferred shedding ink to spilling blood; therefore, when you chose to be a soldier here in America, I was content with the character of a simple merchant at Hamburg; and while I made an ample fortune in *my* pursuit, you lost in yours the little our father had left you.
>
> *Gen.* I am proud of that circumstance.
>
> *Camp.* Very like. Well, the country is now old enough to take care of itself; and the more fools they who trouble themselves about it, say I. [1.1]

Mr. Campdon's justification of himself by the allusion to the parable of the talents is a clever stroke of irony on Barker's part.

But to return specifically to wit and humor, not all of the comedy is a matter of content, of satiric target, as the verbal duel between the Widow Freegrace and Mr. Campdon will demonstrate:

> *Camp.* . . . a daughter's a positive plague; a wife's a worse; and a widow's the torment superlative. There's grammar for you.
>
> *Wid. Fr.* Ha! ha! But why, Mr. Campdon, are you in such haste to marry Louisa, and thus, according to your rules, make her the second degree of bad — a wife?
>
> *Camp.* Simply to get rid of the first, a daughter; and at present I wish I was fairly rid of the last.
>
> *Wid. Fr.* A widow! a palpable hit! Certainly, my dear, your father has

the pleasantest way with him, the most facetious mode of turning one out of doors.

Lou. Nay, do not think any thing my father says —

Camp. Worth attending to — is that it, miss pert?

Wid. Fr. O, child, 'tis a charming morning recreation. If he'd set chairs, I would chat an hour with him in this sociable way.

Camp. I'll not be laughed at in my own house; and let me tell you, madam —

Wid. Fr. Keep your distance; I won't box with you, that's flat: nay, don't burst with passion, I'm going. [2.1]

As in the comic scenes with Fluttermore, Barker shows a sound dramatic skill by exploiting contrasting characters. Fluttermore's wit is perfectly complemented by Rangely's naïveté and by Galliard's dialect and near-intentional malapropisms. Here the widow's good-natured and poised wit is set off against Mr. Campdon's humorslike, angry contempt for all women. Although he rises only to a kind of plodding false-wit in his grammatical analogy, the repartee is still rapid and comical, as it should be in manners comedy. As with Tyler's, Barker's wit is perhaps too forced and certainly too congenial — softened by humor — to be deemed high wit. It is pallid by comparison to that of the Restoration playwrights. But it is wit nevertheless, and it succeeds well. As has already been suggested, such wit, closer in its gentler, good-natured tone to that of Sheridan or Goldsmith — even Farquhar — than to that of Congreve or Etherege, is consistent in tone with the sentimental period in which it arises. Whether such wit is native to American comedy is less easily proved than that it certainly dominates the early comedies.

Barker's comedy demands a fuller dramatis personae than either of the preceding two plays. Not including incidental servants, the characters number eighteen, in comparison to twelve in *The Father* and nine in *The Contrast*. However, sheer numerical superiority is meaningless without adding that Barker uses these characters fully, not simply peopling his scenes with walk-on roles. Here in the matter of dramatis personae, as well as in scene manipulations and plotting, he reveals a competence and maturity at his craft beyond his limited experience. Recall that *Tears and Smiles* was Barker's first completed play, in fact written more or less to order in six weeks. But of more significance than the expanded dramatis personae, even if only tentatively posed as an indication of maturer playwriting in the twenty years since *The Contrast*, is the interesting development of character types. Here the ground is surer, for it is possible to trace that development in certain types since Tyler's comedy. First, the beau.[18]

There are two beau characters, Fluttermore and Rangely. Since Fluttermore has been treated above in the discussion of wit and humor, little need be added except that he is different from Rangely in being both fop and rake. There is nothing foppish about Rangely, who by self-admission is simply "an itinerant rake by profession" (1.3). Rangely is far less interesting than Fluttermore, because Barker makes less effort to treat him comically or to give him much wit. For the most part he functions as a foil, as a straight man in the scenes with Fluttermore, except in making his bid for the Widow Freegrace's hand, when he responds well to her witty challenge.

> *Ran.* — [*Meeting the Widow in Mr. Campdon's garden.*] And bless the little god who bid me jump over here, for I've heard — you can't deny it — like Romeo, I listened; like Juliet, you confessed. You must have me. You will; say you will.
>
> *Wid. Fr.* Heaven help the man, how he runs on! Why, I expected a modest, speechless kind of a body; but I can't get a word in! Lord! d'ye think I'll marry a man who talks more than myself?
>
> *Ran.* I'm dumb, madam; dumb, as when you first knew me. I'll be eternally dumb, if you'll promise always to be talking, for your voice — (*She smiles.*) a hem!
>
> *Wid. Fr.* What a *babillard*!
>
> *Ran.* Cure me, madam. Marry me.
>
> *Wid. Fr.* They say you're a sad rake!
>
> *Ran.* Love has half reformed me; let Hymen complete the good work. Marry me.
>
> *Wid. Fr.* The hazard would be too great: for, if I took you, what assurance could I have of keeping such a rover?
>
> *Ran.* Nay, dear madam, don't make me out quite so great a fool as Lucifer: to run from Heaven! [5.3]

Beneath the wit is Rangely's charming honesty, which contributes to the force of his persuasion with the widow, although she is hardly unreceptive. As we saw earlier, Fluttermore is capable of witty repartee, but the basic distinction between these two beaux is that Fluttermore is stuffed full of "unnatural" foreign affectation. On the other hand, Rangely is a new type in native comedy, a rake who is wholly American. If immoral, his rakishness is posed as an immoderate degree of the natural sexual urge. Even at that, we must accept that reputation at his own say so, for there is no real evidence of it in scene.

Barker's use of a pair of beaux is not new to American comedy, for two had appeared in Samuel Low's *The Political Outwitted* (1789). However, Low's Frankton and Worthnought were two of a kind, both fops in the exaggerated comic tradition. That Barker made a clear distinction, even a contrast, between his beaux is new to native comedy, although it has precedent in the Restoration comedies, which were generously peopled with various degrees of rakes and fops. Such developments — the creation of an American beau, a rake untainted by foreign affectation, and the distinction between fop and rake — seem a clear indication of an emerging maturity in native play writing.[19] Furthermore, Rangely's character reflects none of the comic sterotyping that stemmed from the chauvinism that had affected Tyler's conception of Dimple. This is an indication of cultural maturity, of literary independence, as well as evidence of the direction toward more realistic native types, even those derived from familiar comic types in the British tradition.

Such realistic development in characters may also be seen in Mr. Campdon and his brother, General Campdon. We have already noted how Mr. Campdon, as the man-of-affairs figure, has undergone some change since the first such character, Tyler's Van Rough, in that Barker challenges his materialistic ethic. Furthermore, the conflict between Mr. Campdon's unpatriotic economic motives and the nationalism of General Campdon is heightened dramatically by pitting brother against brother in their brief debate (1.1). Compared to old Van Rough, indeed by any standards, Mr. Campdon is very much a sophisticated man of the world, a traveled American. The shrewd, Yankee practicality and the provincial business acumen of Tyler's merchant have blossomed into the worldly capability of Mr. Campdon, who has made his fortune in Europe. With his countinghouse in Hamburg, he is more than the successful Philadelphia merchant — he is an international tycoon. The rough edges are gone. The homespun shrewdness, comic in its provinciality, has matured into a sophisticated relish for things European, seen clearly in Mr. Campdon's eager approval of Fluttermore. Having misjudged Dimple's good sense, Van Rough ultimately chose Manly as his son-in-law, in part because he felt that Manly would "mind the main chance." Mr. Campdon's choice of Fluttermore for his Louisa is as much motivated by his appreciation of the beau's manners — "Why, he'll be the most diverting husband! a fanciful amour of his, told over a dish of chocolate, will so amuse ye!" (2.1) — as his respect for Fluttermore's estate. For the same reason, General Campdon is just as adamantly against Fluttermore, even though the fop is his own ward. But General Campdon is not the patriotic idealist Manly is, for whereas he reveals an active interest in America's national affairs, and while he is understandably proud of the American naval victory over the Tripoli pirates — particularly young Sydney's role in the victory — his enthusiasm is not exaggerated or sentimentalized. Barker never permits him the excesses of Columbian oratory in which Manly indulges.

Of the remaining male characters, Sydney and Osbert are stock figures from romantic drama or sentimental comedy, characters of refined sensibility and minimal wit — none, in fact, shown. With the three dialect types, O'Connor, Nathan Yank, and Galliard, Barker achieves varying degrees of success. Contrary to expectation, O'Connor lacks the traditional braggart qualities of the stage Irishman, and has apparently never heard of the Blarney stone. Indeed, Barker hardly makes an effort to give him an Irish dialect. He is more positive about Nathan Yank, however, in spite of protestations to the contrary in his letter to Dunlap. The Yankee is a clown, all of his comedy arising from dialect, for he is given no farce scenes of his own like Tyler's Jonathan. But Nathan Yank lacks the cockalorum and spontaneous humor of Jonathan, for as Barker admitted, he had never seen a real Yankee. Yet, his Yankeeisms provide some comic moments during the scene in which O'Connor challenges Rangely to a duel.

> *Yank.* O Lord! you'd better leave it to a justice of the peace.
>
> *Ran.* Silence! Name the time and place, sir.
>
> *O'Con.* Faith, now's the best *time*; but for place, let me see — we mustn't let the peaceable gentleman your servant mentioned hear the arguments of our referees.
>
> *Ran.* 'Tis but stepping into the next state. Yank, you'll attend us.
>
> *Yank.* What! into the next state? I an't afeard to die, sir, only going so lightly into another state, without knowing whether it's a blessed state or no—
>
> *Ran.* Simpleton, I only want ye to cross the Delaware with me.
>
> *O'Con.* Ay, only to step over the river. It's mighty easy, sure.
>
> *Yank.* It must take a tarnal long stride to do it.   [4.2]

Nathan Yank is pure fool, pure clown — we detect no hint of shrewdness behind his mask of naïveté, as with Jonathan. But his importance is in his very presence in the comedy. As Barker's letter to Dunlap indicates, Jefferson, who was a highly popular comedian in Philadelphia, had insisted on there being a Yankee for him to play. As with Tyler's friend Wignell, Jefferson probably contributed more to the role than the playwright wrote by virtue of his comic artistry. Still, there was obviously an audience awareness of if not a demand for the figure. As a dialect character, however, Yank was only moderately successful. Galliard is the best of the three, for Barker achieves in him a superbly comical fusion of accent and attitude. His speech is a hilarious mingling of French and malaproprious broken English, and his pose is one of *seeming* innocence — innocence of his sometimes sharply satirical replies to Fluttermore (e.g., "wherever you are, *de peuple gape at you*," from 1.4, quoted above). What may be concluded about Barker's characters must ultimately be a comment about Barker himself: about his skillful handling of dialect and dialogue, and about his alertness to the people around him in Philadelphia as possible comic types for his drama. Such use of dialect types, although old in the British tradition, was new to the American. Realism through comic dialects — now progressing into foreign types — is a continuation of Tyler's initial impulse to create a realistic stage Yankee, drawn from the life around him. As the nineteenth century drew on, American comedies increasingly continued to reflect, through comic dialect types, our interest in foreign visitors as well as our own native types.

Among the female characters, Louisa Campdon and the Widow Freegrace are the most interesting, not to detract, however, from the fine caricature of the hypocritical busybody, Miss Starchington. There is little to say about Clara and Mrs. Clermont other than that they are stock sentimental types, long-suffering and saddened through underserved misfortune. Even the Widow Freegrace, as her name indicates, is a stock type: the merry widow. Her wit has already been described above. But Louisa Campdon is not quite the stock heroine — at least, the stock sentimental heroine. In the first place, despite her unfortunate (if temporary) treatment at the hands of her stubborn father, she is not the sentimental, moralizing, languishing figure that Maria Van Rough is. She has some of the rebelliousness of Charlotte Manly. She is not meekly passive, but a girl of spirit, as we see in her defiance of her father's wishes.

> *Lou.* Sir, had I never seen Sydney, my aversion to Fluttermore would still be equal to what it is.
> *Camp.* Aversion! These novel-reading misses! And pray what the devil gives you this *aversion*, as you call it?
> *Lou.* An assemblage of every thing disagreeable. Is he not a fivolous coxcomb?
> *Camp.* Hum! A little so. But his estate —
> *Lou.* Besides, he's a libertine.
> *Camp.* No.
> *Lou.* Not a libertine?
> *Camp.* No, I tell you. To be sure the young man does talk of this and of that; but, I dare engage, he's quite a harmless, innocent kind of a gentleman.
> *Lou.* Then the stories he is continually relating?
> *Camp.* All bounce; not a word true.
> *Lou.* How contemptible!   [2.1]

There is an obvious parallel in situation between this scene and 1.2 of *The Contrast*. While more sophisticated than Van Rough, Campdon exhibits the same contempt for sentimental fiction and is just as adamant as Tyler's father in his choice of a son-in-law. The two heroines, on the other hand, are quite unlike in nature, as well as in the nature of their responses. Louisa does not resign herself sentimentally to her fate, but resolves to do something about her heart's choice. And during the conversation itself, while reasonably polite toward her father, she is far from obsequious, taking every opportunity to confront his strong opinion with an equally strong challenge. Moreover, Louisa is equally reluctant to hide from him her dislike for Fluttermore, refusing to hide blandly behind the conventional mask of feminine compliance the sentimental heroine wore.

It is this quality of spirited independence, an ultimate reliance on her own judgment when it conflicts with unjust parental command, that marks Louisa Campdon as an early example in native drama of a type called simply the American Girl. Henry James, perhaps more than any other American author, explored this type in his fiction with such heroines as Daisy Miller and Isabel Archer. It seems unlikely that the genesis of the type is the witty heroine of Restoration comedy, such as Angelica in Congreve's *Love for Love,* or, in earlier romantic comedies, heroines like Rosalind in Shakespeare's *As You Like It.* But even if it is, the American dramatists, in adapting and assimilating the type, tended to stress the independence more than the wit. In Tyler's Charlotte the stress was equal; in Louisa Campdon one sees little evidence of wit. She tends to be, if good-natured, a fairly serious heroine, not unlike many stock sentimental heroines. But her spirited independence is a striking departure from the long line of indistinguishable (because vapid) ingenues of sentimental comedy, stock figures like Sheridan's Maria in *The School for Scandal.*

Certain significant developments in *Tears and Smiles* must be reiterated here. Barker took what is a conventional sentimental plot, included some satire of contemporary manners, and questioned certain social, political, and economic values. Filial obedience, for example, is not enshrined in the conventional sentimental manner, and the American materialism is seen to conflict with a citizen's responsibility for keeping informed and taking an active interest in national affairs. Certainly the comedy relies foremost on the usual love plots, but the presence of issues more serious than manners indicates that Barker had adapted the older form — actually a mixture of manners and sentimental comedy, though largely the latter — to serve his thematic ends. In short, he took a step toward social comedy. Dunlap's *The Father,* only two years after *The Contrast,* had softened the Revolutionary chauvinism of Tyler, but had not really enlarged its focus beyond the contemporary yet conventional themes of home and hearth, flag and country. But Barker had. He apparently recognized the severe limitations of themes that leaned so heavily on a kind of provincial negativism.

Finally, in spite of his sentimental mode, Barker moved closer to realism by limiting highly stylized diction that inflates much sentimental drama. The change may be seen even in the serious scenes (e.g., 3.1, in which Osbert tells Sydney of his unhappy life). Even here the diction is less artificial than in comparable scenes in Tyler or Dunlap. In part the change stems from a less sentimental attitude toward themselves in the serious characters. We have seen, for example, how Louisa Campdon, unlike Maria Van Rough, was not the person to resign herself to her fate, to the hands of her father, in a gesture of sentimental stoicism. Of course the change is most evident in the comic scenes, as any passage quoted above will substantiate. Note, for example, a more informal syntax, a simpler diction, and the use of contractions in verbs — all representative of the more natural rhythms of the American vernacular. Tyler had first pointed in this direction, primarily in the Jonathan scenes, and Barker allowed Tyler's influence to permeate much more of his comedy. When it appears in *Tears and Smiles*, the stylized dialogue seems almost as surprising as the Yankee dialect had in Jonathan's three scenes.

Robert Montgomery Bird, The City Looking Glass *(written 1828)* [20]

Bird's unproduced comedy is included here because, although to study an emerging tradition means to examine primarily plays that saw the boards and were, we may assume, of influence upon contemporary dramatic literature, it is nonetheless important to corroborate findings by looking at some plays that were not produced. Evidence of a tradition in such plays substantiates the influence of that emerging tradition from the professional stage. If *The City Looking Glass* were merely a trivial piece, a closet drama never intended for acting, it would better be treated with other such plays in chapter four to follow. But is is hardly that, for it was clearly written with the stage in mind. Moreover, as the ensuing discussion will show, Bird was writing not only with a keen awareness of the emerging tradition of native American comedy (and with a bold willingness to experiment and innovate), but from a knowledge — if youthfully pretentious sometimes — of the English stage. Bird was to become a successful American playwright soon after *The City Looking Glass,* and is without question of major importance among early nineteenth-century native dramatists. Publication of this comedy waited until 1933, when Quinn edited the manuscript, but seeing the boards is not always infallible proof of a play's intrinsic worth, as both Dunlap and Barker had learned before Bird. Obviously good plays were produced. But, as we have seen, feuds among actors over suitable roles, and the whim of great actors, or the judgment of managers could and did bury plays in the closet. Not all of them were poor plays.

The City Looking Glass is a young play, and one finds it derivative in some ways. It has, for example, some misplaced echoes of Shakespeare in the Iago-like machinations of Ravin. The romantic and melodramatic qualities in what is basically a social comedy may be an indication of Bird's true talents or propensities, demonstrated subsequently in his successful tragedies. Unpublished and unproduced in its time, the play was never an influence on the mainstream of native comedy. Yet, it was and still is a good play, and it clearly reflects the influence of earlier plays in its plot structure, wit and humor, themes, and character types. Having given up medicine after a year of practice to plunge into writing, Dr. Bird was as ambitious and full of energy as he had been studious once. There is no question that he was consciously working within a native tradition in this play. *The City Looking Glass*, obscure though it has been, is in every respect sound evidence of the crystallizing pattern of realism in American social comedy.

Robert Montgomery Bird (1806–54) was born in Newcastle, Delaware, but was educated in Philadelphia, where he settled, becoming a physician, man of letters, and a university professor.[21] Bird was graduated from the School of Medicine of the University of Pennsylvania in 1827. But he only practiced medicine for one year following that, soon turning earnestly to play writing, in which he had dabbled as a student. His apprenticeship at the craft ended when, in 1830, the tragedian Edwin Forrest bought the romantic tragedy, *Pelopidas*. Prior to that Bird wrote three comedies, none published or produced: *News of the Night* (1827); the fragment, *'Twas all for the Best* (1827); and *The City Looking Glass* (1928). He also wrote six romantic tragedies: *The Cowled Lover* (1827); *Caridorf* (1827); *The Volunteers* (1828); *Gionone, The Fanatick*, and *Isadora*, (1828) — none of which was complete. Unfortunately, Forrest never produced *Pelopidas*, because his role was not strong enough. Like Dunlap, Bird quickly learned how to write a "better" play — for the leading actor — and his second effort for Forrest was produced with great success in New York. Forrest liked *The Gladiator* (1831) so well that he used it for his triumphant debut at Drury Lane in 1836, thereafter keeping it in his repertoire until his retirement from the theatre in 1871. *Oralloossa* followed with less success in 1832, although Forrest was still playing it fifteen years later in 1847. Bird's finest romantic tragedy was his last, *The Broker of Bogota* (1834), which Forrest acted with much success in America, taking it abroad on a second trip to London in 1845. Like *The Gladiator*, the play remained active in his repertoire until the end of his career. Unfortunately, Bird's career as a playwright, so promising in 1836, terminated in 1837, following a squabble with Forrest over royalties.[22]

Doggedly refusing to abandon his literary urge, however, Bird continued to write, turning now to the novel. Between 1834 and 1839 he published five: *Calavar* and *The Infidel*, both historical, romantic novels of Mexico at the time of Cortes; *The Hawks of Hawk-Hollow*, a romantic novel of the American Revolution; a picaresque novel, *The Adventures of Robin Day*; and his best, *Nick of the Woods*, a realistic, antiromantic novel of Indians and settlers in Kentucky during the early post-Revolutionary period. Ill health forced him to retire from the demands of writing books after 1839, but in 1841 Dr. Bird was appointed to the Chair of Institutes of Medicine and Materia Medica at the new Pennsylvania Medical College. Although he had not practiced medicine past his first year out of school, Bird nevertheless had maintained an active interest in the science of medicine. In spite of poor health, Bird assumed literary editorship and partial ownership of the Philadelphia *North American*, once more returning to writing in 1847. He continued in this journalistic capacity — off and on, depending upon uncertain health — until his untimely death in 1854. He died at only forty-eight.

The following is a plot summary of Bird's comedy, *The City Looking Glass*: Philadelphia, 1828. Ben Garket, a swindler posing as a wealthy Yankee named Ravin, desires to marry Diana Headstrong, daughter of a wealthy man of affairs. He then intends to discard her to marry Emma Gall — whom he knows to be Emma Raleigh — partly for love, partly because she is heiress to the Raleigh fortune. With forged credentials and a personable, witty exterior, Ravin has won for himself Headstrong's approval as his future son-in-law. But his long range scheme is complicated by Emma's presence as a houseguest in Headstrong's home: she and Diana are best friends from boarding school. Sometime in the past, though, Ravin — then Ben Garket of Virginia, and married to Ned Raleigh's cousin — had embezzled funds from a bank in which he had held an important position because of his connections with the Raleigh family. Thus he knew that Emma Raleigh had been kidnapped by Mrs. Gall, then a servant in the Raleigh home. She had stolen the infant as revenge against Raleigh, Sr., who had seduced her, under the usual false promise of marriage. Furthermore, Ravin had learned — with the villain's instinct for useful information — that Mrs. Gall, who had somehow kept her own identity a secret from Emma during the years in which she had kept the girl at school, was about to make a harlot of her. Mrs. Gall would then return her to Raleigh, Sr., thus effecting her long-awaited revenge and also setting up a blackmail scheme. Mrs. Gall knew that Raleigh would pay her heavily to keep from revealing what she had done to Emma.

Ravin acts swiftly in his own interest, revealing to Headstrong that Emma is the daughter of a bawd, upon which Headstrong throws her out of his home. Mrs. Gall is then forced to remove Emma from school and to take her into the bawdy house to live. But before Mrs. Gall can bewhore the girl, Ravin threatens to inform the police of her kidnapping, for which she would certainly be jailed. Emma, of course, knows nothing of Ravin's Machiavellian maneuvers, and is now safely out of the Headstrong house. Ravin has thus contrived to separate Diana and Emma for fear that they would make confidantes of one another. At the same time, by removing Emma from Headstrong's house, Ravin has insured that she will not marry Diana's cousin, Roslin, who loves her. Roslin would not disgrace his family by marrying a bawd's daughter.

But Ravin's scheme is not wholly successful, for Diana, who has had little interest in him to begin with, now scorns him as a gossipmonger. Therefore, he contrives to "rescue" Diana from an "assault" by his brother, Ringfinger, a pickpocket just released from the penitentiary. Ravin is to drive off the attacker, but he is to be "shot" in the ruse, hopefully to win her sympathy. Unfortunately, Ned Raleigh happens along just as Ravin is "felled" by the attacker's shot, and he rescues Diana himself. When Ravin visits Diana after a brief period of "convalescence," he finds her in Raleigh's arms. Alarmed at this, but more so upon learning that his rival is a Raleigh — the Raleighs had for years been searching for the Ben Garket who had shamed their family — Ravin first insults Raleigh by calling him a relative of Ben Garket. After Raleigh storms out, Ravin then tells Headstrong about Ben Garket's embezzlement, and insinuates that Ned Raleigh is really Garket in disguise. This infuriates Diana, but causes Headstrong, who trusts Ravin, to banish Ned Raleigh from his house. Seizing his momentary advantage and playing upon Headstrong's hot temper, Ravin goads the old man into a rage over Raleigh's impudence at daring to make love to Diana in her own home. He assures Headstrong that he will write to Virginia immediately to obtain proof that Raleigh is indeed the imposter, Garket. In return, the old man assures Ravin that Diana, despite her renewed dislike for Ravin, will marry him on the next day.

Raleigh proceeds to Roslin's apartment (they had been close friends at college) to tell him about the incident at Headstrong's house. He informs Roslin that he has recently seen Ravin coming out of Mrs. Gall's house, saw, in fact, Emma at the window. Emma, he assumes, is Ravin's mistress. Although Raleigh refuses from a sense of honor to show him the house, Roslin locates it. Hearing Emma's screams, he crashes through the door in time to rescue her from a drunken Ravin. He then takes her to his own apartment for protection.

In the meantime, Headstrong has insisted that Diana marry Ravin, stubbornly refusing to listen to her request to bring Ravin and Raleigh together to settle the former's accusations. Diana, faced with an impending marriage to Ravin, takes positive action, going out alone at night to find Raleigh. She is accosted in the street by Ringfinger, in the company of three bucks, Bolt, Crossbar, and Mossrose, who are in search of easy women. Before she is actually molested, Tom Taffrail, a sailor, happens by to rescue her, and she makes her escape while he scuffles with the bucks. Minutes later she accidentally encounters Raleigh, who in returning from her home, having been refused admittance. Diana tells him of Ravin's slanderous accusations, imploring him to bring Roslin with him to see her father. Her father, she knows, would accept her cousin's vindication of his friend, Raleigh. But Raleigh's honor as a Southern gentleman will not permit him to humble himself by taking the first steps to clear his reputation: Headstrong must initiate any such action.

On the following day, Roslin receives a note from Ravin, challenging him to a duel, which he accepts. Later, learning that Roslin is out of town, Ravin sends Ringfinger and Mrs. Gall to his apartment to bring Emma back, but they are foiled by Roslin's servant, Nathan Nobody, aided by Tom Taffrail — who for a second time in the play passes by at an opportune moment. Roslin returns at that moment, learns that Ringfinger is Ravin's brother, and has him released, fearing that to punish him, now that he, Roslin, has accepted a challenge of a duel from Ravin, would be taken as cowardice. He gives Emma a sealed letter which, he tells her, will guarantee her legal assistance in seeking her true identity. He also pledges his love to her, even though she, being uncertain of her identity, cannot return that love yet. But he is forced to leave town that night, perhaps never to return (from his duel with Ravin) to otherwise aid her in unraveling the secret of her birth. Before he leaves, he is visited by his uncle, Headstrong, with whom he leaves two letters, which, he says, will prove to all that Emma is not a bawd's daughter. Before parting, Roslin convinces Headstrong that Ned Raleigh is not an imposter after all.

Headstrong goes to Raleigh to apologize and invites him to his house that evening. Ravin has also been invited, but when he learns, upon arriving, that Raleigh, Sr., whom Headstrong had summoned from Virginia, is expected at any moment, he sees that he cannot afford to remain in Philadelphia long, and leaves the house as Ned Raleigh arrives. No sooner has he left that the elder Raleigh, with his overseer, O'Slash, arrive, and the old Virginian positively identifies Ned as his son. Raleigh, Sr., and Headstrong then argue hotly over the issues of slavery, states rights, and the tariff, and the proud Southerner becomes so angry that he forbids his son to marry Diana, and then leaves. Diana, who is beginning to suspect that Ravin is really Garket, asks that her father get him to come to the house the next day on the pretext that he wants Ravin to personally deliver a large sum of money for him. She is certain Ravin cannot resist this bait.

On the next day, Tom Taffrail and the three bucks are at a tavern, to be joined shortly by Ringfinger, who is subsequently caught stealing from Mossrose. Threatened with the penitentiary, Ringfinger agrees to turn state's evidence and reveal who Ravin really is. They take him to Headstrong's house where he identifies Ravin as Ben Garket. In a desperate effort to save himself, Ravin then tells Raleigh that Emma is his daughter, and that he had saved her from harlotry by taking her from Mrs. Gall. But, he continues, she had run away from him to become Roslin's mistress. Hearing this, Ned Raleigh runs out before Headstrong can prove, by means of Roslin's letters, that Ravin is lying, that Emma is innocent. With Ravin in custody, all hurry to Roslin's apartment just in time to prevent Ned Raleigh from killing Roslin. Emma is reunited with her family and is promised to Roslin, and Headstrong and Raleigh, Sr., overlook their political differences to agree to a match between Diana and Ned Raleigh.

It has been necessary to give a longer summary than with the previous plays to show the complexity of intrigue in *The City Looking Glass*. In its simplest form, however, the plot relies upon the familiar double love triangle, with Ravin, a member of the first, also being a member of the second (Diana-Ned, Raleigh-Ravin, and Ravin-Emma-Roslin). Superficially, the plotting is similar to many comedies, including *The Contrast*, but the difference between Bird's play and Tyler's is strong, and is to be found in the complication and intrigue. Sentimental comedies, with their reliance on action rather than repartee, and their emotional rather than intellectual appeal, provided fertile dramatic soil for melodramatic situations that were seeded into these British plays as the eighteenth century drew on — situations involving, for example, the heartless, unforgiving father, the rejected and suicidal lover, or the brutally rapacious seducer. It was only a short step from these later sentimental comedies — many only remotely comic — to the noncomic, and highly melodramatic domestic dramas of varying tragic and pathetic hue. In generalizing about the mode of these dramatic types in the later eighteenth century, we must not overlook an important fact: as dramatic situations grew more sentimental and melodramatic, the characters and problems tended to grow more realistic, for they were drawn from — to appeal to — the broad middle class. Certainly the complications in the Emma-Roslin love affair are melodramatic, for Mrs. Gall is the epitome of the woman scorned. The naked ruthlessness of her scheme to bewhore the innocent Emma, and then to profit by her deed through blackmail, is as chilling as any revenge concocted by a Webster, Chapman, or Tourneur. Bird was familiar with the Elizabethan and Jacobean dramatists, and there is much evidence in this play alone of their influence on his plot intrigue, his villains, and his scenes in the city streets.[23] But to return to the point, both Mrs. Gall and Ravin, in spite of their Machiavellian scheming, are quite credible as stage characters.

A close examination of the plotting of *The City Looking Glass* reveals the interesting fact that it is structurally more like a tragedy than a comedy. To begin with, the play is longer and is divided into more scenes than any of the previous comedies studied. It contains four scenes in act 1, six in 2, four in 3, six in 4, and four in 5. Secondly, the point of view in the play is largely Ravin's. Our attention is focused again and again upon the villain and his machinations, as it is upon Iago in *Othello*, since Ravin initiates most of the action. Roslin only counters defensively, and Raleigh, until the fifth act, hardly does that. The comic heroes are largely acted upon. It is Ravin's game throughout the first three acts. Even though he is not wholly successful in trying to seduce Emma in 1 (subtly, by offering her pearls) or in 2 (drunkenly, by trying to force himself upon her), he is still in control in act 3. This is the major crisis, in which he, first, challenges Roslin to a duel and, then, sends Ringfinger and Mrs. Gall to Roslin's apartment to kidnap Emma. The second move is thwarted, but the duel is still to follow, and Ravin is certain that he will kill

Roslin, thus removing the only person who for the present can refute his accusation of Ned Raleigh. As in Shakespearean tragedy, the conflicting forces are in stasis at the conclusion of act 3, and the fourth act is comparatively quiet, leaving the inevitable peripeteia and resolution for act 5. Actually, the reversal of fortunes is begun in the last scene of act 4 with the arrival of Raleigh, Sr., at Headstrong's house. But Ravin slips away before he can be identified as Garket, and although he knows then that he will never marry Diana Headstrong, his future with Emma is still undecided.

Bird demonstrates a mature dramatic skill in his manipulation of scenes. The setting constantly shifts, from Mrs. Gall's house to Ravin's, to Headstrong's to Roslin's apartment, and so forth. Also, as we noted in Barker's *Tears and Smiles*, the scene shifts realistically from inside various houses to the streets without. Compared to Barker, Bird is very successful in enlarging the scope of his Philadelphia setting, for in addition to scenes at Mrs. Gall's, Ravin's, Roslin's and Headstrong's, there are four scenes played in the streets (1.3, 2.3, 2.4, and 2.6), one in a tavern (frequented by Tom Taffrail and the three bucks), and one at an inn where Raleigh, Sr., is staying. The play thus sustains interest at one level at least, by presenting a realistic panorama of Philadelphia city life. Yet variety never sacrifices continuity, for the announcement of an intention in one scene, such as Ravin's drunken decision to try Emma's virtue, having been unsuccessful in his sober attempt to woo her with the pearl necklace (1.2), inevitably paves the way for another scene — Ravin's drunken, second assault (2.5).

In spite of certain tragic and melodramatic aspects, *The City Looking Glass* is still a comedy, for Bird sustains the overall comic mood even in his most melodramatic and sentimental scenes. One example, 2.5, will serve to illustrate this point. The scene, which takes place in Mrs. Gall's house, opens with Mrs. Gall trying to gain Ringfinger's sympathy by informing him that Ravin has her at a standstill because of his knowledge of her past, and because of his threat to expose her to the police. The mood, however, is comic, stemming not only from her helpless frustration, but from the dull-witted Ringfinger's indifferent amusement at it all. Trying a new approach, and with the finesse only a bawd could muster, she then asks Ringfinger whether Emma is interested in him.

> *Ring.* I reckon not. I wanted to kiss her t'other day; but she cried and promised to tell Benjamin. So I conclude that she don't fancy much after me: — but that's nothing.

We notice with delight some of Yankee Jonathan's mannerisms in Ringfinger's speech. But suddenly the mood becomes serious as Mrs. Gall proposes that he kill his brother. Yet even this turn is balanced comically by his answer: "I believe, old woman, you are mad. I have resolved never to kill any body in a state where they build penitentiaries." Undismayed, Mrs. Gall later suggests that he could both aid her and satiate his own lust by raping Emma. We are shocked and horrified at her bluntness, and the mood becomes, if melodramatic, deeply serious: "Therefore I hate him, and if you will kill him, you shall make your fortune. Or if you have the spirit, you can aid my vengence by — Do you understand? — she is alone." But Ringfinger's reply,

> You are a damnable old devil, mother Gall, and I suppose you are expounding concerning a rape. But I tell you again, I shall never do a fault that would send me for life to the penitentiary; and besides, brother Ben has as much of the devil in him as you and such a freedom with his own game might lead to a fracas.

immediately violates the seriousness by its very Yankee expression. The pretentiousness of "expounding concerning a rape," and the exquisite anticlimax of "and such freedom with his own game *might lead to a fracas*," anticipate the manner of Southwestern regional humorists. At the end of the scene Ravin attempts to seduce Emma, and although he is obviously drunk, he demonstrates an effective wit in:

> Come, I will kiss thee numerically, by arithmetic: I will skip from addition to the Rule of Three till we be in full practice; and thence from Simple to Double Position; and thence to Promiscuous —

Bawdy, but also as clever as anything a Restoration wit would say. Thus, the melodramatic situation, replete with the heroine's sentimental lapsing into blank verse,

> Who was my mother?
> O take me to her: If she be poor and needy,
> I am young and strong: O take me to my mother, —
> If she resemble not this wretched woman.
> I'll leave this house.

is offset comically, both by Ravin's bawdy wit and the farcical, stumbling chase about the room. While there are serious pathetic and melodramatic moments in this scene — certainly the intentions of Mrs. Gall and Ravin are as villainous as can be, and the plight of Emma as pathetic — they are more than balanced by the dialogue and farcical moments, keeping the overall mood predominantly comic.

The City Looking Glass seems least like the earlier sentimental comedies when one examines its themes. To be sure, there are characters and scenes that are unquestionably sentimental. Emma, as the prime example, is by sentimental standards the perfect heroine: of unknown parentage, and of spotless virtue and heightened sensibility, she is cruelly subjected to the whims of her guardian, Mrs. Gall, who is a bawd, and to the licentious advances of Ravin. To some extent her virtue is its own defense, as, for instance, when she refuses Ravin's gift of pearls:

> *Emma.* When the world will allow my fame to be as spotless, I will accept them. — I cannot take them, sir: My mother supplies me with all necessary apparel; and indigence should not become ridiculous with ornament.   [1.2]

Like many sentimental heroines in similar circumstances, she verges on self-pity, yet maintains a pride in her virtue. But her response is realistic; it is what any upright young lady, educated at a Philadelphia boarding school might say, subjected there, as she doubtless was, to the maxims of Poor Richard.

Roslin, too, is a sentimental character. He has loved Emma before Ravin's disclosure that she is a bawd's daughter, and continues to love her, although perfectly aware that it is socially impossible now to marry her. Yet, not content to languish in self-pity, he sets about to clear her reputation. After rescuing her from Ravin, he offers her financial assistance in unraveling the mystery of her parentage, fearful that he might not return from his duel with Ravin to assist her in person. Emma's response to this generosity is just what we expect.

> *Emma.*   That I am friendless and unfortunate,
> Exposed to danger and to contumely,
> It is heaven's will, and I should repine.
> My grief is deeper than misfortune brings:
> I bear an odious and suspected name;
> Which gives to calumny the show of truth,
> Excuses those who hate me, and constrains
> The kinder to desert me and forget me.
> I did delude myself (for I am yet
> Foolish and ignorant) that all would not
> Misdoubt me, or, like many, misinterpret
> My wrongs and sorrows to make crimes of them:
> I was deceived. — I thank you, much I thank you
> For that you have done, for that you would have done.
> Your gold I need not.
> *Ros.*   By my soul, you wrong me.
> I think, I *know*, ye innocent and blameless.
> Fair fountains bubble from the foulest fens;
> And though the source ye come from be most foul,
> The offspring is most pure.   [3.4]

Roslin's intuitive faith in her virtue is equally sentimental. The blank verse dialogue is an obvious attempt to indicate not only the romantic mood but the rarer sensitivity of the lovers (another device Bird borrowed from tragedy). The presence of an Emma and a Roslin, and the prologation of her undeserved suffering, until she is reunited with her lover, and united with her rightful parent and brother, show the influence of sentimental comedy on Bird. On the other hand, even in this plot there are traces of antisentimentalism.

Ned Raleigh, for example, regards Roslin's love affair with frank amusement. When, after a long separation, the two friends meet, Raleigh asks, "How fares the little angel you wrote about, some six months ago? the mysterious tragedy queen, you made so much fuss about? how fares she?" (1.3), suggesting, by his irony, his own casual approach to romance. Later in the play, after Roslin tells him he is harboring Emma in his apartment, Raleigh scoffs, "What, the bawd's daughter! and innocent! Lord, lord! worse and worse! Why the vengeance did you bring her here?" (3.1). Clearly the whole affair is a crude joke from the viewpoint of a Virginia gentleman. Raleigh has, perhaps, acted impetuously in his own affair with Diana, but the difference is important — she is perfectly respectable. That Roslin's conduct seems foolish to Raleigh is not simply a random viewpoint; it is society's opinion, and Roslin knows it.

Further evidence of antisentimentalism may be seen in Bird's treatment of Headstrong and Diana. Here, of course, was a stock sentimental situation, at least as Tyler and Sheridan had posed it: filial obedience versus the choice of a daughter's heart. But unlike Tyler's Maria, and even more vigorously than Barker's Louisa, Diana openly and without the slightest trace of the conventional sentimental anguish or remorse opposes her father's choice of Ravin. Headstrong has been taken in genuinely by Ravin's forged letters of recommendation, justifying his initial approval of Ravin as his future son-in-law. But once Diana challenges his judgment, claiming that Ravin is "a malignant slanderer venting his hints, his doubts, his regrets, his suspicions behind the back of his victim" (2.2), Headstrong stubbornly refuses to admit even the possibility of an error in his judgment. It suddenly becomes clear that Headstrong's motivation now is essentially selfish: his concern is less Diana's welfare than his own reputation. Such being the case, he has no choice but to insist that Raleigh, as Ravin has insinuated, is the imposter: "Daughter, if you will avoid the eternal disgrace of having it said you married a common swindler, now is the time to give the world the lie by receiving the addresses of a gentleman." And a moment later the truth is out when he shouts,

Hark you, minx; don't talk this way. I give you to know, you shall love anybody I please. What, you jade? — I will cast you off, I will build a church with my money, and leave you to pray in the street, you graceless rebel, I will.   [2.2]

Diana's happiness and welfare, and certainly her affections, have been subordinated to a point of honor: Headstrong's reputation in society and his reputation as the unquestioned head of his family.

The whole matter of honor — or pride — is central to much of the motivation of characters in the play. It motivates, as we have seen, both Emma and Roslin, who love each other, but who are each painfully conscious of the impossibility of a happy marriage without social approbation. Romantic though Roslin is, and as intuitively certain as he is of Emma's virtue, he dare not bring social disgrace upon his family by marrying her before he can prove her innocence. Raleigh's chiding is a continuing reminder to him of what he cannot do. In Ned Raleigh's case, having been falsely maligned by Ravin, and, as a result, having been banished from Headstrong's house, he stubbornly ignores Diana's plea to initiate steps to clear his reputation. As a Virginia aristocrat he considers it a point of honor not to do so. Here again honor, a form of social consciousness, conflicts with love.

Honor, even among the thieves, Ravin and Mrs. Gall, is an important motivation. It is because she was dishonored in her youth by Raleigh, Sr., that the servant-turned-professional-bawd seeks revenge. Granted she would profit well if her scheme succeeded, but revenge, the assuagement of her sense of honor (however warped) is at the core. Honor is likewise central to Ravin's character, for no complex villain is wholly without some pride in his abilities. Ravin had married well, into the Raleigh family, but by embezzling bank funds and abandoning his bride, he had incurred their wrath. To succeed now in marrying Emma, a Raleigh, he would gratify his own passion for her, but more than that, consummate a revenge on the Raleighs: "a bold man might marry her, assume another name, cultivate his whiskers, march off to Virginia, claim her portion, and then march off to the devil" (1.4). How profitable, how sweet the revenge — how proud the revenger.

The familiar theme of patriotism, ranging in intensity from Tyler's anti-British chauvinism, through Dunlap's plea for Anglo-American understanding, to Barker's nationalism, undergoes another significant modification in *The City Looking Glass.* In the first place, and for the first time among these comedies, there is no character created in the image of a patriotic hero; there are no military characters whatsoever. In the second place, although Bird openly portrays the seamier side of Philadelphia city life, dealing very realistically with underworld figures for the first time in native comedy, he never suggests that vice in the city results from any decadent foreign influence. Neither does Bird fall into the conventional sentimental dichotomy of defining city life as synonymous with vice, and country life with virtue. Tyler had implied such a dichotomy, for native worth — the "natural" virtue of Manly and his Jonathan — was a pastoral virtue. It grew naturally in the rocky, Puritan soil of New England. It was foreign to New York. Even Barker had succumbed to this convention, for it is in the pastoral setting of the outskirts of Philadelphia that his characters all find virtue. Fluttermore's reform, it will be recalled, occurred after he had seen Clara and child, as in a vision, on his guardian's country estate; and the denouement, which included the touching family reunion and three betrothals, takes place in or near Mr. Campdon's garden — most of it in the arbor. But chauvinism and pastoral Columbianism are not issues in *The City Looking Glass.*

Yet there is a modulation of the familiar patriotic theme in native comedy. It lies in the argument between Raleigh, Sr., and Headstrong over the contemporary political issues of slavery, states rights, and the tariff. Certainly slavery and the tariff were of some international concern, as any economic issue in a large nation is, but all three were domestic matters, and in fact matters on which there was a broad schism between North and South. Headstrong, with his liberal Whig arguments for Abolition and the tariff, and against states rights, is representative of the Northern view, while the Virginian, Raleigh, takes the opposing Southern view. Such a contemporary issue is perhaps no more realistic than the chauvinism of Tyler had been. *The Contrast* accurately reflected a broad spirit of the time. Moreover, we cannot overlook Tyler's inclusion of the less outstanding domestic issues, such as pensions for war veterans. While Bird's domestic issues were as hotly debated in 1828 as those intense nationalistic issues immediately following the Revolution, they are perhaps more credible — and in that sense more realistic — because they are less sweeping, less ideal, less an outcry of the eighteenth-century optimism that pervaded postrevolutionary letters. Tyler's Manly had to be a mythical figure, the Patriot, or his pronouncements would seem impossibly idealistic. On the other hand, excluding the exaggeration inevitable in caricatures like Raleigh, Sr., and Headstrong, these characters are more realistic, more common, and certainly more palatable to modern taste, even though the issues they embody are now buried in history. What is more, they are comic figures. Manly cannot be.

One finds the familiar stock character types in Bird's play as in the earlier comedies, and as with Tyler, Dunlap, and Barker, Bird has modified stock figures from the comic tradition, adapting them to his own dramatic needs. He has made native persons of them — not a difficult task in most cases, since types like the tyrannical father, the romantic hero, and even the sentimental heroine are universal, as old as Roman comedy, and by no means indigenous to eighteenth-century British comedy alone. But Bird brings some depth to the tyrannical father by scratching Headstrong beneath the surface to reveal a selfish pride at the core of his motivation. He is a caricature in his stubbornness and hot temper, as his very name suggests; nevertheless, he is more fully developed than Tyler's Van Rough. Although just as foolish, he is more complex. So too is the sentimental heroine, Emma, more complex than her counterpart in *The Contrast.* Her sensibility is not the product of sentimental novels, like that of Maria Van Rough (or Lydia Languish). Her problems are not the result of a conflict between a sentimental idealism derived from fiction and life as it is. Her situation, be it melodramatic and sentimental, is one that sighs and patience will not dismiss. She is, however, a product of an upper middle-class boarding school: the well-educated, well-mannered, moral-minded young lady. As such, Emma Gall is an early example of a character who was to become a stock type in the drama and genteel prose fiction of the late nineteenth- and early twentieth-century America.

Bird was indeed sensitive to realistic native types, drawing upon the life materials around him not only for Emma but for his beaux. Bolt, Crossbar and Mossrose are quite different from Dimple or Fluttermore: they are Philadelphia bucks. There is nothing of Dimple's effeminate fastidiousness or Fluttermore's outrageous vanity about them. Their concern is all for easy women, drinking, and gambling — tavern joys. They do not affect a disdain for native fashions, manners, or the theatre. They affect no concern for a decline in social graces or aesthetic taste. They are wholly engrossed in satisfying their own sensual desires, to the exclusion of any social awareness. Unlike Dimple and Fluttermore, they are nothing more than home products: they have not returned from the grand tour to pronounce judgment on America's boorishness from the peak of a newly acquired refinement. Ravin tells Ringfinger, who is posing as a doctor,

> I have introduced you to the circle, where, to be as genteel as the rest, it is only necessary for you to dress well, to drink deeply, to be knowing with the ball and pasteboard, and to swear abominably. Follow them in their frolics, invite them to the tavern, let them be drunk often at your expense, and they will suffer themselves to be gulled out of sheer gratitude. You will find Bolt, the lawyer, an excellent introduction to all the rakes and profligates in town: therefore be tender of his purse. Keep up the Doctor; the character is respectable, and will be an excuse for want of manners.   [1.1]

Ned Raleigh is also a fresh figure, a modification of the stock rake. Barker had been the first to experiment with an American rake in his Rangely, and Bird continues further by introducing the rake as a regional character. Previously, playwrights had explored only the comic possibilities in regional differences. What is engaging about Tyler's Jonathan, for example, is his Yankee dialect. But Raleigh's Southernness is a matter of temperament: our interest is in his attitudes, in him as a person. Like Barker's Rangely, young Raleigh has a reputation as a rake with a devil-may-care outlook, and both are hotheaded, but for different reasons. Rangely challenges O'Connor to a duel with all the impetuousness of a romantic hero — quite out of keeping with his supposed reputation as an easy lover. But Bird is careful to establish that Ned Raleigh is the black-sheep scion of an old Virginia family, implying that his hot temper and his amorous nature are qualities of the Southern gentleman. Raleigh, Sr., says of his son,

> We are now, O'Slash, in the very town that witnesses the young rake-hell's extravagance; we shall be eye-witnesses, incog., of his vagabond tricks. I warrant me, he leaves sore noses and heavy pockets wherever he goes; for the boy is as free with his fingers as his money. [4.1]

And he adds, "Look, you O'Slash, he played the very devil at college, for all 'twas in a Yankee land. The wenches went mad for him" (4.1). The Irishman's reply, "Then he did but follow after the footsteps of his father; and I have heard the wenches went mad for him" (4.1), reveals that Ned's way is to be expected from a young Virginia gentleman — it was his father's way before him. Here in both Raleighs, Bird more clearly establishes a regional type than in the three Philadelphia bucks. Moreover, the proud, rash Southerner was to crystallize later in the century into as popular a figure in American drama and fiction as the boarding school Miss.

Yankee Jonathan undergoes a significant metamorphosis in *The City Looking Glass*, exchanging his farm garb for that of Tom Taffrail, first officer on board the *Liz. Lucky*. Unlike Tyler's Jonathan, Taffrail is given no farce scenes of his own, nor is he, as were Jonathan or Barker's Nathan Yank, a clownish figure. Yet his dialogue is fresh and entertaining, as in his exchange with Bolt in the tavern.

> *Bolt.* . . . my pocket was picked.
> *Tom.* Look ye here, Mr. What-d'ye-call-'em, you're not the only man that has been run foul of by unlawful cruisers in this here cursedty deceitful town. There's sharks and sword-fish enough, though they keep their heads under water, to nibble one's eyes out of his head, and run their snouts into one's keel. I have seen a painted pirate run up into a gentleman's head-quarters as naturally as into a Spanish West-India harbour; and I've found a counterfeiting knave carry his unlawful paper into a gaming house with as little conscience as a New York speculator sends pewter quarter-dollars to Hayti. — But what has that to do with your pockets? and how am I concerned in the matter?
> *Bolt.* I want you to help me take the cheat.
> *Tom.* With all my heart: and I hope you'll sarve me the same turn. You see this here Twenty; 'tis as fair as looking a Twenty as one may look on; but the banks have laid it under embargo, and I am recom-

mended to take the fellow that palmed it on me. I got it at the billiard table of an ugly knave, a cheating land rat, who, I am told is a great lover of this here tavern.   [5.1]

Some of Yankee Jonathan's speech mannerisms are here — the pronunciation of "sarve," the coining of "cursedty," the fondness for metaphorical elaboration, although the similitudes are now nautical. Moreover, Taffrail's view, beneath the gruff seaman's exterior, is essentially as moral and Puritanical as Jonathan's. He is as sternly disapproving of city vice as Jonathan was, even though as a sailor he has seen a great deal more of it. Although he is a little more guarded than Jonathan was in making friends, as in the scene above, he is nonetheless friendly and helpful like his progenitor. The contrast between Jonathan's simple, naïve honesty and Jessamy's affectation has been modified, now appearing as a contrast between Taffrail's rugged strength, physical and moral, and the character and appearance of the Philadelphia bucks.

This is not to suggest that he is excessively moral. The virtuous soul beneath a salty exterior is perhaps more romantic a concept than ever Tyler's Jonathan was. But Tom indulges his minor vices: he gambles in the taverns, and he enjoys his pipe and a gin sling. In fact, he finds Philadelphia rather dull, and sings "a dull song, which is about as good for a serenade as any that these caterwauling dandies sing under their sweethearts' windows."

> Oh Kitty Kid,
> Hilloa ho!
> Poor soul, she's dead,
> Hilloa ho!
> Have ever ye heern the tale or no?
> If not, give ear, hilloa ho!
>
> Sweet Kitty Kid, she was beloved
> By cruel Bobby Bullet,
> Who one day pulled his jackknife out,
> And stuck it in her gullet.
> And then he took her body up,
> And hove her in the river,
> The nasty mud to be her bed,
> The noisy wave her kiver.
> Poor Kitty Kid, Etc.   [3.3]

"Yankee Doodle" has undergone a fitting transformation.

Most inportant of all, however, is the role of this Yankee, for he is not a clown. He is not included simply for comedy, however amusing he is. Tom

Taffrail has an important dramatic function in the plot, since it is he who appears in time to rescue Diana from the assault of Bolt and his friends in 2.3, and later to thwart the kidnapping attempt upon Emma by Mrs. Gall and Ringfinger in 3.3–4. Thus, he functions to advance the plot, linking the doings of the underworld characters and their profligate friends to the love plots of Emma-Roslin and Diana-Raleigh. The point is, that Bird, while retaining those fresh comic qualities of the stage Yankee, has expanded his role, which up to this time had been more or less static as a clown. As simply a clownish type, the stage Yankee was obviously limited. Bird experimented beyond these limits observed by earlier playwrights.

Nathan Nobody is a new and intriguing type in native drama, a comic and witty servant whose prototype may be found in both the wise fool of tragedy, such as the fool in *King Lear*, and in the witty servant of comedy, such as Valentine's Jeremy in *Love for Love*. That he is a foundling, symbolized by his name, gives Nathan Nobody that detached objectivity one expects in the Greek chorus, and he functions both as a commentator upon and a participant in the action. One of the most delightful scenes of repartee occurs in the first act between Nobody and Roslin, who, under the spell of Nathan's impish raillery, momentarily drops his usual romantic, melancholy pose.

Ros. Will you be my servant, my squire, my page?

Nath. With all my heart, if you are not aristocratical.

Ros. And why not, if I am aristocratical?

Nath. Because I hate an American aristocrat as much as I hate an English travelling lord, or a French travelling count. They brag, talk of their ancestors, and show their coats of arms; which gives an honest man reason to suppose, that they have formerly had in the family more arms than ears; that their titles were registered in a jail book; that their family house was a dunghill, and their tree of genealogy a gallows.

Ros. A very republican spirit! Your observation should have shewn you that, in this land, no one enveighs against an aristocracy, unless he is poor. Give him a fortune, and he finds no rank above him to rail at. Properly understood, aristocracy means wealth, and republicanism poverty; and there is always a natural enmity between the poor and the rich. — Can you do anything besides joking and railing?

Nath. I can thresh your jacket, and dust your coat; I can ring your bell, say your prayers, and write your love-letters.

Ros. Indeed!

Nath. I can dun your debtors, lie to your creditors, speak evil of your enemies, and slander you with much praise.

Ros. Your wisdom is beyond your years and condition. — What wages will you have?

Nath. A new suit when my old one decays, which may be monthly; pocket money when I want it, which must be daily; and a theatre ticket when I like it, which shall be nightly.   [1.3]

Although the wit is excessive by Restoration standards, it is nevertheless bright, clever, and rapid. Bird reveals, through Nathan Nobody's quickness, a sense of fun, of pun — of sheer enjoyment of witty language for its own sake. None of the native playwrights before Bird rose to quite this level of ease and spontaneity.

Diana Headstrong is a far less captivating figure, yet in her own right she is charming and certainly important in the native tradition, emerging after 1800, of the willful heroine, the American Girl. By contrast with the passive Emma, Diana is remarkably vigorous, even more so than Barker's Louisa Campdon. Louisa, when pressed by her father to marry Fluttermore immediately, had resolved to find a way out, to rebel; but shortly afterward, when Sydney had proposed elopement, she was reluctant, agreeing only after he had taunted her with heartlessness. Diana Headstrong reveals no such uncertainty, for after a similar scene in which her father demands she marry Ravin at once, she not only decides to take action, but does. She goes out alone into the city streets at night to find Ned Raleigh and to urge him to clear his slandered name with her father. She is a heroine with wit and quick ingenuity.

For example, she reveals a capable control of the situation in 1.4, in which Ned Raleigh, having "saved" her from Ringfinger's mock assault of a week before, has called at the Headstrong home. Headstrong is polite and grateful to Raleigh, but his choice for Diana is Ravin, and he is somewhat upset by her obvious interest in the dashing Virginian.

Headstrong. And, so, Mr. Raleigh, you don't know Mr. Ravin?

Raleigh. I have not that honour, Mr. Headstrong.

Head. Why then, my excellent dear boy, you shall have that honour tonight.

Diana. Tonight! Bless me, Pa, I thought Mr. Ravin was secure for another week.

Head. How! secured for another week! Secured! Is this your gratitude? Is it thus you express your thanks to the man whose blood was shed in your defence?

Diana. My dear father, I am the most grateful woman alive; and it is my very tender regard for Mr. Ravin's health, that makes me dissatisfied with his premature visits. — I beg Mr. Raleigh's pardon for appearing to neglect his. I should certainly have expressed a similar anxiety; but —

Head. [*Aside.*] Good. I fear he grows particular. I like the boy well, but discourage him.

Diana. Fear me not, dear sir.

Head. We are pledged in honour to Mr. Ravin. Be civil, but distant — [*Exit.*]

Diana. I will, sir — Mr. Raleigh, my father was saying, I was rude in not expressing my anxiety for your health.

Ral. Be not uneasy. The indifference which keeps me at your side, is more agreeable than the solicitude that drives me away.

Diana. A false construction and a vain one.

Ral. Pr'ythee now, be not coquettish, or I shall be tantalizing. I know you are terribly fond of me.

Diana. We are told that knowledge is vanity and vexation; and we know that vanity is always vexatious.

One sees that Diana plays the game cleverly, matching insults with her admirer. A moment later, however, Raleigh ends the game by kissing her, just as Headstrong and Ravin walk in.

Head.⎫
Ravin.⎭ Humph!

Diana. The impudent wretch! I'll never forgive him.

Ravin. My dear Miss Headstrong, has your memory paid me the ill compliment —

Diana. Mr. Ravin! I beg your pardon. I am excessively glad to see you. How is your arm? You are pale, very pale: I declare you look very ill. You must have lost much blood. I am afraid you were incautious, to expose yourself so soon. You are very weak. [1.4]

The situation itself is farcically contrived, and much humor stems from the element of surprise — at the unexpected entrance and initially at Raleigh's bold kiss. Yet the composure of Diana, so quickly regained, and her ability to turn what seems a hopeless disadvantage into a minor victory dominates our attention. In a single ironic speech to Ravin she reveals her perfect control, and of course her wit.

But easily the most fascinating character in the play is Ravin. Here, for the first time in native comedy, a playwright has created a rake, in fact a villain, who is more than a flat stereotype. We have already, in the discussion of the tragic and melodramatic aspects of the plot, explored Ravin's motivation. In brief, he is as much motivated by the sheer love of intrigue and of power as by the usual greed and lust. Then too, there is the matter of revenge and honor.

Bird's conception of his rake as a villain seems evidence of the influence of Elizabethan and Jacobean drama. Ravin is melodramatically conceived, but so is Iago, and Ravin is never less — or more — than human. He is as frustrated and angered by his schemes gone wrong as he is invigorated by success. After his drunken attempt to seduce Emma is foiled by Roslin's effort, Ravin thirsts for revenge, but he blames no one but himself.

> This is it to be drunk!
> Drunk, drunk and mad! Lost, ruined, blown, and ruined!
> Game gone, — Diana, Emma, lost! both lost! —
> This cursed Roslin! — Out, ye hag, and get her;
> Fetch her again, or I will wring your neck;
> Fetch her: begone [*Exit Gall, terrified.*] But you shall
>   rue it well,
> Meddlesome boy! if there's in steel or lead
> A medicine will help me to revenge!   [2.6]

Beneath the comical bombast, Elizabethan in mode, lies realistic motivation.
 Yet the fustian bluster, after all, is but the impassioned extreme of Ravin's cleverness with language, the same wit we admire in other scenes, as when Ringfinger asks him whether he has been "sucked dry again."

> As dry as a fool's wit, and by a fool's wit too. There's an ass of a sailor, in citizen's clothes, that gets into all the decent hell-holes in town; and he makes as free cargoes of my pockets, as you did of your neighbor's before you went to grind marble at Auburn: And the fool won't deal in *domestics* neither; nothing but genuine prints or hard coin will serve his purpose. And tonight he has plucked and drawn me like a partridge.
>   [1.1]

It is Ravin's unaffected nature, the frankness of his response whatever the situation, that makes him convincing. We are able to empathize with him, to be concerned about him and of course about those around him because of this realism. Dimple and Fluttermore, while realistic in the sense that they reflect affected tendencies in city beaux of the period, remain caricatures, a means to a satiric end. Too much concern for the dramatis personae of a comedy, it is true, may destroy the comic mood, but this question has been met in the discussion of plot above. The mood remains comic overall.
 Wit and humor have been pointed out already throughout the discussion of this play; to quote further passages here would be redundant. It should be said, however, that almost every character, excepting only Emma, who is always serious, and Headstrong, rises to some wit or humor. *The City Looking*

Glass deserves praise as a comedy for its quality of diction, in spite of certain melodramatic or serious sentimental moments in it. Nathan Nobody, Ravin, Diana, Ned Raleigh — even Roslin — are consciously articulate. They entertain us by saying things cleverly. Others like Tom Taffrail and Ringfinger are just as entertaining, although the risible exists more in dialect or satiric character. The point is this: Bird never forgot the importance of language to the mood of comedy, and in spite of what are obviously youthful experiments with tragic elements in plot and character, the clever language of the play sustains its comic mood.

To sum up the contributions of Robert Montgomery Bird to native American comedy is to sum up generally the steady movement toward realism in character, plot, and theme in the forty years of native comedy since *The Contrast.* Following Tyler's experiments with a native type in Yankee Jonathan, Bird and his predecessors all drew upon the life materials around them for characters. Until Bird, however, no playwright had used a regional type other than as a novelty, whether in dialect or dress. Regional types like the Yankee and the New York burgher provided authentic local color, and by their very strangeness in contrast to the other characters, entertained the audience. They functioned principally as dialect types, such as the Irishman in British (and American) drama. But Ned Raleigh, the hot-blooded Southerner, is different from his fellow dramatis personae only in temperament and personality, and is in no way comically outstanding in dialect or dress.

The language of native comedies since *The Contrast* has moved toward realism, if one defines as realistic, middle-class characters in an American city sounding like middle-class characters in an American city, rather than cultured Europeans in a Paris or London drawing room. Stylized, artificial diction had been the rule in the comedies of Tyler and Dunlap, but it is minimized in Barker and Bird.[24] Yankee Jonathan's mannerisms had seemed so fresh, so different in the stilted environment of dialogue by Maria Van Rough and Manly. But Barker's stage people, for the most part, do not sound like characters in an eighteenth-century sentimental novel. Nor do Bird's except in the most sentimental scenes. More characters speak like native Americans, although not in as exaggerated a fashion as Jonathan. Yet there is some of Jonathan in several of Bird's characters, namely Tom Taffrail, Ringfinger, Mrs. Gall, the three bucks, and even Ravin at moments. In general, more of the dialogue flows naturally in the vernacular.

Another advance in the treatment of character, to be seen somewhat in Barker and strongly in Bird, is greater attention to realistic psychological and social motivation. Barker's heroine, Louisa, acts in defiance of her father, not because this is the role of the sentimental heroine — it is in fact the opposite — but because she is an independent, willful person: the girl of spirit, the American Girl. Maria Van Rough and Caroline Felton are flat, sentimental characters; they are predictable; they are sentimental ideals personified. While the same ideals motivate Louisa Campdon and Diana Headstrong, they conflict with other more practical matters. Social approbation, for example, is of first importance in the major decisions Roslin, Emma, Ned Raleigh, Raleigh, Sr., Diana, and Headstrong make. The actions of these characters are accelerated or retarded by their social consciousness, by their awareness of society about them. An erring Charlotte Manly was immoral in Tyler's play, as was Racket in Dunlap's. But an erring or rash Diana, or Roslin, are less conscious of the immorality of their behavior than of the possible social disapprobation it might incur.[25] An honorable reputation and a good family name were not to be risked for the hasty passion of the moment. By rounding out his characters more than his predecessors, by dealing with them as complex human beings, Bird encourages interest in them as such, and not merely as the dramatic means to thematic ends. In particular, perhaps, a class consciousness, a sense of social as well as moral responsibility motivates these characters, and because of this the play is really the first example of social comedy. The ways of society were primarily satirical targets for those playwrights before Bird, whose interest was chiefly in defending certain ideals, whether sentimental (as all were), patriotic and chauvinistic, or whatever. But an examination of Bird's themes finds him tending away from the general and the ideal, and moving toward the concrete, the particular, and the social.

For example, the favorite theme of vanity and affectation is barely present in *The City Looking Glass.* One might possibly consider Ned Raleigh's hellfire ways as an affectation, but Bird makes little of this, and within the play the only one concerned is Ned's father, Raleigh, Sr., whose principal worry seems to be that Ned might be disgracing his family. As to the three bucks, they represent Philadelphia beaux, and Bird devotes a scene to their activities on the street at night (2.4). They are on the prowl for women, and after first encountering a Negress by mistake, providing some broad humor, they then accost Diana Headstrong. These three are not conventional drawing-room fops, and the scene paints a realistic if frightening picture of Philadelphia streets in that period. Furthermore, the taverns they frequent prove to be the hangouts of counterfeiters and pickpockets like the Garket brothers (Ravin and Ringfinger).

Or take the familiar theme of patriotism. Tyler viewed decadent foreign affectation as not only immoral but unpatriotic, and although Chesterfieldian libertinism is singled out as the chief enemy, the accusation is a sweeping, general condemnation of European sophistication. For Tyler, morality and patriotism were all but synonymous. Turning away from patriotism as anti-British chauvinism, Dunlap sought to heal the rift between England and America. Colonel Duncan fought bravely as a patriot — he who was not even born in the colonies — but now urges peace and love, the international brotherhood. In Barker's play the broad patriotic theme reappears as General Campdon praises the American navy for its victory over the Mediterranean pirates. Yet General Campdon also argues that it is the responsibility of every patriotic citizen to keep informed of national affairs — a practical, realistic maxim to insure an intelligent electorate.

But in Bird's play there are no military characters, no patriotic sentiments, no democratic idealism, except in a brief passage (1.3) in which Nathan Nobody criticizes the so-called American aristocracy as much as the English and French visitors. The issue is as much a matter of social class consciousness as of American republicanism: the haves viewed from the gutter of the havenots. And finally, what political issues there are, are concrete internal, domestic affairs. The inclusion of the brief debate on the issues of slavery, states rights, and the tariff realistically reflects contemporary national interests. Perhaps most important is that such broad national themes in both Barker and Bird do not interfere with the comic business at hand. Barker, like Dunlap and Tyler, is somewhat interested in inculcating the moral through sentimental situations of betrothal and family reunion. Bird, on the other hand, is far more interested in his characters as people. Entertainment rather than moral edification is primary.

Certainly the stage settings have moved away from the limiting confines of the drawing room and the mall. Dunlap, by getting the most out of his household setting (Mr. Racket's home in New York) had conveyed a more realistic picture of upper middle-class domestic life in that city than Tyler had been able to. Both Barker and Bird moved out even further from the traditional drawing-room setting. Barker succeeded in painting a realistic portrait of what was suburban domestic life in Philadelphia of the early nineteenth century, while Bird, peopling his cast with some underworld characters in addition to "rakes and profligates," explored the seamier side of life in the Philadelphia streets, taverns, and bawdy houses. Bird was in fact well ahead of his time in drawing upon this realistic material, since credit for the first play about lower life in the city is given to Benjamin Baker, whose *A Glance at New York* did not come out until 1848 — twenty years after Bird's unpublished and unproduced comedy.

In conclusion, it would seem that Bird, and Barker before him, were consciously working in a native tradition of comedy. Tyler, to be sure, had no native precedent to guide him, and the wonder is that he did draw so successfully upon native materials for theme — anti-British chauvinism and Columbian idealism were the spirit of his time — but more especially for character. Dunlap, fresh from London, and with a knowledge of contemporary British drama as well as of the British tradition as a whole (a knowledge that Tyler was surely deficient in), recognized the vitality of native materials in Tyler's comedy, and was able to incorporate them into the form of the British sentimental comedy with more skill and polish than Tyler had. Barker and Bird were unquestionably sensitive to that native tradition, as brief as it had been, aware of the fresh appeal of realism, most particularly in character type and dialogue, and they sought consciously to develop it. To Bird must be given the credit for bringing a greater depth and complexity of motivation to characters, and for sensing that realism would be ettered until character motivation ceased to be dominated by sentimental or patriotic idealism. A pervading social as well as moral awareness marks *The City Looking Glass* as the first true native American social comedy. It is ironic that it should have been unperformed professsionally, and unpublished for so long. Because of this, the play was never an influence on dramatic literature of its time. But this does not cancel out the fact that Bird was consciously working within the emerging tradition of native American social comedy.

4

Forty-Five Years of Experimenting
Nine Minor Comedies, 1789–1834

THE nine plays to be considered now are of somewhat lesser quality than the three examined in chapter 3. Although they are of miscellaneous form — including comedies, farces, musical farces (or farcical operettas), and even one semihistorical drama — they are representative of native "comedies" in the period between *The Contrast* (1787) and *Fashion* (1845) and are important as evidence of the developing tradition. Six of the nine saw the stage (designated by an asterick in the list below), and three of these remained popular for a number of years.[1] Obviously these six plays, especially those which survived for a time, were an influence per se — or at least could have been — upon the developing tradition. But this does not discount the importance of the remaining three unproduced plays, which serve by their substance to corroborate the presence of an emerging native tradition and that their authors were aware of and clearly working within it. It is unnecessary to examine each play in any depth. To touch lightly and go on will suffice to flesh out the skeleton of development we have seen thus far, substantiating what has already been outlined as the mainstream of realism in the emerging native tradition. The nine plays include: *The Better Sort* (anonymous, 1789), Samuel Low's *The Politician Outwitted* (1789), J. Robinson's *The Yorker's Stratagem* (1792),* John Murdock's *The Triumphs of Love* (1795),* Lazarus Beach's *Jonathan Postfree* (1807), A. B. Lindsley's *Love and Friendship* (1809; performed during the 1807–8 season at the Park Theatre),* Mordecai M. Noah's *She Would Be a Soldier* (1819),* Samuel Woodworth's *The Forest Rose* (1825),* and Cornelius A. Logan's *Yankee Land* (ca. 1854; first performed 1834).*

Six Produced Comedies

J. Robinson, author of *The Yorker's Stratagem; or, Banana's Wedding* (1792),[2] was a member of Hallam and Henry's American Company. He him-

101

self played the role of the West Indian Negro, Banana, in the two-act farce's only performance, at the John Street Theatre on April 24, 1792. Quinn mentions the play only briefly, noting accurately that its importance is in being the first native play with a Negro character to reach the stage.[3] However, the Negro had appeared in drama in Low's comedy, to be discussed below, and even earlier. John Leacock had used Negro slaves in *The Fall of British Tyranny* (1776).[4] But neither of these plays was produced. Leacock was the first to explore the comic and pathetic possibilities of the type by grossly caricaturing certain Negroid features (e.g., large mouth) and by attempting the "Guinea" dialect, as the following passage shows:

> *Lord Kidnapper.* . . . What's your name?
> *Cudjo.* Me massa cawra me Cudjo.
> *Lord K.* Cudjo? — very good — was you ever christened, Cudjo?
> *Cud.* No, massa, me no crissen.
> *Lord K.* Well, then I'll christen you — you shall be called Major Cudjo Thompson. . . .
> *Cud.* Tankee, massa, gaw breese, massa Kidnap.
> *Sailor.* [*Aside.*] What a damn'd big mouth that Cudjo has — as large as our main hatch-way —
> . . . .
> Aye, he'd tumble plenty down his damn'd guts and swallow it, like Jones swallow'd the whale.   [4.4]

The plot of *The Yorker's Stratagem* relies on a Yankee trick — in fact a number of them — and, simply, is this. Amant, a New Yorker, comes to the West Indies, seeking Miss Bellange, a beautiful heiress he had met at her New York boarding school. Fingercash, her cruel and avaricious guardian, hopes to gain control of her fortune, and in the meantime will not give his permission for her to marry. Furthermore, he is forcing his own daughter, Louisa, into a marriage with a West Indian Negro, Banana, who is heir to a large sugarcane plantation. Disguised as a foolish Yankee named Jonathan Norrard, Amant manages to dupe Fingercash, with the help of that merchant's young accountant, Ledger, who is Louisa's true love. In the end, Amant gets Bellange and her fortune, Louisa and Ledger are united, and Banana happily returns to his mistress, Priscilla ("Prissey"), and their child, Quacka.

While Robinson's farce has none of the emotional loading of the slave issue, being set in the West Indies and involving West Indian Negroes, we can see that his concept of the Negro is shaped by some familiarity with the American Negro, slave or not, as he appeared to most whites then, and as he was to be portrayed in much literature of the coming nineteenth century. Banana is a carefree lad, and he is naturally tenderhearted, as we see in his deep love for

Priscilla and Quacka. But he is not very intelligent or stouthearted. He fears his mother, who forces him to agree to the marriage with Louisa, obeying her largely because it is the easiest way out of a situation too difficult for him to solve: "Niber mind, I will marry de fine lady Louisa for please my mumma, and go lib wid Prissy and poor little Quacka for please myself" (2.1).

When he approaches Louisa, Banana is awed and frightened by being in the white home as a suitor, and while the "Guinea" dialect is difficult to read, the scene would provide some broad humor on the stage.

> *Ban.* [*Timidly approaching Louisa.*] Suppose you no bex [i.e., box my ears], I will tell you one tory; I lobe a you, I lobe a you, like a peppa pot my heart do burn, a burn a like a fire coal, put you yi [i.e., eyes] sweet upon me, sorry fo' me, sorry fo' me, sorry fo' me do, or I da go dead like a one pig.
> [*Enter Ledger from a closet with a pistol.*]
> *Ledg.* Say that again, you scoundrel, and I'll send this bullet through your head.
> *Ban.* O Lord, Oh! — [*Falls down on his face.*]
> *Ledg.* Offer to squall and I'll — [*Points the pistol at him, Banana looking up with terror.*]
> *Ban.* Lod, I dead a ready. [2.2]

Pure farce of course, but effective, and dependent wholly upon the dialect type. Banana's comic qualities are very much those of the stereotyped Negro in American literature during the nineteenth century and up until very recently.[5] His emotions are close to the surface, he laughs and cries easily, and his eye-rolling, head-bobbing, and yassuh-ing were the trademark of the stage Negro from Mister Bones of the minstrel show to Step-'n'-fetch-it of the motion picture. The comic type, then, sees the stage for the first time in Robinson's *The Yorker's Stratagem* in 1792.

The first true American Negro character on our stage was Sambo, in John Murdock's *The Triumphs of Love; or, Happy Reconciliation* (1795), a social comedy in the sentimental mode about Philadelphia Quakers.[6] Produced at the Chestnut Street Theatre on May 22, 1795, this four-act comedy was one of two native dramas that season. The other, *The Female Patriot* (1795), was by Mrs. Susannah Rowson, a well-known British author of the novel, *Charlotte Temple* (1791). It is likely that Mrs. Rowson, then a member of Wignell and Reinagle's company, and who had been sympathetic all along with the American cause, was instrumental in persuading Wignell to produce Murdock's awkwardly constructed play. But in fairness it should be said that *The Triumphs of Love* was a highly occasional play, for its themes ranged over such contemporary issues as slavery, Quakerism, the whiskey rebellion, patriotism, and the security of America under a democratic system; and, too, it provided a good role for Wignell himself in Peevish, a caricature of the jealous husband.

The plot is based on the theme of the prodigal son. In this play he is George Friendly, Jr., who has been "given" to his uncle (after whom George is named) for upbringing. The uncle is not a Quaker, and the main story involves his efforts to convince George's father, Jacob Friendly, that the young man will turn out all right, that it is natural for any young man, Quaker or not, to sow his wild oats. Jacob, however, banishes and disowns his son, having seen him drunk. But in the end father and son are happily reconciled. In one of the second plots, George's friend, Maj. Harry Manly, a revolutionary hero, seeks to marry Rachel, George's sister. But Jacob Friendly refuses to sanction her marriage to anyone but a Quaker. The crux of this problem of Quakerism is amusingly summed up in the uncle's comment:

> Parents have not a positive right in every instance, to cross their children in marriage matters: — Here are two young people whose affections are mutual; and who are ready and willing to pull off their shoes and socks together, and you won't let them. [2.1]

When Jacob retorts that it is the Quaker law, his brother adds: "You are a virtuous and valuable people; but you should not set yourselves up in opposition to other people so much" (2.1). Rachel's problem is, of course, happily resolved at the end. It is clear even from this brief synopsis that Murdock is aware of social problems — realistic problems in the city around him. The stock tyrannical father is here religously motivated, and not socially or economically, as is more usual in the British tradition. Using the form of traditional comedy, Murdock has drawn realistically on native characters and themes for his play.

Yet Murdock was also drawing from the new native tradition as well, particularly in conceiving his fops and his military figure. Trifle and Careless are both patterned after Tyler's Dimple: dandies in the American hybridized version of the rake-fop. (So is George Friendly, but he "reforms" at the play's end.) The essence of Trifle's vanity and effeminacy is captured in his first grand entrance. He sweeps onto the stage, minces up and kisses George's hand with a flourish, and then proceeds to babble on about a captivating mulatto girl, a "yellow piece of perfection" he had been pursuing, before he was overturned by a dog chasing a hog. George teases him about this, and in the same scene drolly accuses his sober friend, Maj. Harry Manly, of vanity in "dangling that fine affair [sword]" at his side. As we might suspect, Manly — drawn in the image of Tyler's revolutionary hero — replies in dead earnest:

> No, George . . . I feel a conscientious pride in wearing it, for these reasons: — it has been my trusty friend in the hour of danger; and the

first moment I girded it on this side, I subscribed my name to our glorious independence, which I will support while I have breath.   [1.2]

Later, when George suggests that Manly elope with Rachel as a solution to Jacob Friendly's antipathy, the major is shocked by what he sees only as a dishonorable plan, to which George cavalierly replies: "Ha, ha, ha, honour indeed! do you talk of honour in love matters? Love is not to be restricted" (1.2).

Murdock's treatment of the Negro slave, Sambo, is as perceptive as his probing of Quaker customs. Sambo is of course presented as a comic dialect type, but with some pathos, arising perhaps from Murdock's own abolitionist sympathies. As a dramatist, Murdock was interested in the Negro as a comic stage type, but he was also interested in the social problem of Negro slavery, as the following excerpt will show. George has ordered Sambo to carry a note to one of his mistresses, and as he leaves the room, Sambo observes him singing:

> Sweet let me trifle time away,
> And taste of love 'ere I grow grey.

Sambo. Eh, eh, eh, dare he go sing like a mocky bird. Massa George berry good to poor foke; he gib great deal money away; but he drom rogue for gall; he keeps he tings berry close too: he not tell Sambo he secrets; but Sambo be drom cunning for all dat. Now I take dis to Missey Sopey Suds; berry well; den Missey Sopey Suds gib it to somebody else; Sambo know all about it; how Sambo wish he had a rich quaretoe old uncle, like Massa George. He be a drom rogue among fair sex too. [*Looks at himself in the glass.*] I tink I berry handsome fellow: — look much like a gemmen; we Negro improbe berry much. [*Dances and sings.*]

> Sweet let me trife time away,
> And taste of lub fo I grow grey.   [1.2]

Later, in act 3, George returns to his lodgings to find Sambo, whom he had recently freed, cavorting drunkenly in front of the mirror. He defends Sambo's behavior against the criticism of Trifle, who views the Negro as typical of the irresponsible, freed slave. Since the three bucks, George, Careless, and Trifle, had themselves been drunkenly baiting a watchman on the street, George maintins that, as a human being, Sambo has as much right to carouse as they do.

The Triumphs of Love, then, may be seen as drawing upon the native tradition newly established by Tyler, yet experimenting with more native types, some of them dialect (there is a German watchman and an Irish servant), and moving toward more particular social and political themes. As in the case of most comic playwrights after Tyler, Murdock took his play out of the drawing room and, in some scenes, into the streets of the city, searching for greater social realism in scene as well as in character and them. Unlike many comic dramatists since Tyler, though, he includes no Yankee character.

A. B. Lindsley's *Love and Friendship; or, Yankee Notions* (1809) [7] is not a typical "Yankee play" (a play whose action revolves solely about the Yankee character), but is representative of many that worked the refreshing Yankee figure into an otherwise stock sentimental comedy. Lindsley, who was a member of Cooper's company at the Park Theatre, succeeded in having his three-act comedy produced during the 1807–8 season.[8] Although the play is amateurish and relies on stock sentimental situations and characters in large measure, it is interesting in that the scene is in Charleston, South Carolina, and in that Lindsley has increased his Yankee characters to four from the usual one.

There is the Bostonian gentleman, Seldreer, who is stranded in Charleston without funds. Other than being a New Englander, though, he exhibits no real Yankee characteristics. His man, Jack Hardweather, is a Yankee sailor who has been put out of his seaman's work by the embargo of 1807–9 (a realistic contemporary detail). There is also Captain Horner, the Yankee skipper, who is, like Seldreer, destitute of funds and hopeful of peddling his cargo of notions to get underway once more. Finally, there is the clownish Jonathan, Horner's man, and a swapper of sorts himself.

The play also has a college fop, possibly the first of this native type on our stage. Dick Dashaway is a hot-blooded, Southern gentleman — the forerunner of Bird's Ned Raleigh in *The City Looking Glass* — who is vain, whose speech is fashionably punctuated with "demme's," who is quick to challenge a rival to a duel, and who spends his money recklessly and his days drunkenly at his "Club." His Negro slave, Harry, provides some broad humor in aping his master.

> Eh! he de gone; I s'pose he no could wait. Now if I no feara ole massa come and play de debil wid me for true, I do like young massa Dickey, and make little julep for myself. [*Mixes liquor, sugar, etc.*] — Heigho! bess for me for happy I can; so now no massa bin here, I 'joy myself, and do de same like massa, on'y I no git drunk.   [1.2]

Yet Harry's conception is also somewhat sentimental and pathetic, for later, when he sees Dashaway reel drunkenly back from his club, he sighs, "Heigho! what wicked worl dis white man worl be for true do! No like de negur countrey; no do such ting dere; no hab rum for git drunk and fight. I wish neber bin blige for lef it. I bin happy dere" (2.3). Here, and in earlier passages of "Guinea" Negro dialect quoted above, one misses the consistent touch of later masters of "plantation" Negro dialect, such as Joel Chandler Harris and Mark Twain. But it is still the beginning of the tradition, and these early playwrights at least recognized the inherent comic possibilities in the stage Negro.

The plot of *Love and Friendship* is a version of the familiar pattern in sentimental comedy. Seldreer, stranded in Charleston without funds, is in love with Augusta Marcene, but she is to marry Dick Dashaway, whose unscrupulous father (he had cheated Seldreer's father in Boston in the past) is eager to marry his son into the fine old Marcene family. Seldreer, upon learning that his rival, Dashaway, is the son of the man who had cheated his father, challenges the fop to a duel. But the duel is never fought, for Dashaway's father, learning that Augusta refuses to marry Dick because she loves Seldreer, has Seldreer jailed for failure to pay up a note he holds. Nevertheless, Portrain, a friend of Seldreer's manages to get him released, and Horner promises to lend Seldreer the passage money so that he and Augusta can sail to Boston. A last minute effort by Dashaway's love, Miss Lightlove, who shows Augusta a forged certificate of marriage between herself and Seldreer, is exposed. In the denouement, Marcene is convinced that he has been taken in by Dashaway, and consents to a marriage between Augusta and Seldreer. Seldreer generously forgives the Dashaways, and Mr. Dashaway, touched by this gesture, seriously repents his ways and returns the cheated money to Seldreer. At the very end Jonathan delivers a letter from Seldreer's father in Boston, announcing that he will be coming to Charleston for the nuptials.

The love intrigue is rather busy, and the whole play hastily put together. Its real comic strength lies in the excellent Yankee dialect.

> [*Enter Capt. Horner, Jonathan following with a basket on one arm, containing some apples and potatoes; in one hand, a string of dried apples and onions; in the other a piece of cheese and a bottle.*]
>
> *Capt. H.* Come along, I say, Jonathan; what dewe you walk so nation slow for? Staren and gapen at everything you see, I s'pose, bayn't you? — You rotten fool you, ayn't we got as fine things in Boston and Newport as any on 'um here? And then there's New-York outshines um all; she's the capsheaf. Take special care of the examples and don't lose none on 'um, Jonathan.
>
> *Jon.* Why, Capun Horner, you walk so tarnation fast the old dragon couldn't keep up with you; I'm sure I kayn't; and no wonder 'f I dewe lose sonethen' — why you'd beet daddy's old leaden hoss all holler; darn my skin, 'f you wouldn't dewe it clear as mud.
>
> *Capt. H.* Never seem tewe mind it, Jonathan, you'll git yuste tewe me byme bye, my heart 'f wax; but we're got enamost up tewe the shops, and it's time for um tewe open; and 'f I sell my notions well, Jonathan, we'll buy a dram. [1.1]

Lindsley, with his actor's eye for costume detail, included the splendid description in the initial stage direction above, capturing the image of the Yankee
peddler so well. The dialect here in the dialogue between two Yankees is
excellent. A few moments later, the Yankee sailor, Hardweather, joins them,
and Jonathan, hoping to barter his notions, offers him a taste of them.

> *Jon.* I'll venture tewe draw the tap, and let you jist taste on't.
>
> *Hard.* Oh the land lubber! talk about taps. [*Aside.*] Don't trouble
> yourself, brother Jonathan, I'll set all trim for you before you'll say Jack
> Robinson. [*Takes his bottle, stuffs apples and cheese in his pockets, breaks
> neck off bottle.*] Here's success to Columbia's sons, commerce and free-
> dom, and may the eagle have a shot in the locker 'till doomsday, and a
> jolly tar to heave it ahead, with a gallant officer at the ensign halyards
> of all our national ships, to stand by and bouy up, but never to haul down.
> [*Drinks off the liquor and sets the bottle down.*]   [1.3]

In this scene the Yankee peddler is tricked — outwitted by a Yankee tar, a
familiear comic device in Yankee plays. Through Hardweather's vigorous
dialect, Lindsley has captured another fresh, realistic native type: the American (or Yankee) tar. It is interesting to note that the Yankee, whether New
England peddler or sailor, has penetrated into the South by the early nineteenth century, bringing with him his unique gifts of dialect and humor. These
rough, bumptious farce scenes are indeed the real strength of Lindsley's play.

Mordecai Manuel Noah's *She Would Be a Soldier; or, The Plains of Chippewa* (1819),[9] which premiered at the Park Theatre on June 21, 1819, is a
three-act comedy set against the background of the American campaign on
the Canadian plains, in which Generals Jacob Brown and Winfield Scott were
triumphant over the British. It captures some of the moment of the actual
battle in both scene and summary, particularly in 3.1, in which the romantic
hero, Lenox, describes the victory in precise detail to his commanding officer.
But the main plot is a love triangle set in Christine's village and in the
American camp. Like Barker and Woodworth, Noah is successful with his
romantic, pastoral effects of the village setting, the peasants, and the rustic
feast, including "pastoral and fancy dances." Noah's comedy reveals the urge,
seen in the comedies and tragedies (or romantic melodramas) of other native
playwrights (James Nelson Barker and Henry J. Finn) during the first quarter
of the nineteenth century, to exploit national and patriotic themes.[10] Earlier
playwrights had alluded to contemporary national issues of course, but had
not based their plays entirely upon them. The obvious exceptions are Tyler
and Low, whose work in one sense may be seen as representing the *end* of
the period of revolutionary drama (e.g., John Leacock, Mercy Warren, Hugh
Henry Brackenridge), in which the plays were political satires — closet
dramas.

The plot of *She Would Be a Soldier* is refreshingly simple, in spite of being conventionally sentimental. It relies upon the old device of romantic disguise. Jasper, an American farmer of French birth, who had fought for America while in the French army, is marrying his daughter, Christine, to a prosperous Yankee neighbor, Jerry Mayflower. But Christine detests the bumpkin, who, although he is "a *brevet* ossifer in the militia," is really a cowardly lout. Her love is all for Lieutenant Lenox, an American officer, who has been residing with Jasper while recuperating from his wounds. Lenox is summoned back into service to fight in the coming battle of Chippewa. Determined to avoid a marriage to Jerry, Christine disguises herself as a man and secretly slips off to follow her lover to camp. When she arrives she observes Lenox, once a schoolmaster, talking with the general's daughter, Adela, a former pupil of his. Not realizing that they are old friends rather than sweethearts, Christine silently denounces Lenox as false and enlists in the army. During her first guard duty, outside the general's tent, she hears Lenox within singing a love ballad to the general and Adela. In a rage she throws down her weapon and attempts to enter the tent, but she is seized by other soldiers, who suspect her of being a British spy. Subsequently court-martialed and sentenced to execution, Christine stubbornly maintains her male disguise, sentimentally choosing to die rather than endure life, as she thinks, without her Lenox. But of course all ends well, for her identity is discovered an instant before the scheduled execution, and she is happily reunited with Lenox, with the consent and blessings of Jasper and Jerry, who have both turned up at the camp.

In the subplot Noah introduces without a doubt the most memorable British fop in American drama since Tyler's Dimple: Captain Pendragon, who, with his French servant, LaRole, is placed in a hilarious farce situation. The two are ordered by an Indian chief to discard their uniforms and to don war paint and full Indian regalia for the coming battle of Chippewa. Pendragon objects vociferously:

> Why, this is the most impertinent and presuming savage in the wilds of North America. Harkee, sir, I'd have you to know, that I am a man of fashion, and one of the fancy — formerly of the buffs, nephew of a peer of the realm, and will be a member of parliament, in time, . . . Mr. — Red Jacket. Paint my face, and fight without my clothes? . . . Put rings in my nose? a man of taste, and the *ne plus ultra* of Bond-street, the very mirror of fashion and elegance?

But threatened with being roasted alive if he does not obey, he takes some comfort in resolving to "caricature" the Indian, and almost cheerfully agrees: "Come along — courage, LaRole. We'll fan the Yankee Doodles in our best style, and then get a furlough, and be off to White-Hall, and the rings in our noses will afford anecdotes for the bon-ton for a whole year" (2.l). The even

funnier consequences of all this nonsense occur after the two have been captured by the Americans and are being interrogated in the presence of the
beautiful Adela. Not in the least dismayed by his grotesque appearance or his
ignominious capture, Pendragon rises to heights of vanity.

> *Adela.* As I live, an Indian dandy!
> *Pen.* A lady? [*With an air of fashion.*] Ma'am your most devoted slave
> — inexpressibly happy to find a beautiful creature in this damn'd wilder-
> ness. You see, ma'am, I am a kind of prisoner, but always at home, always
> at my ease, a-la-mode St. James — extremely rejoiced to have the honour
> of your acquaintance. A fine girl, LaRole, split me!
> *LaR.* Oh, oui, she is very fine, I like her ver mush.
> *Adela.* Pray, sir, may I ask how come you to fancy that disguise?
> *Pen.* Oh, it's not my fancy, 'pon honour, though I am one of the fancy;
> a mere *russe de guerre.* We on the other side of the water have a kind
> of floating idea that you North Americans are half savages, and we must
> fight you after your own fashion.
> *Adela.* And have you discovered that any difference exists in the last
> affair in which you have been engaged?
> *Pen.* Why, 'pon my soul, ma'am, this Yankee kind of warfare is
> inexpressibly inelegant, without flattery — no order — no military ar-
> rangement — no *deploying* in solid columns — but a kind of helter-skelter
> warfare, like a reel or a country-dance at a village inn, while the house
> is on fire.
> *Adela.* Indeed?
> *Pen.* All true, I assure you. Why, do you know, ma'am, that one of
> your common soldiers was amusing himself with shooting at me for
> several minutes, although he saw from my air, and my dodging, that I
> was a man of fashion? Monstrous assurance, wasn't it?   [3.1]

While Noah is successful with Pendragon's British speech mannerisms and
with LaRole's French dialect, he makes no attempt to give the Indian any kind
of dialect. Dialect was used largely for comic effect or to delineate characters
of a lower — usually economic — order. Conceived in the romantic image of
the noble savage, the chief speaks the flawless, dignified English of a schoolmaster. When, for example, Pendragon is irately puzzled by the Indian's
reference to the king as "my father" and demands an explanation, the chief
calmly responds: "What should I mean, young man, but to inquire after the
health of my father, who commands my respect, who has honored me with
his favours, and in whose cause I am now fighting" (2.1).

The Yankee, Jerry, is in the tradition of the clown, but he plays an important
role as a suitor for the heroine in the Lenox-Christine-Jerry triangle. This is

the first time that a Yankee is given such a role. What Jerry lacks, however, is the hint of winning shrewdness behind his country naïveté, nor does he reveal the usual fundamental moral goodness inherent in most stage Yankees. Furthermore, while most stage Yankees are more bluster than actual courage, he is shown to be a genuine coward, having retreated ignominiously at the Battle of Queenstown — which he regards, without any qualms of conscience, as a joke. He has, as we might expect, that gift of extended rationalization, and he is thus in the tradition of stage Yankees who prefer talking to fighting, given the choice. At times his dialect can be convincingly realistic: "O, fiddle-de-de, I don't mind how larned she [Christine] is, so much the better — she can teach me to parlyvoo, and dance solos and duets, and such elegant things, when I've done ploughing" (1.1). But he lacks the consistent freshness and verve of Tyler's Jonathan or even Low's Humphry. Noah seems curiously ambivalent about his status, too, for although as a wealthy young farmer, Jerry is seen as the social equal of the other principals (Jasper regards him as a desirable son-in-law in most respects), he is relieved at the end when Lenox wins Christine. Jerry is quite happy to be returning to his own village to marry Patty, the weaver's daughter, "though she can't crack a bottle nor bring down a buck" as Christine can (3.4). Yet Noah gives him a full part in the plot, and his presence contributes in the traditional way to the play's broad humor, with one exception. Jerry is not a means of satirizing (through contrast) manners, foreign or domestic.

Both women in *She Would Be a Soldier* are interesting figures, although Christine is obviously the more remarkable. In her brief role, however, Adela is seen to be a spirited, imaginative, and witty girl. When Lenox, her old master, first meets her at camp, she responds to his teasing greeting with some flippant irony:

> *Adela.* I am delighted to see you, dear Lenox; you are still as gay and amiable as when you taught your little Adela to conjugate verbs, and murder French; I heard of your gallantry and wounds, and imagined I should see you limping on crutches, with a green patch over one eye, and a wreath of laurel around your head, a kind of limping, one-eyed cupid.   [1.3]

When Lenox asks if she is prepared to "endure the privations of a camp," she replies:

> Oh, it is delightful! it is something out of the common order of things, something new — such echoing of bugles — glistening of firearms, and nodding of plumes — such marchings and countermarchings — and such pretty officers too, Lenox.   [1.3]

She goes on to describe a skirmish she had witnessed, during which she had been fired at by Indian, the bullet shooting off her hat plume. Admitting she had been frightened at first, she maintains that she had quickly recovered, for "courage is something like a cold bath; take the first plunge, and all is over" (1.3). Adela is a charming mixture of witty coquettishness and enthusiastic tomboyishness — a new native character.

But Christine, the heroine, is easily the most unique character in the play. The daughter of an old soldier, she has been taught to shoot. Yet she is capable of wit, as when she twists the sighing Lenox, who who wishes to sketch her before he leaves for battle:

> Why, what a statue you are making of me. Pray, why not make a picture of it at once? Place me in that bower, with a lute and a lap dog, sighing for your return; then draw a soldier disguised as a pilgrim, leaning on his staff, and his cowl thrown back; let that pilgrim resemble thee, and then let the little dog bark, and I fainting, and there's a subject for the pencil and pallet.   [1.1]

At camp, in disguise of course, she enlists as a soldier in the ranks, scoffing at the suggestion that she should be a drummer or fifer — "though small, you will find me capable" (1.3) — and she is able to perform the musket drill with ease. Early in the play, Jenkins, a friend of Jasper's, refers to her intelligence and education as a possible deterrent to any happiness in a marriage with someone like Jerry.

The passive sentimental heroine was simply an inadequate type for native dramatists, largely because she could not personify the essence of American independence, of common sense in other words. Christine is, granted, a kind of frontier woman in her physical capabilities, but in other respects she is a sentimental figure. Filial obedience is a major consideration for her, yet good sense will not permit her to accede passively to her father's wishes merely because he is her father. By training her in soldiership, Jasper has encouraged her independence. Reason is all, and reason tells her she cannot love someone like Jerry. In a broad sense, reason and good sense send Jerry back to Patty, a more suitable mate; and at the patriotic and nationalistic level of meaning in the play, good sense convinces the captured Indian chief to return to his tribe and to keep the peace with the Americans henceforth.

The significance of Christine's character is not that she is a bold, spirited heroine alone, but that Noah has given her a part in which these various qualities are revealed in the action. That the American Girl must make up her own mind has been a theme seen in earlier comedies, but that she is able to do something about it, or at least try to act independently and not just talk about it, is an important dramatic advancement in this play. The Yankee and the fop, who in earlier plays were good comic types, were nonetheless rather static figures, not given much participation in the plot. By expanding their roles, the dramatists were reaching for greater realism. It was inevitable that playwrights move in this direction once they had taken their comedies out of the drawing room.

One of the most popular Yankee plays in the pre-Civil War period was Samuel Woodworth's *The Forest Rose; or, American Farmers* (1825),[11] which premiered at the Chatham Theatre in New York on October 7, 1825. The play was acted periodically throughout this country, as well as in London, until 1866.[12] Woodworth called it a pastoral opera in the 1825 edition, and it is representative of the genre of musical farce, increasingly popular after 1800, for it uses incidental and occasional solos and duets. Unquestionably, the enduring success of this two-act farce may be attributed to the Yankee character, Jonathan Ploughboy, first played by Alexander Simpson, and later by such renowned Yankee actors as George Handel ("Yankee") Hill, Henry Placide, J. L. Silsbee, and Dan Marble.[13] As one might suspect, the humor is broad and farcical, resting primarily upon a Yankee trick in the second act. But the dialogue is surprisingly good in general, natural and lacking the stylized, stilted quality of many plays in the period. It must be added, too, that much of the comedy's charm (like that of Noah's) lies in its pastoral setting, for Woodworth sets his plot in the New Jersey farmlands, on the farm of Miller. In the background may be seen the village spire, complete with clock, which strikes periodically during the play, tracking the course of the action from dawn till dusk.

The plot follows a stock romantic formula, involving the reuniting of separated lovers and the unmasking of the licentious villain, the hybridized rake-fop common to many early native comedies. The heroine, Lydia Roseville, with her brother, William, have been living on the Miller farm since they were orphaned. Both have known something of city life but are happy in their pastoral environment — particularly William, who is in love with Miller's daughter, Harriet, a witty and somewhat coquettish country maid. While Harriet is fond of William, she is unwilling to marry a farmer, for she longs to see the fashionable city Lydia often speaks of. Lydia had experienced an unhappy love affair with Blandford in New York: his family had refused to let him marry a girl of "plebeian blood," and Lydia would not consent to his proposal of a secret marriage, returning instead to the farm, without telling him of its whereabouts.

To the nearby village come Blandford and his foppish friend, Bellamy, in search of Lydia. In brief, Bellamy falls in love with Harriet's virginal freshness, and after failing to get Miller's permission to take her to New York with him, plans to abduct her. To this end he gives Jonathan some money, ordering the Yankee to lure Harriet (Bellamy's "Forest Rose") into the woods, where he plans to seize her and take her to his sloop, moored nearby. As much as Jonathan wants the money, however, his conscience will not permit him to do such a thing. But his sweetheart, Sally, suggests that they substitute her Negro servant, Lydia Rose, disguised of course as Harriet.[14] In this way they will deliver to Bellamy a "Forest Rose" and "keep the purse instead of the promise" (2.4). Harriet is told of the plan and agrees to play a part. That evening, during a village dance held at Miller's farm, Harriet is heard screaming for help in an adjoining woods. Miller and William rush off, to return with Bellamy and "Harriet" — the Negro in veiled disguise. Accused of villainy, the fop maintains that "Harriet' has consented to run off with him, to which "Harriet" nods silent assent. Miller and the rest are shocked, but at the last minute the "Forest Rose" is unveiled — to Bellamy's horror — after which the real Harriet appears. In the denouement, Jonathan and Sally keep the money, Bellamy is driven off in disgrace, and Miller unites William and Harriet, and Blandford and Lydia. Closing in song, Miller and company sing praises of American farmers, "lords of the soil."

Jonathan Ploughboy is really the heart of the play, for his comic presence not only enlivens the action and serves as a native contrast to the vain fop, but it acts as a dramatic catalyst, an agent in forwarding the action of the love plots. He is formerly from Massachusetts, and when his sweetheart, Sally, teases him, he threatens to "burn . . . [his] shop, pack up . . . [his] duds, and go back to Taunton to catch herrings for a living" (1.2). He is the adventuresome Yankee, now settled prosperously in New Jersey, working: "a little in the marchant way, and a piece of a farmer besides" (1.3). But while he is shrewd beneath his naïve exterior, and while he can "calculate" as well as the next fellow, he is honest, or protests he is.

> *Bland.* What do you sell?
>
> *Jon.* Everything; whiskey, molasses, calicoes, spelling-books and patent gridirons.
>
> *Bland.* With which you contrive to shave the natives?
>
> *Jon.* No sir; everybody shaves himself here. There is no barber nearer than Paris.
>
> *Bland.* You don't understand me. By shaving I mean making a *sharp* bargain, or what your parson or deacon might denominate cheating.
>
> *Jon.* I wouldn't serve a negro so. But as to the parson or deacon, folks say they are pretty cute that way themselves.   [1.3]

Blandford does not quite know how to take Jonathan: "Confound your stupidity or shrewdness, I know not which to call it" (1.3). But the British fop, Bellamy, concludes he is "a clodhopper that knows his letters. Been to Sunday-school, I suppose. A real aboriginal, 'pon honor. Wonder where he was caught?" (2.2). Jonathan simply "calculates" that the two gentlemen are "a little cracked" (2.2), and in spite of Bellamy's judgment, manages to outwit the "white-gilled, baby-faced gentleman from New York" (2.4). Despite his clownish, muddling way, Jonathan wins Sally, outwits the city fop to keep the purse, and brings together the two pairs of romantic lovers. In creating this amusing character, Woodworth has molded many of the traditions of the stage Yankee into one, for Jonathan is the naïve-but-shrewd clown, the Yankee trader and swapper, the stammering yet eventually successful lover, the moral yet skeptically critical citizen, and the straight-faced, yarn-spinning comedian.

Woodworth's basic theme, suggested by the play's subtitle, *American Farmers,* is romantic and nationalistic. Its long life on the stage is an indication of the play's strong appeal to America's tastes in character, setting, and themes. The romantic triumph of the American farmer over the British fop may also be seen as a reflection of American reaction to the sharp criticism by foreign visitors in the early-nineteenth century. Bellamy is, as most stage fops before him, both an object of and an agent of social satire, as when Harriet, pretending utter naïveté, asks him where city folks keep "their creatures — the geese, the calves, and the pigs" if the houses are "so close together."

> *Bel.* The geese, you must know, are mostly seen in termtime, flocking round a marble house in the Park, where they generally get confoundedly plucked before they are aware of it, in which particular your little city much resembles my native London. The calves and donkeys, are principally found in your Broadway, and in our Bond-street. As for the other animals you mentioned — the pigs — I believe New York is the only place where they enjoy the freedom of the city.
>
> *Har.* You spoke of *donkies,* sir; does that mean the same thing as dandies?
>
> *Bel.* [*Aside.*] Humph! Not quite so simple as I imagined. Perhaps you, sir, can answer the lady's question.
>
> *William.* The two words, I believe, are derived from the same *root.* The real genuine dandy, however, is an *imported* animal; and, the breed, having been crossed in this country, the full-blooded bucks command but a low price in the market at the present time. [1.1]

The witty double entendre is very effective here, and somewhat surprising in the rural setting. William and Harriet, who embody both pastoral virtue and the gift of wit, are of course romantically conceived characters. Harriet is a strong-minded, intelligent, and witty heroine. At one point she asks her father, with tongue-in-cheek, for permission to go to New York with Bellamy, whom she has known for only a matter of minutes. Even the wordly Bellamy is disarmed by this maneuver. She is another figure in the emerging tradition of the American Girl, or the girl of spirit.

Beneath its idyllic charm, and not to detract from that engaging quality, the play's theme is a restatement of the familiar old one of native worth, but here dressed up pastorally, suited to the romantic taste of the nineteenth century. William, Harriet, Miller — even Jonathan, who farms as well as keeps shop — are glorified American farmers, embodying such virtues as honest industry, social equality, and moral uprighteousness; and these positive, Columbian virtues are contrasted to the evils of the city, whether the social snobbery of Blandford's family, or the vanity, affectation, and licentiousness of the London fop. In spite of Woodworth's deliberate romanticizing of rural Americana in character, scene, and theme, the play is not wholly unrealistic, for it is drawn from native materials and is thus in the mainstream of American social comedy. Woodworth, like many playwrights after Tyler, had not only taken comedy out of the drawing room into the city, but into the country as well. And successfully.

The last play of the six considered in this first section of produced comedies is Cornelius A. Logan's *Yankee Land* [ca. 1854],[15] a two-act farce that was first produced in 1834 at the Park Theatre, New York. Although it survived in its original form until about 1854 (it was completely rewritten in 1846 by Leman Rede, and called *Hue and Cry*, with an entirely new dramatis personae except for the Yankee),[16] it is at best a poor sentimental farce. Nevertheless, it deserves attention here because it is typical of the numerous Yankee plays in the first half of the nineteenth century.[17] Seizing upon the great popularity of the stage Yankee, the Yankee comedians were paying playwrights well for almost any sort of a stage vehicle that had a strong Yankee figure in it. The plot mattered little so long as the play offered a dramatic setting for the Yankee role. It is therefore unimportant to give any plot synopsis of *Yankee Land*, except to say that it is built upon the device, common to much farce, of mistaken or lost identity. In the denouement, following numerous complications, the Yankee, Lot (Launcelot) Sap Sago, who has been told he was a foundling — discovered nude in an apple orchard — turns out to be the illegitimate son of Sir Cameron Ogleby, an English peer now residing in America. Lot is of course the whole play, and invites some attention.

The edition of the play used here gives a full costume description of Lot, showing him to be much in the usual image of the eccentrically dressed stage Yankee. He wears a "drab long tail coat; broad striped vest; eccentric trousers; straps and boots; yeoman crown hat; bright colored cravat." He does not deviate from the traditional clownish, semishrewd, semifoolish figure. At times the comedy is broad farce, when Lot, like Beach's Jonathan Postfree, stumbles into a room or bumps awkwardly into others. But at other times he is consciously witty in the usual earthy way, triumphing over the fop, Manikin. The newest development is in the Yankee's bawdy streak, and in this respect Lot differs strikingly from his Puritan forebears. For example, in a conversation with the elderly Miss Starchington, who affects a stiff prudishness to conceal her eagerness to snare a husband, Lot is amusingly insolent.

> *Miss S.* . . . What did you mean by calling me the mother of that bear?
> *Lot.* We call a bear's mother a dam —
> *Miss S.* What!
> *Lot.* Dam if we don't.
> *Miss S.* Did you say I was your mother?
> *Lot.* I don't know nothing about it. I was found in an apple orchard. You don't think I growed there like a tree, do ye? — Something must have been done with me afore I got there any how, and you might as well had a hand in it as any body else, you know. [1.4]

While the bawdy aspect is interestingly new, though not surprising considering the full exploitation given the stage Yankee as the nineteenth century drew on, the most significant feature is, as almost always, the dialect.

Lot's Yankee drawl, his exaggerated naïveté, and his superb way with the Yankee story, related to the tall tale, is superior to anything yet in native drama, as in the following elaboration of a bear hunt.[18] Josephine, the heroine, asks him what he did when the bear charged.

> *Lot.* Du? What I dun jest now.
> *Jos.* What was that?
> *Lot.* Shoved a bullet through his head with such all-fired force that I driv the ball clean through, and picked it up behind him.
> *Jos.* O Launcelot, my friend, that is stretching it too far. . . .
> *Lot.* Why, yes, I had to stretch considerable. — I had to gin the trigger an almighty hard pull.
> *Jos.* Now, Launcelot, I am certain that you did not even shoot at the bear; for I know that when you were here this morning, you left your rifle standing in that corner. How could you shoot without a rifle?
> *Lot.* I had a fowling piece, and the infernal machine never had a bullet in it afore, and its stomach seemed to turn agin it, for it squirmed and twisted so like the devil, that I was glad to fire it off to ease it. [1.3]

When pressed for a true account, Lot only exaggerates more delightfully.

Why, you see, there was nine of us, including your father, and we surrounded that animal. When he seed himself hemmed in, he wanted to sneak out the worst kind. He kept turning round and round, jest to make us think he wanted to chastise his tail; but he was only looking for an opening to get out of. I know'd what was passing in that feller's mind; so I jest stretched out jest so [*Acting it out*]. He come towards me, and I blazed away. I meant to hit him in the eyeball, but that crocodile hunter's gun was crooked, so I bored a new hole in his nose. That staggered him; and just then your father let slip, and that wound up his airthly affairs; and Harvy and I had him skun and slung on our shoulders before the sarpent know'd he was hurt.   [1.3]

The mannerism is close to that used by the Southwestern humorists of a little later period (Twain himself could have written it). It is lamentable that Logan, with his gift for Yankee dialect, could not have used it for more probing social satire; Lot Sap Sago is wasted in such a trivial farce. But insofar as he has developed even one aspect, native dialect, Logan has contributed something to the tradition, drawing upon the past and looking toward the future.

Three Unproduced Comedies

In 1789 there was published anonymously in Boston a comic operetta, *The Better Sort; or A Girl of Spirit*.[19] The music is more than incidental for there are in all eighteen songs, duets, or airs in the ten scenes of the play, each reflecting the thematic business in the plot at that moment. Boston had no legally sanctioned theatre until 1792, but aside from that historical fact, the author of this trifling afterpiece obviously had no intention of writing for the stage. He promises that if his reader has the patience "to read these fifty pages clean through,"

> his good nature [will] be awakened, when he finds that the conversation of the parties tends to some general point, that the unities of the Drama are not altogether violated, and that a PLOT is pursued and brought about.   [Preface, p. iv]

Yet, as insignificant dramatically as this "Operatical, Comical Farce" is, there are some developments in character and theme worth noting.

The plot involves Mira Lovemuch, a "girl of spirit." Her father is forcing her into an unhappy marriage with Alonzo Hazard, a sixty-year-old miser (Mira is only fifteen), whose reputed wealth Lovemuch admires. Mira, on the other hand, loves the poor but worthy Harry Truelove, and she is also much admired by Captain Flash, a British fop. In spite of her stubborn verbal resistance to her father's wishes, Mira's betrothal to Alonzo seems inevitable, when it is suddenly learned that the miser has lost his property "by dealing too extensively in the usury business." Moreover, Harry Truelove has just become a gentleman of means by drawing "the highest prize in the North Mills Lottery." The scene of the play is laid entirely in the home of Mr. and Mrs. Sententious, a wealthy middle-class couple, who are entertaining all the others that evening.

Mrs. Sententious is the most intriguing person in the play. Even though she is sketchily drawn in such a brief farce, she is the archetypal middle-class parvenu, the matriarchal ancestor of a race of stage wives who "mean to be remarked for splendour and luxury" because these are the steps "to the pinnacle of politeness and the tip top of the bettermost genii." Her misprounced French — "canal" for "canaille" — and her frequent grammatical blunders — "them is" — wound the sensitivity of her husband, who lectures her at every opportunity. But she only galls him further with such replies as, "The bettermost genii don't place the ton in mere words — it is in actions, and actions of high life and grandeur too — It is these that distinguish the better sort from the *canal*" (scene 1). And she gets her way, whether by winning in the bout of repartee, or as a last resort by pretending to faint, thus appealing to her husband's tender sensibility. Here in Mrs. Sententious, then, is an early conception of the middle-class parvenu, and down to the last detail, the mold for Mrs. Tiffany in Mowatt's *Fashion* and the many culture-starved caricatures to follow in American drama.

In Mira we have the American Girl, or the girl of spirit. Because the play is largely song and talk, with minimal action, we see Mira's resolve to "exercise my spirit" only during an argument (sung as a duet) with her father, in which she proclaims:

> *Alonzo!* the miser I cannot abide,
> To a whipping post, father, I'd sooner be tied:
> . . . .
> With my hand goes my heart, Sir, whenever I find,
> A youth of an open and generous mind   [Scene 2]

She concludes the verse with:

> In short, 'ere I'll wed such a fellow as he,
> A virgin I'll live to E——ter——ni——ty.   [Scene 4]

Fortunate circumstances, as one can see from the synopsis above, cheat us from ever seeing such steadfast independence tested, but this does not keep us from seeing the playwright's interest in the type of heroine he has created: the American Girl. The emphasis is on Mira's independence, her freedom to choose, to make up her own mind, and not on her wit or her ingenuity at finding a way out of difficulties imposed necessarily by social custom (i.e., a tradition of filial obedience). Such independence is the general pattern for later heroines of this type, although there is an increasing interest in wit and ingenuity.

Yorrick, in spite of being named for the traditional clown of British comedy, is a good Yankee, and is not really a clown. As traditionally, his dialect is spiced by vigorous, homespun colloquialisms — "can't hold a candle to," "of the first water," and "clean as a whistle" — and he sings a delightful ballad about a winter frolic, which ends with the following two stanzas:

> Now for Boston we prepare,
> And the night is cold and clear,
> And we're stowing close, we're stowing close, because it's
>   chilly weather
>   O then what fun we feel,
>   When the sleigh it takes a heel,
> And we're huddl'd, huzza! and we're huddl'd, huzza! and
> we're huddl'd brave boys, altogether.
>
> 'Tis then the ladies cry
> O lud! — O dear! — O my!
> And we scrabble, boys — we scrabble, boys, all from the
>   snowy weather:
>   Then in the sleigh again,
>   Do we scamper o'er the plain,
> And tantarra, huzza! and tantarra, huzza! and tantarra
>   sings ev'ry brave fellow.   [Scene 5]

A bit more genteel than Jonathan's version of "Yankee Doodle" in *The Contrast*, but it captures the Yankee spirit nonetheless. Yorrick takes a leading role in an argument with Captain Flash (the familiar contrast of native and foreign types) about the merits of American music, the conclusion of which sounds the theme of cultural (broadly, artistic) independence: "and ought not a *new nation* to have *new songs*? I wish some clever fellow would sit down and write us half a hundred" (Scene 5). But the most significant thing about this Yankee is that he is the social equal of the other characters. He is an invited guest at the soiree of Mrs. Sententious, along with Captain Flash, the (presumedly) wealthy old Alonzo, and the rest. His dialect is not always consistent in its Yankee flavor. But in its best moments it smacks of rural New England. Yet he does not play the foolish clown, and he more than matches Flash in their argument. His refusal to fight a duel with Flash reflects a touch of the clownish cowardliness increasingly seen in later stage Yankees, but he talks and laughs his way out of what would be a foolish duel. Dueling is, after all, foreign to the New World. Finally, it must not be thought that Yorrick's new social status in this play detracts from his Yankee-ness, for he abounds with the usual good-natured cockalorum, colloquialisms, and zest for life.

Samuel Low's *The Politician Outwitted* (1788)[20] is a political drama in the guise of a manners comedy. Low was obviously influenced by *The Contrast* in creating a Yankee character and in somewhat imitating the gossip and raillery scenes of Tyler. The play is not a good one, being rather talky, and it was, as Dunlap tells us, rejected by Hallam and Henry of the Old American Company.[21] Yet it reads fairly well, and as uneven as it is, the play reveals an experimenting with native characters and themes beyond its prototype.

Almost from the opening speech by Old Loveyet — "Ugh, ugh, ugh [*coughing*], — what a sad rage for novelty there is in this foolish world!" (referring to the new Constitution, to which, as an advocate of the Articles of Confederation, he is dogmatically opposed), we recognize that the play is a Federalist tract, with Trueman as the spokesman through whom Low defends the proposed Constitution. "The Constitution you hear so much noise about," Trueman tells Loveyet, "is a new government, which some great and good men have lately contrived, and now recommend for the welfare and happiness of the American nation" (4.1). Low's theme is as intensely polemic as Tyler's was chauvinistic. But Low's characters are not mere personifications of political sympathies. Trueman, who is politically an enlightened liberal, is otherwise satirized. He is a caricature because he is overenlightened, tediously spouting Latin phrases, alluding to classical authors, and using pretentious diction and tortuous syntax. Loveyet is also a caricature, for his arch political conservatism is far exceeded by his foolish refusal to admit his true age, which is upward of seventy. But Old Loveyet (the conservative "politician") is foiled ("outwitted") in his peevish efforts to prevent the marriage of his son to Trueman's daughter by a spiteful plan, motivated largely by his political differences with the more liberal Trueman, but also because Trueman openly scoffs at the old fool's efforts to conceal his true age. Loveyet not only refuses to admit his age (he is humorslike in his obsessive fear of being thought old), but he goes to ridiculous and uncomfortable lengths to prove he is under forty.

> *True.* Mr. Loveyet, you run on in such a surprising manner with your narrations, imprecations, admirations, and interrogations, that, upon my education, sir, I believe you are approaching to insanity, frenzy, lunacy, madness, distraction, — a man of your age —
>
> *Love.* Age, sir, age! — And what then, sir, eigh! what then? I'd have you to know, sir, that I shall not have lived forty years till next spring twelvemonth, old as I am; and if my countenance seems to belie me a little or so, why — trouble, concern for the good of my country, sir, and this tyrannical, villainous Constitution have made me look so; but my

health is sound, sir; my lungs are good, sir, [*Raising his voice.*] ugh, ugh, ugh — I am neither spindle-shank'd nor crook'd-back'd, and I can kiss a pretty girl with as good a relish as — ugh, ugh, — ha, ha. A man of five and forty, old, forsooth! ha, ha. My age, truly! — ugh, ugh, ugh.   [1.1]

Even in this brief passage we can see amusing possibilities for farce, for Low is not afraid to satirize Trueman's pompousness any more than he is Loveyet's humor. Moreover, the political theme, while clearly central, does not weigh the comedy down. Low sensed the humor even in serious political matters, which is as it should be in comedy. Nothing should be sacred, neither exaggerated patriotism nor reason.

However, all is not political in the play, for there is much effective satire of both the fashionable and the more domestic social life of New York in the period. Low achieves this in a number of ways. First, and most directly, Maria and Harriet, the two belles of the play, comment about social life. Fashionably bored by winter amusements, Maria complains: "You know, Harriet, I do most cordially hate dancing at any time; but what must one do with one's self these irksome, heavy, dreary Winters? If it were not for cards, visits to and from, and . . . " (1.3). A moment later she rails at "the sweets of domestic life" as

The large portion of comfort arising from a large winter fire, and the very pleasing tittle-tattle of an antiquated maiden aunt, or the equally pleasing (tho' less loquacious) society of a husband, who, with a complaisance peculiar to husbands, responds — sometimes by a doubtful shrug, sometimes a stupid yawn, a lazy stretch, an unthinking stare, a clownish nod, a surly no, or interrogates with a — humph? till bed time, when, heaven defend us! you are doom'd to be snor'd out of your wits till daybreak.   [1.3]

The satire, while more humorous than witty, is nevertheless effective. Maria's similitudes are as labored as those of her prototype, Charlotte Manly: "I am half of my time as motionless as Pitt's statue; as petrified and inanimate as an Egyptian mummy, or rather frozen snake, who crawls out of his hole now and then in this season to bask in the rays of the sun" (1.3) It is not effervescent wit, but it is wit. As we have seen, native playwrights were often more successful with less intellectual humor, and in the case of the Yankee character, Low is successful.

Humphry Cubb is a well-drawn stage Yankee. Always somewhat clownish, he nevertheless reveals a hint of shrewdness, and certainly a coarse honesty. Through Humphry's observations on what he sees as the awesome life about him in New York, Low achieves not only an amusing satire of the naïveté of this New England Yankee, but also criticizes city manners. The Yankee's commentary, like that of Jonathan before him, is the second method of social satire in the play. His best scene is that in which he converses with Worthnought, a dimple-like fop.

> *Hum.* My proper sirname is Humphry Cubb; why our family is the most largest family within the circumroundibus of fifty miles, and the most grandest too.
> *Worth.* Yes, the world abounds with Cubbs, just such unlick'd ones as you are; — there is a profusion of them in this city. — You must know, *I* am Dick Worthnought, esquire; a gentleman, a buck of the blood, and a — you understand me?
> *Hum.* Why, your family must be as big as mine, then; for I've seen hundreds of such Worth-nothing bloody bucks as you, since I've been in town. [4.2]

The farce follows the pattern set by Tyler's Jonathan, for Humphry amuses us by his long-windedness, his eagerness to relate his family affairs, his fondness for quoting proverbs — seldom accurately — his seeming inability to understand others, and his malaproprious diction. But Low's Yankee plays a more extensive role than did Jonathan, and his function in transmitting messages to and fro between the main characters furthers the plot.[22] As we might expect, his rough humor is refreshing in scenes which would otherwise bog down because of the stylized language of much of the dialogue.

This Yankee scene above, typical of many, reveals a time-tested comic pattern of repartee: the straight man's query (or comment) followed by a comic reply, which is always quick, and often puns on or otherwise satirically distorts the form or content of the query. Today the quick comic reply is often called the one-liner, yet it dates back as far as the call and response pattern of the leader and chorus in ancient Greek drama. More directly, it came from the witty repartee of Restoration comedy, and in America it was the very backbone of the minstrel show and, later, vaudeville comedy. Indeed, many so-called situation comedies on radio and television today rely heavily on this device, and in early native comedies the best scenes are generally those which use it. Granted that most of the early comedy was broad humor rather than wit, but such humor was successful, and we must conclude that it was indigenous to America, appealing naturally to our native sense of the comic. The early native playwrights took from the British tradition the technique of repartee, of verbal exchange, and adapted it to native comedy, making it, in a sense, peculiarly American in the process: American not in form, but in content — in the stuff of its broad, often farcical, humor.

Low's third means of presenting a comprehensive social satire is to increase the variety of scenes and to extend the range of character types, that is, by comparison to Tyler. *The Contrast* seldom leaves the drawing room, giving the audience only a limited view of city life. And, there are no street scenes, for the two outside scenes are set in "The Mall." *The Politician Outwitted*, however, contains seven different scenes in the street, one in a barber shop, and the rest in a total of seven different houses or lodgings. Through variety of scene, Low strives to create the illusion of a busy city. He does so likewise by offering a range of character types among the thirteen dramatis personae. *The Contrast* has nine. (Both figures exclude incidental servants.) Sheer number is, of course, no guarantee of dramatic success, but among his characters Low includes two elderly gentlemen, Old Loveyet and Trueman; two beaux, Charles Loveyet and Frankton; a Chesterfieldian fop, Worthnought; two belles, Harriet and Maria; two gossipmongers, the younger, Miss Herald, and the elder, Miss Tabitha Cantwell, who is also a vain, superannuated coquette; two Yankees, Humphry and Dolly, his former sweetheart, although she has renounced her New England heritage since coming to the city; a city-bred servant, Thomas, who contrasts well with Humphry, and who is Dolly's new boyfriend; and a French barber, Toupee, who is a good comic dialect type. Among the incidental servants is a Negro, Cuffee, who appears in two scenes but speaks only once in one. He is told to put down a trunk that he carries on his head as he walks along barefoot, and says to Humphry,

> Tankee, massa buckaraw; you gi me lilly lif, me bery glad; — disa ting damma heby. [*Puts down the trunk.*] — An de debelis crooka tone in a treet more worsa naw pricka pear for poor son a bitch foot; and de cole pinch um so too!   [5.1]

(As if the devilish — "debelis" — cobblestone streets weren't troublesome enough, the winter cold — "de cole" — hurts his bare feet.) The profanity contributes something to the comedy. Since the play was never produced, though, we can only speculate about the success of the dialect, which appears conventional. But Low's urge to experiment with a fresh source of comedy is noteworthy, and that source, the Negro dialect (West Indian or "Guinea"), is native and realistic.

The last of these three trifling, unproduced plays to be looked at is Lazarus Beach's *Jonathan Postfree; or, The Honest Yankee* (1807)[23] a three-act musical farce but not, like *The Better Sort*, a comic operetta, because the eight songs are chiefly decorative. According to his preface, Beach had written the "*petit* piece" for the stage, but he had submitted it too late in the season of 1806 for production, presumably at the Park Theatre in New York. It seems improbable, though, that Dunlap, then manager, would have accepted it earlier, for while the songs are fresh enough, the characters, other than Jonathan, are thinly drawn even for a light farce. The plot contains only one real incident, and there is not much farce humor — and none at all except when Jonathan is onstage. Nevertheless, as trifling a play as it is, the characters of Jonathan, the Negro servant, Cesar, and the aggressive mother, Mrs. Ledger deserve some brief attention here.

The scene is New York, around 1800, and the plot involves the Ledgers, once a family of means but now poor as the result of Mr. Ledger's bankruptcy. Mrs. Ledger, eager to retain her former status, is forcing her daughter, Maria, into an unhappy marriage with the wealthy Fopling, who has no intention of marrying the girl, only of seducing her. Living with the Ledgers is Maria's bosom friend, Sally Herdy, the daughter of a prosperous Connecticut farmer. Her board fee and what Young Ledger earns at a counting house are the sole income for the Ledgers. To New york comes Jonathan Postfree, Old Herdy's farmhand, to sell some cattle for Herdy, and incidentally bringing some letters from his neighbors to the city. Upon his arrival, Sally learns that her father will be coming soon to take her back to Connecticut, which disturbs her because she loves Young Ledger.

Fopling tries to hire the elderly Yankee to help him abduct Maria, but Jonathan angrily refuses any part in his immoral scheme. Later, Jonathan beats off the ruffians Fopling does hire, thus saving Maria. In the meantime, Jemmy Seamore (really Sally's brother, Jemmy Herdy) returns, having made his fortune at sea. He had once been an employee of Ledger's and had asked to marry Maria. But Mrs. Ledger had refused her consent to an impoverished nobody, driving him off. Now that Fopling's foul nature is revealed, however, she welcomes Jemmy as a suitor. Finally, Old Herdy arrives, overjoyed to find his son, whom he had believed lost or dead. Jemmy offers a generous portion of his fortune to the bankrupt Ledger, and at the end Sally and Young Ledger, and Maria and Jemmy are happily united, while Jonathan Postfree hastens back to Connecticut, bearing the joyful news to the homefolds.

Mrs. Ledger is a strong figure. As a woman who had known luxury and social prominence before her husband's business failure, she is now ruthlessly determined to regain that status at the expense of Maria's happiness, though of course she does not see it quite that way.

> *Mrs. L.* . . . Would you not be glad to see your mother in better circumstances? Would you not prefer a house opposite the Park, to this dirty lane we now live in? And would you envy me the pleasure of a coach ride with my dear son-in-law, Mr. Fopling? [She refers to him as her son-in-law before the marriage, it should be noted.]
>
> *Young L.* Dear mother, heaven knows I wish you all the happiness you can possibly enjoy; — but I presume, dear madam, to make yourself happy, you would not wish to make your daughter miserable.

> *Mrs. L.* Certainly not. I mean to make her happy too: she will have a great house to live in, a coach to ride in, and servants to wait on her; will not that be happiness?   [I.1]

When, a moment later, her husband ventures a timid questions, she cuts him with:

> *Mrs. L.* I say, sir, hold your tongue; you are no longer able to support me, and of course I am no longer under your control.
> *Old L.* I know *you* are not willing to acknowledged my authority; but my children—
> *Mrs. L.* You talk of authority over a family, when you have squandered the property that ought to support it. Fie on your authority! Let me hear no more of it.   [I.1]

Jemmy shares his fortune with the Ledgers, but in spite of this happy ending, Beach questions the value of the American Dream. He does so in the characters of the Ledgers and their situation, as well as in the figure of young Jemmy. The materialistic ethic that equates prosperity with happiness is clearly suspect. Mrs. Ledger is in some respects a descendant of Mrs. Sententious's, and another step toward Mowatt's Mrs. Tiffany and the many Mrs. Tiffanys to follow in later nineteenth-century drama and fiction — that tribe of aggressive, materialistic, often culture-mad mothers who are endlessly prodding their adamant children into "good marriages" or nagging their husbands toward "success." Whether or not Beach was sincerely disenchanted is not important. That he saw the comic potential in the social situation is what concerns us. The aggressive mother was obviously not an original type, for the British tradition is peopled with such matrons. But native playwrights successfully adapted the comic type to their own society because it was one in which social rank was largely determined by economic standing.

Of Cesar, the Negro servant, it need only be pointed out that he is treated in a comic yet sympathetic manner. He is the faithful old family servant, loyal to the Ledgers in good times and bad, and he is selflessly devoted to his "younga missee" Maria's welfare. Jonathan Postfree proves to be a little different Yankee in that he is an older man, devoted to his family, and not in any way interested in showing the girls what a virile lover he is (as Jonathan and Humphry were). Yet he is very much in the clownish tradition of the stage Yankee in his appearance — his rustic suit and bell hat, in which he carries his letters, tied up with yards of twine — and in his awkward behavior, as in tripping over the rugs when he enters the room.

> [*Getting up.*] What a posset do you keep these kiverlids on the floor for? a body can't go a step about your fine houses here, but he must be tripped

up by your plaguy kiverlids. Why, Sal, you have got proud enough, that you can't go without these plaguy kiverlids to walk on.   [1.3]

Without sacrificing his freshness as a unique comic figure, native playwrights like Beach were beginning to give the stage Yankee a more active role in their plays. Jonathan Postfree (like Humphry Cubb in Low's comedy) is given a larger share of the action, and in fact is involved in the single important incident of the play, in which he thwarts Fopling's plan to abduct Maria. These tendencies in character and theme, even in such trifling farces as this, are evidence of the emerging native tradition.

To sum up what we have learned from an examination of these nine minor comedies, first we have noted a strong urge to use whatever native materials were available — whether regional types, settings, or contemporary national issues, external and internal. But the earlier patriotism, synonymous with a kind of moral chauvinism, has given way to a more realistic awareness of social values, of problems to be solved at the practical level of common sense and social morality rather than the level of patriotic idealism. Adapting the British form of manners comedy, native playwrights quickly took the comedy out of the drawing room and into the city streets or the country.

They likewise modified stock comic types from the British tradition, peopling their plays with vigorous Americans, interested in their maturing society, oversensitive to foreign criticism (yet never deaf to it), and striving to promulgate the democratic principles for which the Revolution was fought. There are two interesting native characters to emerge. The first is the new American heroine, the intelligent, and often witty American Girl. Unlike the stock sentimental heroine, she is active rather than passive, and although she is a rebellious figure (usually against parental desires for her marriage), her inherent virtue and sound reason effect a happy compromise with the social forces against which she rebels. Such compromise is the democratic process. The second interesting figure is the social parvenu of one form or another. She is usually energetically pushing her children into wealthy, unhappy marriages, and her husband into greater debt with her lavish expenditures. In some cases she tongue-lashes him on to greater business success in her unceasing ambition to rise economically and thus socially — the two are synonymous for her. With wealth, of course, she can surround herself not only with material splendor but culture as well. Her rage is to be as chic and cultured as the prized European visitors she courts socially.

Of course the Yankee continues to stride ebulliently across the comic stage, and while he is given an ever-larger role in the plots, ceasing to be purely a dramatic novelty, he still reflects the same dualism of Tyler's Jonathan. He is always the caricature, yet at the same time he is the effective means of responding to satirical criticism of Americans by foreign visitors through the contrast of his appearance, manner, and views to those of Europeans (or Americans with foreign affectation). Fighting satire with satire, the Yankee always maintains his irrepressible good nature, his American humor.

Finally, the mode of comedy remains principally farce, with humor stronger and more successful than wit. Wit is, however, never wholly absent, although it never rises to the polished, intellectual level of the best European manners comedy. American types seem more concerned with *doing* than with talking elegantly.

5

Cultural Maturity and the Flowering of Native American Social Comedy: Mowatt's *Fashion* (1845)

ON March 24, 1845, only a few weeks short of fifty-eight years after *The Contrast*, Mrs. Mowatt's *Fashion; or, Life in New York* [1] premiered at the Park Theatre in New York. It is, of course, the terminal play in this study. We will therefore examine Mrs. Mowatt's comedy to find to what extent its dramatic structure, themes, characters, and wit or humor are in the mainstream of the emerging native tradition, hitherto traced from shreds of evidence in a motley assortment of comic pieces — yet nonetheless an emerging tradition when seen in total. All of these plays, in one way or another, owe something to *The Contrast*, and perhaps *Fashion* more than any, since it returns to the form of the drawing-room comedy of manners, a form which most of the interim playwrights must have regarded as either too restrictive, artificial in view of the social reality about them, or simply unsuitable for their peculiarly American humor. Mrs. Mowatt, however, returned to that form (although much of the comedy depends on farce humor), demonstrating a surprising competence in her first professional attempt.

Novice playwright though she was at twenty-six, Mrs. Mowatt had been busily supporting her ailing husband as a hack writer in New York since 1842. Under the *nom de plume*, Helen Berkeley, she had been contributing prose to such popular journals as The *Columbian*, The *Democratic Review*, *Godey's Lady's Book*, *Graham's Magazine*, and The *Ladies' Companion*.[2] In 1842 she published her first novel, a social satire like *Fashion*, although much inferior. Even this was hackwork — a novel written to order: The *New World* had offered a one-hundred-dollar prize for "the best original novel in one volume. The title must be *The Fortune Hunter*, and the scene laid in New York. The novel must be completed in one month, or within six weeks at the latest.[3] At about this same time Mrs. Mowatt wrote *Evelyn; or, A Heart Unmasked*, a sentimental romance she called "a domestic tale in two volumes." [4] Interestingly, it was not published until three months after her debut as an actress in 1845. The success of *Fashion* elevated Mrs. Mowatt's name above the mediocrity of her earlier reputation as a hack writer.[5]

In her *Autobiography* Mrs. Mowatt speaks reverently of the stage as the career "for which she was destined," referring to her keen lifelong interest in drama.[6] She was born Anna Cora Ogden, the tenth child of American parents, then residing in Bordeaux, France, in 1819. At five she made her debut in a French translation of *Othello*, playing a walk-on part she describes as "the sedate and solemn character of a judge." [7] The production was one of many she, with her brothers, sisters, and playmates, undertook as family entertainments. She did not, however, attend the professional theater until she was thirteen, for her family pastor had taught her that playhouses were "the abodes of sin and wickedness.' " [8] But her adolescent religiosity vanished immediately when, on her first visit to the theatre, she saw Fanny Kemble in James Sheridan Knowles's *The Hunchback* (1832). After her marriage to James Mowatt at fifteen, she continued her ardent childhood interests in reading and in writing verse and dramatic pieces, turning these talents into profit not many years later, when her husband's illness and business failure forced her to become a hack writer.

She was encouraged by the immediate success of *Fashion*. Moreover, she had already gained some experience in histrionics by giving public "readings" for some months with apparent success.[9] Thus Mrs. Mowatt took the advice of friends who urged her to take up acting. Her debut at the Park Theatre, on June 13, 1845, as Pauline in *The Lady of Lyons* (1838), Edward Bulwer's romantic comedy, launched a successful if brief career on the boards. Edgar Allan Poe, whom Mrs. Mowatt calls "one of my sternest critics," criticized *Fashion*, according to Mrs. Mowatt, as resembling "*The School for Scandal* in the same degree as the *shell* of a locust resembles the living locust." [10] But Poe praised her acting warmly.[11] There is, therefore, some credence to her own report, that after her debut performance, "it *rained* flowers; for bouquets, wreaths of silver, and wreaths of laurel fell in showers around us. Cheer followed cheer as they were gathered up and laid in my arms." [12]

For the next eight years, interrupted only by periods of illness, Mrs. Mowatt pursued her new career throughout many of the major cities in America east of the Rocky Mountains, as well as in the British Isles.[13] *Fashion*, which had run initially in New York for three weeks — and during the third, simultaneously for a week at the Chestnut Street Theatre in Philadelphia — ran for two weeks at the Olympic Theatre in London in 1850, during Mrs. Mowatt's engagement there.[14] Upon occasion she did act in her own play, playing Gertrude. But Mrs. Mowatt was reluctant to do so because she disliked the role.[15] In spite of her enthusiastic reception in other roles in London, she declined to play Gertrude there.

After eight hard yet successful years of acting on both sides of the Atlantic,

Mrs. Mowatt retired on June 3, 1854. Interestingly, her final role was as Pauline in *The Lady of Lyons*, the one in which she had made her debut and with which she had enjoyed a continuing success.[16] Mr. Mowatt had died in 1851, and Mrs. Mowatt, upon retiring from the stage, married William F. Ritchie of the Richmond *Enquirer.*[17] After 1861 she lived abroad, and died in London on July 28, 1870. During her years as an actress, Mrs. Mowatt wrote a second play, *Armand; or, The Child of the People* (1847), which was first produced at the Park in New York, September 27, 1847. Three years later at the Marylebone Theatre in London, Mrs. Mowatt's company played it for twenty-one consecutive nights as *Armand; or The Peer and the Peasant*, with many of the "offensive" antimonarchial lines expunged.[18] She continued to write after her retirement, publishing, among other works, two romantic narratives of stage life (drawn of course from her own experiences), *Mimic Life* (1856) and *Twin Roses* (1857). Both are sentimental narratives in the mode then popular. But her most valuable work is her *Autobiography of an Actress; or, Eight Years on the Stage* (1854).

The plot of *Fashion* is as follows. New York, about 1845. Mrs. Tiffany, a social parvenu, is impoverishing her husband, once a wealthy merchant (and still seemingly so), but now resorting to forgery to conceal his debts. Determined to be among the "eelight," the "upper ten-thousand," she has employed Millinette as her French "femmy de chamber," to instruct her in "*les modes de Paris*," as she entertains with lavish receptions and balls. To the Tiffany home comes old Adam Trueman, at the invitation of his old friend, Antony Tiffany. But the Catteraugus farmer's blunt, critical manner and his coarse garb immediately embarrass his hostess, who is entertaining two "drawing room appendages," T. Tennyson Twinkle and Augustus Fogg, and more important, Count Jolimaitre, to whom she is determined to marry her daughter, Seraphina.

Complications arise in that Mr. Tiffany is being blackmailed by his confidential clerk. Snobson knows of his forgery and demands Seraphina's hand. Moreover, Millinette has threatened to expose Jolimaitre, who is neither French nor a count. Thus, he must keep her silent until he can elope quickly with Seraphina. Yet he is intrigued by Gertrude's virginal freshness, and he suggests that she "remain in the family" after his marriage to Seraphina. Gertrude, Seraphina's governess, becomes suspicious of Jolimaitre's ungentlemanly behavior, particularly after he tries to force a kiss and then proposes that she become his mistress. Later, overhearing the count make a tête-à-tête with Millinette, her doubts are strengthened. Accordingly, she devises a bold plan to expose him in time to prevent his marriage. Contriving to get Millinette out of the way at the appointed time, Gertrude herself meets Jolimaitre in the darkened housekeeper's room, disguising her voice to sound like the French maid.

Unfortunately, they are followed there by the suspicious Prudence, Mrs. Tiffany's old maid sister, who then summons Mrs. Tiffany, Trueman, and Colonel Howard. Bluffing it through, Jolimaitre insists that Gertrude has had designs upon him all along and had lured him to the private rendezvous. His story is accepted, to the dismay of Trueman, who had hoped to find his granddaughter pure, and to the dismay of Gertrude's lover, Colonel Howard. Mrs. Tiffany, fearing that Gertrude is competing with Seraphina for the count, angrily dismisses her. On the following morning, however, after Gertrude has convinced Trueman of her innocence, he then bluntly smooths out the misunderstanding between her and Colonel Howard.

In the final act, Prudence gleefully announces that she has discovered a note from Seraphina, revealing that she has eloped with Count Jolimaitre. Although Mrs. Tiffany is disappointed at being cheated of a gala wedding, she is delighted to have the count for her son-in-law. Trueman is now assured that Gertrude is virtuous and that Colonel Howard loves her for herself (and not his fortune, about which neither Gertrude nor Howard know). Tearfully he informs her that she is his grandchild and unites her with the colonel. Gertrude then tells Mrs. Tiffany that Jolimaitre is an imposter, which she refuses to believe. But the matron is convinced when Millinette bursts in to confirm the truth, whereupon Mr. Tiffany moans that he is ruined. At this point, a drunken Snobson, furious at the news of the elopement, arrives to expose Mr. Tiffany's forgery, but his revenge is short-lived, because Seraphina returns, as yet unmarried, to get her jewels for Jolimaitre. In desperation, Mr. Tiffany implores her to save him by marrying Snobson. Then Trueman intercedes to save the day for all. First he drives off Snobson by informing him that, as a witness, he is an accomplice in the forgery. Next he generously guarantees Mr. Tiffany's debts, offering to reestablish him in business — but in a small town upstate. Finally, when Jolimaitre returns, Trueman promises to set him up in the restaurant business if the imposter will call upon all of his society friends in his proper attire: as a cook. The rogue cheerfully agrees, and all ends happily as Trueman thus abolishes fashionable affection of one sort or another.

As the summary reveals, *Fashion* reiterates Tyler's theme of native worth, but with some interesting modifications and advancements. Mrs. Mowatt is not just contrasting native worth, represented principally by Trueman and Gertrude, to fashionable, imported folly, represented by Mrs. Tiffany, Seraphina, and Count Jolimaitre. Such a fundamental contrast, as between Tyler's Manly and Dimple, is of course prominent. Certainly Mrs. Tiffany's headlong plunge into what she deems Continental customs, and the imposter-count's outrageous, foppish vanity provide the major situations for satire. Yet the fashionable practice of reckless spending, or, in modern terms, conspicuous consumption, is sensed as a widespread folly in New York (as Trueman's blunt, choruslike commentary indicates).

Mr. Tiffany, representative of one type of the new American man of affairs, has "melted down . . . [his] flesh into dollars, and mortgaged . . . [his] soul in the bargain " (2.1). He is desperately trying to keep up with his wife's lavish spending and to keep ahead of his numerous creditors. Mrs. Tiffany's hunger for the "jenny-says-quoi" in everything, while deliciously funny, is merely the frosting on the cake. The Negro servant, Zeek, apishly assuming foppish airs in his resplendent scarlet livery, knows nothing of foreign manners, beyond what little Millinette can teach him. He seems to represent the new Negro (perhaps the newly liberated Negro), whose status among his own race is a matter of gaudy dress, which will " 'stonish de colored population" (1). He is hardly a step beyond the crude stereotype of his primitive, bauble-infatuated ancestors in West Africa.

Even the "drawing room appendages" are home products. The bored pose of Augustus Fogg, scion of "one of our oldest families," as Mrs. Tiffany trills, bears no explicit foreign imprint. He is clearly the epitome of the idle American rich. His Philistine affectation, plus his single interest — food — echo those redoubtable virtues Washington Irving caricatures in the stolid citizenry of New Amsterdam.[19] Or, what could be more American that the poetaster, T. Tennyson Twinkle, whose new and utterly nonsensical philosophy of composition is founded upon the principle of mass production? "The true test of a poet is the *velocity* with which he composes" (1). And above all, Snobson's narrow greed, his hunger for the power and luxuries of wealth, seems peculiarly American. There is certainly the lightly satiric in his fashionable dissipation: "Bless me! eleven o'clock and I haven't had my julep yet?" (2.2). Yet mirrored in his clerk's dream of marrying the boss's daughter, and in his vow that "Six months from today if I ain't driving my two footman tandem, down Broadway — and as fashionable as Mrs. Tiffany herself, then I ain't the trump I thought I was!" (2.2), is the ugly image of the American-dream-gone-sour. It is a decadent extreme of the Jacksonian promise.

Foreign affectation, as it has been pointed out above, defines Mrs. Tiffany's character: her blatant denial of her own middle-class origins (she had been a milliner in upstate New York) and those of her husband (he, a peddler) now that she is numbered socially among New York's "upper ten thousand" is sufficient proof. So too is her absurb dependence on the coaching of her French maid in all matters of fashion. Yet her determination to marry Seraphina to Count Jolimaitre, to gain thereby the prestige of having a count for her son-in-law, or better still, a countess for a daughter, is not entirely a matter of foreign affectation. It is again a reflection of that same misguided aspiration seen in Snobson's dream, the energetic struggle of the New World "aristocracy" to graft on status that could never be hereditary, that had to be bought. Mrs. Tiffany's dream was of a cash-and-carry countess.

The satire of these affectations, some obviously imported but many just as clearly indigenous to the new American society, reveal Mrs. Mowatt's concern for a social problem rooting deeper than the surface of universal foibles and follies, the traditional target of comic playwrights. Examining the play's positive values, such as sane social conservatism, romantic (or sentimental) love, the dignity of honest labor, the republican principle of individual merit regardless of social class, and above all common sense — all embodied in Trueman and Gertrude, one finds it difficult to agree with Poe's criticism, that the play was merely a facile imitation of *The School for Scandal* and that its success was attributable to its theatricality: "the carpets . . . the ottomans . . . the chandeliers . . . and the conservatories." [20] Perceptive critic as he often was, Poe was perhaps too close to the problem of the jaded American Dream to see it beneath the bright glitter, which is, after all, part of the show in the tradition of manners comedy.

But *Fashion* is more than manners comedy. The heroine, Gertrude, and the hero, Adam Trueman, function as characters fully aware of the seriousness of the corrupted ethics underlying certain fashions in their society. Both are, in a sense, outsiders and therefore able to bring a more objective judgment to the pursuits of New York society. Both are independent, freed from the necessity of any compromise with folly as they see it. To them, the doings of Mrs. Tiffany's circle are not an artificial game, the rules of which they seek to learn, but a sign of moral corruption: the enemy. Gay though its comedy is, and preposterously happy though its ending is (almost inevitable in the light of Truman's romantic and sentimental conception as the old patriarch whose gruff exterior conceals a tender heart beneath), the play takes a serious view of folly and seeks to reform the attitudes responsible for it. Thus, *Fashion* is a social comedy.

In this respect it is closely related to *The Contrast*, yet it is, although not sixty years apart from Tyler's play, continents apart in its sophistication — in wit and humor, dramatic structure, and characters, indeed, in themes. One further point concerning theme must be stressed here, before proceeding to these other matters.

While Mrs. Mowatt is concerned with the contemporary problem of heiress-hunting in her mid-nineteenth-century society, her portrayal of Count Jolimaitre is never less than good-natured. He is perhaps no more comical than Tyler's Dimple, for all of Dimple's foppishness, vanity, and greedy opportunism are certainly Jolimaitre's. But there is no malice, no real evil in the cheerful rogue. He is not the enemy, as was Dimple, who represented Chesterfieldian libertinism. Instead, the satire points at American society, at the Mrs. Tiffanys, whose distorted materialistic values have led them down the paths of senseless fashion. It is an extravagance antithetical to the older materialistic ethic, that embodied such solid virtues as usefulness, industriousness, and thrift. Moreover, without the shield of an older nationalism and chauvinistic suspicion of foreign entanglements — social of course — the parvenu was vulnerable to the invasions of European fortune hunters.

Such a condition was central concern of Mrs. Mowatt's. Yet she reveals, particularly through Gertrude, an unusually tolerant attitude toward European customs. It is the parvenu's grotesque aping of such manners, mere mode without intelligence, that she views as misdirected. Trueman is likewise brusquely critical of such gross foolishness on the part of Mrs. Tiffany and her circle, but he is as severely critical of Mr. Tiffany's business practices, which are not imitative of Continental fashions. And Trueman, it must be remembered, is a caricature. His nature is to be testy and critical of any innovations, good or bad, that challenge his conservative, materialistic, and sentimental ethics. One cannot overlook the fact of his comic role, his satirical conception. Gertrude, on the other hand, reveals none of his righteous indignation, although her actions denote her sympathy with many of his views.

But hers is not the chauvinistic suspicion of all things European, an attitude one might expect had she been Tyler's heroine. Gertrude's sophisticated cosmopolitanism (admittedly somewhat unrealistic in view of her upbringing in Geneva, New York) reflects Mrs. Mowatt's own childhood in France and her later travels to Europe. In her *Autobiography* Mrs. Mowatt writes sharply of the American imitation of European manners as "mere caricatures." [21] Her criticism is dramatized well in the behavior of Mrs. Tiffany, who loudly reminds herself not to introduce her guests to one another (1) and in the extravagant overdressing of Seraphina, who, for example, wears a headdress, "a *lady's tarpaulin . . .* the exact pattern of one worn by the Princess Clementina at the last court ball" — at an afternoon drawing-room reception (1).

The point is then, that in the matter of theme, Mrs. Mowatt reveals what may be called a greater cultural maturity than we have seen in any of the earlier playwrights. Whether her own experience in Europe is responsible, or whether American society was finally beginning to outgrow the painful self-consciousness so marked in some of the early plays — or both — is not the concern of this study. That such cultural maturity exists, and in fact has been seen emerging from the beginning, from Dunlap's first conciliatory overtures toward England in *The Father* (1789), is what matters. Mrs. Mowatt's is indeed a sensible treatment of the old problem of foreign affectation, and she places the blame where it belongs. She does not resort to long, defensive harangues of a patriotic or sentimental nature. The Polonius of the piece, Trueman, is just that, a *comic* figure, who is himself at times aware of his hortatory excesses. With true comic spirit, Mrs. Mowatt rises above the inevitable prejudice of emotional nationalism, so frequent in earlier playwrights, to point out folly wherever she sees it, in Mrs. Tiffany, in Zeke, in Count Jolimaitre — even in Adam Trueman.

The dramatis personae of *Fashion* are an assemblage of delightful comic types, most of whom fulfill the promise of development in native types, in some cases in the native adaption of stock British types, traced in this study since Tyler's *The Contrast.* It would be difficult if not impossible to single out any one of the major characters — Gertrude, Mrs. Tiffany, Count Jolimaitre, Adam Trueman — as the best, for each has his special charm and all are successfully drawn. But first, the heroine.

Gertrude's situation is typical of the stock sentimental heroine since the creation of Indiana in Steele's *The Conscious Lovers.* She stands as the symbol of virtue, filial obedience, and patient, though not prolonged, suffering — she is too vital, too active to remain a passive victim of unfortunate circumstances for long. In adddition to these stock sentimental qualities, her character reveals those strong virtues of intelligence, independence, and a capacity for decisive action, which are identified with the girl of spirit, or the America Girl, seen emerging as a native type since Louisa Campdon in Barker's *Tears and Smiles* (1808). Moreover, she demonstrates a bright sense of humor and some wit, although the latter is minimally displayed, because Mrs. Mowatt's comic emphasis is on the farce scenes with Mrs. Tiffany, Count Jolimaitre, Snobson, and the like.

Her wittiest display, if brief, comes in the scene in which the bland Colonel Howard struggles to express his love for her. Secretly pleased, for she loves Howard, Gertrude is yet feminine enough to take advantage of his vulnerability, recognizing the age-old comic nature of the situation.

> *Gertrude.* . . . I think I informed you that Mrs. Tiffany only received visitors on her reception day — she is therefore not prepared to see you. Zeke — Oh! I beg his pardon — Adolph, made some mistake in admitting you.
> *Howard.* Nay, Gertrude, it was not Mrs. Tiffany, nor Miss Tiffany, whom I came to see; it — it was —
> *Gert.* The conservatory perhaps? I will leave you to examine the flowers at leisure!
> *How.* Gertrude — listen to me. If only I dared to give utterance to what is hovering upon my lips [*Aside.*] Gertrude!
> *Gert.* Colonel Howard!
> *How.* Gertrude, I must — must —
> *Gert.* Yes, indeed you *must*, must leave me! I think I hear somebody coming.   [2.2]

The situation itself is basically amusing, yet Gertrude's quickness to twit the mooning, stammering Howard is genuinely witty. Moments later, Count Jolimaitre finds her alone in the conservatory and clumsily attempts an embrace. But he is driven off by Trueman's hickory staff. Gertrude is quite capable of fending for herself, but she assumes the conventional pose of the helpless maiden. Thus she allows old Trueman his moment of glory, but not without a wittily ironic, "I do not know what I should have done without you, sir." (It is to Trueman's credit that he sees good-naturedly through her remark.)

Gertrude's almost fierce, independent spirit is the source of her strength and, as she confides to Colonel Howard, was her sole motivation for coming to New York. She wished to free herself from having all her wants supplied by the "two kind old maiden ladies" who had brought her up in Geneva. Although sharply aware of the folly, termed fashion, about her, she is in no way disenchanted with life itself, or in any way despondent. She adapts to the requirements of her new social environment without forfeiting any of herself. And more than this, Gertrude has a strong sense of duty and loyalty to her employer, Mrs. Tiffany. It is this, coupled with a sense of obligation to see that justice is done, that moves her to expose Jolimaitre, thereby protecting Seraphina, her foolish ward. Gertrude has no personal stake in the matter. Nor does she hold any personal animus toward the fraudulent count, whose affectation and scheming she regards with some ironical amusement, even though her sympathy for the possible plight of Seraphina is genuine. Although she is a country girl, and embodies therefore the romantic idea of pastoral virtue, Gertrude's shrewd assessment of Jolimaitre is remarkably objective: "This man is an imposter! His insulting me — his familiarity with Millinette — his whole conduct — prove it" (3.2). Her judgment reflects of course Mrs. Mowatt's own sophisticated cosmopolitanism, acquired in her travels abroad. It is this evaluation of fashion, and not the more usual categorical condemnation of European manners — all foreign influence — that marks *Fashion* as different from some earlier comedies, that makes it, in fact, genuine social comedy. Furthermore, in the historical line of girls of spirit, Gertrude is the first heroine to have been given the peculiarly objective role as defined above. The tradition of the American Girl has crystallized in her person: person, because Gertrude is that and not merely a stage convention.

Since we have already said much about Mrs. Tiffany in the preceding discussion of themes, it remains only to place her as the fulfillment of a development of the type seen emerging in native drama since Mrs. Sententious in *The Better Sort* (1792). Her social ambitions and pretensions, her bad English and worse French, and her domination of her husband all earn her the comic distinction of being the archetypal middle-class parvenu in American drama, the matriarch of her stage race to follow.[22] But Mrs. Tiffany, with her central role in the comedy of *Fashion* and her utterly ludicrous character, remains both the descendant of the race and the ascendant Queen Matron of them all. Even though Mrs. Tiffany is a satiric caricature, Mrs. Mowatt has fleshed out her person realistically — Mrs. Tiffany *is* New York parvenu society — and has expanded her role beyond the earlier sketchy presentation of a comic type. In spite of her shortcomings, which are the satiric target of the play, her driving energy, though misdirected, must not be overlooked. It is the wellspring of her life, that traditional middle-class virtue of aggressive industriousness that has been at the root of America's economic system since the Pilgrims abandoned communal farming in 1623.

There is no need, then, to elaborate further on what Mrs. Tiffany represents. Some brief attention may now be turned to how she behaves, particularly in terms of her dialogue, which, with farce situation, is a rich source of comedy. Her first entrance, as she sweeps onstage "dressed in the most extravagant height of fashion" to take charge of her domestics, is as representative as any scene.

> *Mrs. T.* Is everything in order, Millinette? Ah! very elegant, very elegant indeed! There is a *jenny-says quoi* about this furniture, — an air of fashion and gentility perfectly bewitching. Is there not, Millinette?[1]

And a few speeches beyond,

> *Mrs. T.* This girl is worth her weight in gold [*Aside.*] Millinette, how do you say *arm-chair* in French?
> *Millinette.* *Fauteuil,* Madame.
> *Mrs. T.* *Fo-tool!* That has a foreign — an out-of-the-wayish sound that is perfectly charming — and so genteel! There is something about our American words decidely vulgar. *Fowtool!* how refined. *Fowtool! Arm-chair!* what a difference!
> *Mil.* Madame have one charmante pronunciation. *Fowtool!* [*Mimicing aside.*] charmante, Madame!
> *Mrs. T.* Do you think so, Millinette? Well, I believe I have. But a woman of refinement and a fashion can always accomodate herself to everything foreign! And a week's study of that invaluable work — "*French without a Master,*" has made me quite at home in the court language of Europe! But where is that new valet? I'm rather sorry that he is black, but to obtain a white American for a domestic is almost impossible; they call this a free country! What did you say was the name of this new servant, Millinette?
> *Mil.* He do say his name is Monsieur Zeke.
> *Mrs. T.* Ezekiel, I suppose. Zeke! Dear me, such a vulgar name will compromise the dignity of the whole family. Can you not suggest something more aristocratic, Millinette? Something *French*!
> *Mil.* Oh, oui, Madame; *Adolph* is one very fine name.
> *Mrs. T.* A-dolph! Charming!   [1]

The comedy in such a scene is, as is traditional in satire of vanity (whether in fop or society matron), the result of irony. It arises from a tension between the character's self-view and the character viewed by other characters and the audience. But always undermining her delusions of refinement — unknown to her, of course — is Mrs. Tiffany's unmistakable American twang, "French without a Master" notwithstanding.

Like Mrs. Tiffany, Count Jolimaitre stands at the end of a developing native tradition (within the limited period of this study) of rake-fops. He too wears the comic laurel of his lineage. To review that tradition, one can profitably compare Tyler's Dimple to Woodworth's Bellamy. Tyler had of course initiated the tradition of the hybridized rake-fop, combining the two stock types from the British tradition. Dimple reveals the necessary sexual cynicism of the true rake, but that harshness is tempered by his foppish vanity, so extreme as to approach silliness. While Tyler stressed moral decadence and vain affectation more or less equally, later playwrights tended to play down the rakishness, though never eliminating it entirely, and to emphasize the absurd vanity. Such was true of Woodworth in creating Bellamy. Other rake-fops, like Barker's Fluttermore and Noah's Captain Pendragon, retain their essentially foreign affectation (that much of Dimple's blood flows in their veins) yet lose their vicious sexual cynicism. Virgin hunting, while never quite disappearing, becomes more and more fortune hunting, and while the stock rake in the British tradition displays a cynical sexual vanity, in the native American hybrid that vanity is transmuted to an exaggerated pride in the rake-fop's manner — his tastes, his dress, and his speech.

Count Jolimaitre thus considers himself absolutely irresistible to the ladies — God's gift to womanhood. But coupled with this is his awareness of the inherent comic situation of his own disguise. His clever asides spoof his real origin as an English menial.

> *Mrs. T.* Count, I am so much ashamed, — pray excuse me! Although a lady of large fortune, and one, Count, who can boast of the highest connections, I blush to confess that I have never travelled, — while you, Count, I presume are at home in all the courts of Europe.
>
> *Jol. Courts?* Eh? Oh, yes, Madam, very true. I believe I am pretty well known in some of the courts of Europe — *police courts.* [*Aside.*] In a word Madam, I had seen enough of civilized life — wanted to refresh myself by a sight of barbarous countries and customs — had my choice between the Sandwich Islands and New York — chose New York!
>
> *Mrs. T.* How complimentary to our country! And, Count, I have no doubt you speak every conceivable language? You talk English like a native.
>
> *Jol.* Eh, what? Like a native? Oh, ah, demme, yes, I am something

of an Englishman. Passed one year and eight months with the Duke of Wellington, six months with Lord Brougham, two and a half with Count D'Orsay — knew them all more intimately than their best friends — no heroes to me — hadn't a secret from me, I assure you, — *especially of the toilet. [Aside.]*   [1]

Mrs. Tiffany's naïveté naturally contributes to the comedy in this farce situation, yet the imposter's cheerful impertinence, capitalizing on that innocence, while at the same time ridiculing himself in the Falstaffian asides, gives the satire a double edge. No previous rake-fop in native drama has revealed Jolimaitre's comic awareness of his role, which is an innovation. His aristocratic affectation is as fraudulent as the "French" manners of his hostess. Mrs. Mowatt's "Continental import" is indeed the comic Crown Prince of his roguish predecessors, and the difference between his good-natured satirical conception and the semimalicious conception of Dimple is evidence of Mrs. Mowatt's purer comic spirit. As it has been suggested, this comic spirit is an indication of America's new cultural maturity. Jolimaitre is not the enemy, not Satan's agent; he is a pure comic figure.

One of the currents permeating nineteenth-century drama, whether comedy or (particularly) romantic "tragedy." was romanticism. It had generated a fresh native type, the American farmer (Miller and the Rosevilles, both William and Lydia) in Woodworth's *The Forest Rose* (1825), which had glorified rural Americana. Earlier, Barker had experimented with the theme of pastoral virtue and a near-pastoral setting in *Tears and Smiles* (1808). The resolution, involving among other matters the moral reform of the rake-fop, takes place at a villa on the rural outskirts of Philadelphia — symbolically far enough out from the decadent city so that natural virtue could operate freely. A few years later, Noah had relied on a bona fide rural setting and numerous rural types in his historical comedy, *She Would be a Soldier* (1819). In this play the heroine, Christine, is a remarkable combination of beauty, masculine courage and physical ability, wit, and pastoral innocence and virtue. Yet the romantic impulse can be traced back to Tyler himself, for certainly Jonathan and Manly's native worth is a pastoral virtue, homegrown in rural New England. Thus, there is a traditional romantic association of the pastoral with the naturally virtuous in native American comedy from the beginning. That tradition is clearly present in *Fashion* in the person of Adam Trueman.

Yet, even though Mrs. Mowatt romanticizes pastoral virtue, she keeps the seventy-two-year-old Catteraugus farmer as a comic type by means of caricature. What he represents is of course sacred, but as a stage person Trueman is comic enough to challenge the dominion of Jolimaitre and Mrs. Tiffany. He is endlessly spouting aphorisms and chiding others. He sheds patriarchal tears for the supposed decadence of his granddaughter and the real enough folly of his old friends. And he walks through the play brandishing his hickory staff as if single-handedly to beat down moral decadence. In spite of his combination of exaggerated traits, this Catteraugus Quixote is somehow very real, very appealing, perhaps because of the warmth present beneath his crusty exterior.

According to Mrs. Mowatt, he was the "only character [in the play] which was sketched from life," and the original, she was told, "was seen in the pit vociferously applauding Adam Trueman's strictures on fashionable society." [23] Yet one wonders just how seriously Mrs. Mowatt had intended her audience to take his salutary proposals in the denouement, to save the Tiffanys by returning them to their natural and virtuous pastoral origins in upstate New York? Coming as it does, immediately after the drunken Snobson's own hilarious suggestion that he and Mr. Tiffany, a pair of jaded Huck Finns, "light out for the Territory" ahead of the law: "They want men of genius at the West, — we're sure to get on! You — you can set up for a writing master, and teach copying *signatures*; and I — I'll give lectures on *temperance!*" (5.1). Trueman's romantic and sentimental "solution," — essentially only another kind of escape — is hardly more feasible.

But then, it all ends in fun, for as Mrs. Mowatt maintains in the *Autobiography*, the satire on American parvenuism "was intended to be a good-humored one," [24] a judgment supported by the conclusion of the play's prologue.

> While we exhibit but to *reprehend*
> The social vices, 'tis for *you* to mend! [25]

Adam Trueman, then, is a kind of latter-day Yankee in much of his exaggerated, clownish mannerism, his native shrewdness, and his rural virtue. But he is a sophisticated Jonathan for all that. While retaining much of the Yankee's freshness and vigor, he has none of his "nat'ral" twang in dialect. This seems evidence that the novelty of the Yankee dialect, popular for so long, was not the sole reason for the stage Yankee's comic success. It may have been that American audiences had become too sophisticated for this dialect by 1845. His appeal was deeper than an Eastern twang. He mirrored, comically of course, what Americans liked to think of as their best selves.

Mrs. Mowatt demonstrates a competence with dialogue, not only in repartee and other exchanges, but in special dialects. Since she spent her early childhood in Bordeaux, French being her first language,[26] it is not surprising that Mrs. Mowatt succeeds with Millinette's accent. She succeeds also with Count Jolimaitre's English speech mannerism (he is, of course, really Gustave Treadmill, an Englishman posing as a French aristocrat), for prior to writing *Fashion*, Mrs. Mowatt had traveled in England and the Continent. Jolimaitre's frequent "demme's" and his habit of speaking in fragmentary sentences punctuated by numerous "aw's" (verbal pauses), is typical of the stage Englishman in the British tradition. Discovered, for example, in an embarrasing situation with Gertrude, Jolimaitre stammers to Mrs. Tiffany —

> You see, madam, hoping to obtain a few moment's private conversation with Miss Seraphina — with *Miss Seraphina* I say — and — aw — and knowing her passion for flowers, I found my way to your very tasteful and *recherché* conservatory. [*Looks about him approvingly.*] *Very* beautifully arranged — does you great credit, madam! Here I encountered this young person. She was inclined to be talkative; and I indulged her with — with a — aw — demme — a few *common places!* What passed between us was mere *harmless badinage* — on *my* part. You, madam, you — so conversant with our European manners — you are aware that when a man of fashion — that is, when a woman — a man is bound — amongst nobleman, you know — .   [2.2]

The squirming is itself a clever stroke of farce, and it is enhanced by the realistic speech mannerism, which had always delighted American audiences.

Mrs. Mowatt's ear, like those of her predecessors in the native tradition, is sensitively tuned to native speech rhythms and mannerisms, and her success with both the Negro dialect, in Zeke, and the middle-class vernacular, in Snobson (or for that matter, Mrs. Tiffany, whose Parisian affectation only points up her American accent) is outstanding. Zeke is very much a burlesque figure, and thus in the tradition of the stage Negro. Nevertheless, he is a dramatic conception grounded on realism in his dialect and attitude. In dismissing Zeke as "a Negro with dialect as impossible as the Negro dialect then in vogue among American writers,"[27] Moses failed to see that the realism is inseparable from the burlesque manner. Whether the Negro had assumed a burlesque role, almost a caricature of himself, because a predominantly white society had forced him to — a matter of sheer social and economic survival — or because of other reasons, is irrelevant to the point here. But that such a role has been the Negro's until the very recent social revolution, is a matter of historical fact. It has been reflected in the drama, as in all fiction.[28] Exploiting the comic and pathetic possibilities of this role, American playwrights allowing for some dramatic license, were searching for realism by drawing upon the rich sources of native types. Tyler had done no less with the Yankee, beginning the search and setting the pattern.

By comparison with the previous stage Negroes in this study, Zeke's dialect is remarkably true to life, as the tradition moves closer to the perfection that is Twain's. Mrs. Mowatt achieves a greater phonetic accuracy in spelling than earlier playwrights, obviating the need, at least in reading the play, for one to supply so much of the dialect in his imagination. For example, "th-" in the initial position is written "d-" as in "de," "dis," and "dat," and "v's" are written "b" as in "ob" or "gib ebidence." As we might expect, Zeke's sentences are riddled with malapropisms, such as "your *publicated* opinion," "a bery *lucifer* explanation," or "dese superfluminous trimmings." And his dialogue is rich in then-current Negro expressions, like "Wheugh, am dat *all*?" (1) and "Can't answer, Boss — neber git a word out ob dis child — Yah! Yah!" (4.2). Coupled with these realistic details of character portrayal is the essential fidelity to life of his attitude and behavior, even within the conscious comic distortion.

With Snobson, Mrs. Mowatt finds less need to exaggerate the typical traits of the struggling, lower middle-class clerk, although he is of course something of a caricature, particularly in his drunken scene in act 5. The central theme of fashion permeates every character except Gertrude and Trueman, no matter how minor, and Snobson distinguishes himself as much as Mrs. Tiffany in his pursuit of such folly. He bristles with self-righteous republicanism in insisting that he is as good as his social superiors, yet the desire for social equality thinly conceals his real lust for the advantages wealth will bring him. His mouth fairly waters at the dream of riding down Broadway in his "two footman tandem," while at the same time he pretends to eschew Mrs. Tiffany's "French lingo." In Snobson, as with Zeke, Mrs. Mowatt has fused the inner and the outer character, attitude and manner.

> *Snob.* How dye do, Marm? How are you? Mr. Tiffany, your most! —
> *Mrs. T.* [*Formally.*] *Bung jure. Comment vow portè vow, Monsur Snobson?*
> *Snob.* Oh, to be sure — very good of you — fine day.
> *Mrs. T.* [*Pointing to a chair with great dignity.*] *Sassoyez vow, Monsur Snobson.*
> *Snob.* I wonder what she's driving at? I ain't up to the fashionable lingo yet! [*Aside.*] Eh? what? Speak a little louder, Marm?
> *Mrs. T.* What ignorance! [*Aside.*]
> *Mr. T.* I presume Mrs. Tiffany means that you are to take a seat.
> *Snob.* Ex-actly — very obliging of her — so I will. [*Sits.*] No ceremony amongst friends, you know — and likely to be nearer — you understand? O.K., all correct. How *is* Seraphina? [3.1]

Snobson is as unmistakably American as he is a petty clerk. His language, rich in the contemporary slang, *is* the language of the lower middle-class, urban American. His language is his character.

Of the remaining characters, none are as outstanding as those already discussed. With the exception of Mr. Tiffany, whose role is one more usually found in noncomic domestic drama or more serious sentimental comedy, all are stock comic types. One feels, as Mrs. Mowatt doubtless intends, both pity and scorn for the poor husband who, little by little, has lost his self-respect as well as his fortune in paying for the fashionable extravagances of his wife. He is given no real comedy, rising only to a little sarcasm in an exchange with his wife (3.1). Whereas Mrs. Mowatt is satirically critical of Mrs. Tiffany, Jolimaitre, Seraphina, and the rest, her approach to the folly of Mr. Tiffany is quite different. Only Trueman criticizes him, and then in his blunt, direct and noncomical manner, for their relationship is one of old friends. Mr. Tiffany becomes a pathetic figure in act 5, when, fearing for his reputation if his forgery is revealed, he is reduced to a sniveling beggar for Snobson's mercy. He shamelessly offers his daughter's hand as the price for Snobson's silence, much to the disgust of all. Fortunately, and to the credit of Mrs. Mowatt's skill, or maybe because of her better judgment as a dramatist, the melodramatic mood is very brief. It is interrupted by the commencement of the denouement, in which Trueman dispenses justice among all, but only after the comic mood has been restored by Snobson's hilarious suggestion of flight to the West.

Mrs. Mowatt protested that she had made "no attempt in *Fashion* at fine writing" and that she had "designed the play wholly as an *acting* comedy," [29] which it certainly is. Although she was a novice at her craft, her play reveals a sound structure. This may seem, as it is not intended, like faint praise, for the same comment has been made about several earlier native comedies. If by "fine writing" Mrs. Mowatt meant the highly stylized and decidedly unrealistic diction of much late eighteenth- and early nineteenth-century drama and fiction, than we can feel only grateful that she avoided it. Much of the comedy's vitality, even today, is in its diction, which so genuinely mirrors the rhythms and idioms of the American vernacular. Mrs. Mowatt returned to the form of drawing-room manners comedy, a form rarely used by native playwrights following Tyler's initial experiment with it. Tyler had thus linked American comedy with the British tradition, and we need, therefore, to compare the structure of *Fashion* to that of *The Contrast*, tying up the tradition between the limits of this study.

Architecturally, the structure of *Fashion* is modeled on that of the British tradition of manners comedy. It is a comedy in five acts, divided into eight scenes: one scene each in acts 1 and 5, which are half again as long as the others to allow for matters of exposition and denouement, and two scenes each in acts 2, 3, and 4. In this respect it does not differ significantly from *The Contrast*, but the resemblance is skeletal, for where *The Contrast* did not, *Fashion* does indeed connect the action between scenes. Not only are the two main plot lines closely interrelated but they are inseparable from the subplot.

An examination of the plot reveals that Mrs. Mowatt uses the familiar double love triangle. In plot A we have the triangle of Howard-Gertrude-

Jolimaitre, and in plot B the second triangle of Jolimaitre-Seraphina-Snobson. (To be completely accurate, we might include Fogg and Twinkle, along with Snobson, in this second triangle. But neither is a serious contender. Or, from another point of view, we might designate the second triangle as Jolimaitre-Seraphina-Millinette because of the count's clumsy dalliance with the French maid. This is not the business of the main action in plot B, however, which is simplified properly as Jolimaitre-Seraphina-Snobson.)

Plot A is perhaps equal in importance to plot B only because of what Gertrude's good sense and virtue stand for in contrast to the fashionable folly of other characters. Yet plot A is far from mechanical, for there is the complication of Gertrude's identity to sustain interest. Furthermore, her difficulty in extricating herself from the awkward situation with Jolimaitre in act 4 provides some genuine excitement and suspense. At one level the play represents the ordeal of Gertrude, even though Mrs. Mowatt's focus is properly on the more interesting and amusing comic business in plot B. To a large degree the movement of the main plots flows from Gertrude's decisions and actions. She is thus the heroine. Yet, because of her suspicion of the count and her sense of duty to see that justice is done, that Seraphina is protected from fraud, Gertrude also functions as a complication in the Jolimaitre-Seraphina-Snobson triangle (plot B). For that matter, considering Jolimaitre's interest in her, she is a part of it. Like Dimple's plan to mary Letitia for her fortune yet to keep Charlotte as his mistress Jolimaitre's interest in Seraphina is purely economic, and in Gertrude, sexual.

Snobson is likewise a complication in plot B. He is not merely another suitor, but with his power over Mr. Tiffany he can force him to resist Mrs. Tiffany's plan to thrust their daughter into wedlock with Jolimaitre. There is no equivalent complication in Tyler's play. A more serious complication to the plans of Mrs. Tiffany and Count Jolimaitre in plot B, however, is the threatening presence of Millinette, who is the discarded lover of Jolimaitre, né Gustave Treadmill. Her desire to regain him, to thwart his scheme of eloping with Seraphina, forms the third love triangle, or the subplot. But due to Millinette's power over Jolimaitre, whose real identity she knows and may momentarily reveal, the subplot is at the same time another complication in plot B. Again, no such intrigue or complication exists in *The Contrast.* Because of these intricacies, *Fashion* is much more in the tradition of conventional manners comedy.

Some earlier native playwrights — Bird in *The City Looking Glass* (1828) being possibly the outstanding example — had demonstrated their competence with busy intrigue, perhaps as much as Mrs. Mowatt, but none had sustained the overall comic mood with quite her finesse. None quite had her hilarious comic sense. Her good-humored satire never drops below the level of spirited comedy yet her blade cuts keenly just the same. Her vision, that of true comedy, sees first the risible in human affairs. The moral outrage, so close to the surface of Tyler's satire, has been transmuted by Mrs. Mowatt's comic spirit. Thus her dramatic energies are turned chiefly, as she said, to the business of writing a good "acting play" and not to hammering didactically at imported fashions in New York, which she viewed in the proper comic perspective: with cultural maturity and without the provincial fears of earlier playwrights. It is inconceivable to imagine *The Contrast* surviving on a London stage past the opening night. *Fashion*, on the other hand, ran for two weeks in London at the Olympic Theatre in 1850, and if we may take Mrs. Mowatt's word for it in the *Autobiography*, twenty out of twenty-seven critical reviews were favorable.[30]

A good play opens with a clear statement of the issues in the exposition, as does *Fashion*, but not merely in the exchange between Millinette and Zeke about imported fashions, followed by Mrs. Tiffany's fussy preparations for the arrival of the imported guest of honor, Count Jolimaitre. It also announces the fashion motif in setting, with careful attention to the fashionable, the "jenny-says-quoi" decor of Mrs. Tiffany's drawing room, to the impressive conservatory, and to the extravagant gowns and headdresses of Mrs. Tiffany and Seraphina. And of course it does so in the manners of the characters — most important of all in manners comedy — from the clownish airs of Zeke right up to the fastidious affectation of Count Jolimaitre. Here then is thematic statement in scene — brilliantly so — and not in summary, which is the failing of Tyler's first gossip scene. In fact the gossip motif is never carried out in *The Contrast*, but fashion holds the center of the stage throughout Mrs. Mowatt's comedy, until it is vanquished by Trueman's hickory staff in act 5. The promise of the satiric hilarity in act 1 is fulfilled by the rest of the play.

A good play also exploits the act and scene division, building climaxes and sustaining our interest by maintaining suspense through fresh complications. With Tyler, one feels that the division into five acts, two scenes per act, is mechanical, a dutiful imitation of form without full function. Nothing could be less true of *Fashion*. The conflict of thematic antagonist and protagonist is begun in act 1 with the arrival of Trueman into Mrs. Tiffany's drawing room. Bu even before that, the central suspense device — Count Jolimaitre's disguise — is hinted at by his own ironic punning in conversation with Mrs. Tiffany. It is heightened climactically at the end of the act by Millinette's shocked gasp when she first sees him, recognizing him as her former lover. The play proceeds maturely, building to some climax in each scene: Snobson's threats to Mr. Tiffany in 2.1; Count Jolimaitre's attempted embrace of Gertrude in 2.2; Millinette's insistence on a private meeting with Count Jolimaitre, thus motivating him to suggest an immediate elopement to Seraphina in 3.1; and so forth until the major climax late in act 5, which simultaneously resolves the two main plots and the subplot. Gertrude, proving to Trueman that she is virtuous and that she is loved by Colonel Howard for herself, is told of her real identity. Jolimaitre's true identity is revealed, fortuitously before any elopement with Seraphina occurs, at a double stroke saving the Tiffanys from disgrace and freeing the imposter for Millinette. Snobson's threats have of course been countered and eliminated, and the denouement, while happy enough, allows some poetic justice to be achieved. All the characters guilty of fashion live happily ever after, but only at the cost of relinquishing their fashionable ways. Even the thwarted Snobson, stealing drunkenly off, is grateful for his freedom and eager to seek a future in California.

Where Tyler, through inexperience, had often failed in dramaturgy, Mrs. Mowatt succeeds. She sustains the comic mood throughout *Fashion*, and satisfactorily connects the action in her plot lines. The movement from scene to scene is thus even. Moreover, she is able to create the social illusion at the heart of manners comedy through her use of the "big scene" — one involving rapid interplay and spirited dialogue among several characters rather than between pairs of characters. Also, she further enlarges this illusion thematically by infusing affectation throughout most of the characters rather than by showing it, as Tyler had, less realistically in somewhat cut-and-dried pairs. Then too, she carries off the modification of (Sheridan's) screen scene well, and she convincingly presents an American setting. (Tyler's drawing room and mall could as well be in London as New York, it will be recalled.)

That she was simply more gifted as a playwright than Tyler, though both were novices, seems undeniable. Then too, she had had the advantage of a lifelong interest in drama: in reading it; in acting in it as an amateur; and in seeing it on the stages of Europe and America. On the other hand, Tyler had had no cosmopolitan experience, no travels abroad, and no contact with the stage until he had gone to New York and attended the John Street Theatre, only a month before he wrote *The Contrast*. For him there *was* no native tradition to shape his ideas. He founded it, in general clumsily when he tried to imitate the polished devices of the British tradition, but with sureness and honesty when he drew from his own native resources for character and when he sought for comedy through humor and farce rather than in the more artificial and intellectual wit, with which, as one views the native tradition emerging in the years following, American playwrights and audiences evidently felt less comfortable.

That Mrs. Mowatt was working, consciously or not, in a sixty-year-old native tradition of comedy is beyond doubt. Cosmopolitan experience notwithstanding — reflected perhaps in her successful adaptation of the difficult manners form for the first time in the tradition — Mrs. Mowatt's *Fashion* stands, not falls, upon its foundation of the native tradition begun by Tyler and developed by generations of playwrights soon forgotten. It is a tradition which is marked by realism of character and dialogue; by realism of setting; by a formlessness of structure until Mrs. Mowatt proved that the European manners form was adaptable, that there was an American drawing room and a drawing-room class by 1845; by an ease and spontaneity with farce humor, although wit — perhaps not a highly polished wit — is never absent; by a serious concern rather than a fastidious contempt for folly — hence that corrective, didactic impulse inherent in sentimental comedy and its many-fathered offspring, social comedy; and by a continuing involvement in contemporary social problems, realistic social problems as opposed to the more generalized problems of universal human frailty attacked in the European tradition of manners comedy.

All of these are clearly present in Mrs. Mowatt's comedy. In one sense, the tradition culminates in her play, for native American social comedy comes of age in *Fashion*. But in another sense, looking ahead to the social comedies of Bronson Howard and Clyde Fitch, or later to those of Langdon Mitchell, Jesse Lynch Williams, and Philip Barry, or still later to those of S. N. Behrman, Mrs. Mowatt has herself shaped the old tradition toward the newer, more sophisticated and polished tradition of social comedy on the American stage today.

Notes
Selected Bibliography
Index

NOTES

1 Introduction: The Quest for Literary Independence

1. E.g., histories by William Dunlap, T. Allston Brown, Arthur Hornblow, Joseph Ireland, William Clapp, George O. Seilhamer, George C. D. Odell, Montrose J. Moses, Arthur Hobson Quinn, Barnard Hewitt, Hugh F. Rankin, and others. See Bibliography for titles.
2. Montrose J. Moses, *The American Dramatist* (Boston: Little, Brown and Co., 1925), pp. 72–74, implies that Sheridan's *The School for Scandal* was the major influence on Tyler's *The Contrast*, although insisting that "the witty character of his later writings would indicate that it was not an imitative thing but was something native with him." But Allan Gates Halline, ed., *American Plays* (New York: American Book Co., 1935), p. 7, says Tyler "by his own admission" used Sheridan's *The School for Scandal* as his model, but Halline offers no citation in support of this claim. Halline may be influenced by Arthur Hobson Quinn, *A History of the American Drama from the Beginning to the Civil War*, 2d ed. rev. (New York: Appleton-Century-Crofts, 1951), pp. 69–70, who quotes Jonathan's description of his visit to the theatre (*The Contrast*, 3.1), and then comments, somewhat misleadingly: "This scene reveals directly — and indirectly — the models upon which our first comedy was written. As had been the case with our first tragedy, the main source lay in the best English playwriting of the type. Tyler tells us that *The School for Scandal* was one of his models and the relation of Dimple to Joseph Surface is not hard to see." G. Thomas Tanselle, *Royall Tyler* (Cambridge: Harvard University Press, 1967), pp. 49–81, is the most recent and most accurate, scholarly treatment of *The Contrast*. Tanselle concedes that Tyler probably saw a performance of *The School for Scandal* in New York 21 March 1787), but offers no evidence to support Halline's claim. The evidence of influence is internal, no doubt as Quinn intended to say, however misleadingly. Tanselle, p. 54, speculates that Jonathan's description of " 'The School for Scandalization' may be a fictionalized account of Tyler's own first visit to the theatre." It is clear from this amusing description that Tyler knew something about Sheridan's play, whether from seeing it played or from reading it. As a Harvard graduate Tyler would have been aware of English drama of his age, particularly in view of his own literary interests. See Arthur H. Nethercot, "The Dramatic Background of Royall Tyler's *The Contrast*," *American Literature* 12 (May 1941): 435–46. For a discussion of sentimental aspects of *The Contrast* that indicate Tyler's familiarity with the literary conventions of his day see Herbert R. Brown, "Sensibility in Eighteenth-Century American Drama," *American Literature* 4 (March 1932): 47–60.
3. Quinn, *American Drama to the Civil War*, p. 10.
4. I am indebted for this full definition to Milton J. Levin, "S. N. Behrman: The Operations and Dilemmas of the Comic Spirit" (Ph.D diss., University of Michigan, 1958), pp. 42–43.
5. Quinn, *American Drama to the Civil War*, p. 323.
6. Allardyce Nicoll, *An Introduction to Dramatic Theory* (London: George G. Harrap and Co., 1923), p. 193. By "pure" manners comedy Nicoll obviously refers to the stylized comedy of Etherege, Congreve et al. in the Restoration, or to the rational comedy of Molière.
7. Nicoll, *An Introduction*, p. 193.
8. Allardyce Nicoll, *A History of the English Drama, 1660–1900: Restoration Drama, 1660–1700*, 6 vols. (Cambridge: Cambridge University Press, 1952–59), 1:196.
9. Nicoll, *An Introduction*, p. 198.

151

10. Ibid., pp. 47–48.
11. George C. D. Odell, *Annals of the New York Stage*, 15 vols. (New York: Columbia University Press, 1927–49), 1:50–74.
12. Nicoll, *A History* 1:196.
13. Arthur Hobson Quinn, *A History of the American Drama from the Civil War to the Present Day*, 2 vols. in one, 2d ed. rev. (New York: Appleton-Century-Crofts, 1936), 2:62.

2 Enter Jonathan

1. Arthur Hobson Quinn, *A History of the American Drama from the Beginning to the Civil War*, 2d ed. rev. (New York: Appleton-Century-Crofts, 1951), p. 6. It is interesting that three members of the cast of *The Prince of Parthia* — Mr. Hallam, and Mr. and Mrs. Morris — also performed in the premiere of *The Contrast* eighteen years later.
2. Quinn, *American Drama to the Civil War*, p. 65.
3. See, for example, George C. D. Odell, *Annals of the New York Stage*, 15 vols. (New York: Columbia University Press, 1927–49); Joseph N. Ireland, *Records of the New York Stage from 1750 to 1860*, 2 vols. (New York: T. H. Morrell, 1866). G. Thomas Tanselle (*Royall Tyler* [Cambridge: Harvard University Press, 1962] p. 52) says that four performances in one month "was a record which no other American play had thus far attained, and it would have been unusual even for the most popular of the English plays." Part of *The Contrast*'s appeal was, as Tanselle points out, the publicity connected to its authorship; that Tyler was an American was much in his favor. Moreover, Wignell's popularity as a comedian with the American Company must have helped. Although one can only speculate, Tyler's own popularity as a dashing young lawyer-turned-soldier, and as a parlor wit among New York society may have contributed to his play's favorable reception. His wife's memoirs suggest this. See n. 11 below.
4. William Dunlap, *A History of the American Theatre* (New York: J. & J. Harper, 1832), pp. 71–72.
5. Actually fifteen performances and one reading: in addition to the five performances in New York, cited in the text, there were productions in Baltimore, 12 November 1787; Philadelphia, 10 December 1787; Baltimore, 19 August 1788; Philadelphia, 7 July 1790; Boston, 19, 29 October 1792 (George O. Seilhamer, *History of the American Theatre before the Revolution*, 3 vols. [Philadelphia: Globe Printing House, 1888–91], 3:21; Seilhamer lists both 19 and 29 October for 1972, but Tanselle, *Royall Tyler*, p. 243, n. 8, records only 29 October; Charleston, 25 February 1793 and 11 February 1794; Boston, 11 May 1795; Philadelphia, 27 June 1796; Richmond, 1799. There may have been unauthorized productions, following the publication in 1790, in such Southern cities as Alexandria, Frederick, Georgetown, Hagerstown, and Williamsburg, according to Tanselle, p. 243, n. 8. For dates of authorized performances see also Quinn, *American Drama to the Civil War*, p. 65; Thomas C. Pollock, *The Philadelphia Theatre in the Eighteenth Century* (Philadelphia: University of Pennsylvania Press, 1933), pp. 141, 158, 303; and Eola Willis, *The Charleston Stage in the XVIII Century* (Columbia, S.C.: State Co.; 1924), pp. 163, 196.
6. A Citizen of the United States [Royall Tyler], *The Contrast* (Philadelphia: published for Thos. Wignell by Pritchard & Hall, 1790). There has been some speculation as to whether Tyler might not have written some or all of the play before coming to New York. According to Helen Tyler Brown, it seems unlikely, especially in the light of the satire of New York society in the play. Miss Brown says: "Whether the statement of a New York correspondent to a Boston Paper under the date of April 16, 1887 (the centennial anniversary of the first performance of *The Contrast*), that 'Royall Tyler arrived in New York from Boston, bringing with him the unfinished play,' is true, I cannot prove." Helen Tyler Brown, "Introduction," *The Contrast*, ed. James B. Wilbur (limited edition; Boston: 1920), p. xxvii.
7. I am indebted for much of this biographical material to Frederick Tupper, "Royall Tyler,

Man of Law and Man of Letters," *Proceedings of the Vermont Historical Society* (1928), pp. 65–101; see also Tanselle, *Royall Tyler*, pp. 1–48.

8. Following his graduation from Harvard, Tyler "entered at once, with great zeal and zest, into the dissipated habits and manners which . . . characterized the younger men of Boston." But he had a "brilliant wit and great powers for amusing conversation." Jeremiah Mason, *Memoirs and Correspondence of Jeremiah Mason* (Cambridge, Mass.: Riverside Press, 1873), p. 32. Quoted in Marius B. Peladeau, ed., *The Verse of Royall Tyler: Collected and Edited* (Charlottesville: University of Virginia Press, 1968), p. xv, n. 6.

9. This is less remarkable than it may appear. A second degree could be purchased — a medieval custom of intercollegiate courtesy still observed by some universities in the colonies. Cf. Peladeau, p. xv, n. 5.

10. From *The Autobiography of Colonel John Trumbull*, ed. Theodore Sizer (New Haven: Yale University Press, 1953), pp. 44–46, quoted in Tanselle, *Royall Tyler*, p. 23.

11. The courtship, involving, among other things, Adams's misgivings about Tyler's past "Dissipation" and "Taste for Poetry," is fully chronicled in Tanselle, *Royall Tyler*, pp. 10–18. While Adams may seem unduly harsh, his attitude toward literature was common then.

12. Frederick Tupper and Helen Tyler Brown, eds., *Grandmother Tyler's Book, The Recollections of Mary Palmer Tyler (Mrs. Royall Tyler)* (London: G. P. Putman's Sons, 1925), p. 107.

13. Quoted in Wilbur, "Introduction," p. xxxi. The letter was from Congressman William J. Grayson to James Madison (24 May 1787). Cf. Tanselle, *Royall Tyler*, p. 83.

14. Quoted in Odell, *Annals*, 1:256–57.

15. Tupper, "Royall Tyler," pp. 68–69.

16. Quoted in Samuel Eliot Morison, *Three Centuries of Harvard, 1636–1936* (Cambridge: Harvard University Press, 1936), p. 138.

17. Ibid., p. 140.

18. Of a possible 147 poetical works varying in length from 1 poem of more than 740 lines to brief epigrams, only 5 bore Tyler's signature at the time of original publication. Peladeau, *Verse*, p. xl.

19. Tanselle, *Royall Tyler*, p. 55, commenting on Tyler's literary anonymity, says "He enjoyed . . . a high literary reputation, and his squeamishness about its effect on his legal reputation has sometimes been overemphasized." However, the incontrovertible fact remains that he signed nothing but his legal writings, and whether or not he enjoyed his reputation, without risking his name, is irrelevant. It must be remembered that his reputation as a poet, among other things, had led to the dissolution of his engagement to Abigail Adams less than two years before. Moreover, Tyler was on active duty in the army during his stay in New York, and his mission, for the Boston Council, was administrative and quasi-legal — he was acting partly in his capacity as a lawyer. Cf. Tanselle, pp. 22–23. It is common knowledge that writing was not widely regarded as a "respectable" profession in Tyler's day. Cf. Peladeau, *Verse*, p. xiii.

20. Tanselle, *Royall Tyler*, p. 85.

21. Quoted in Tupper, "Royall Tyler," p. 82.

22. Arthur W. Peach and George F. Newbrough, *Four Plays by Royall Ryler*, vol. 15 of *America's Lost Plays* (Princeton: Princeton University Press, 1941).

23. A comparison with *The Contrast* shows that Tyler's craftsmanship had improved by 1800, the approximate date of the unpublished play. For a full discussion, see Tanselle, *Royall Tyler*, pp. 86–96.

24. Dr. Updike Underhill [Royall Tyler], *The Algerine Captive* (Hartford: Peter B. Gleason, 1816), pp. v–vi. The preface, quoted here, is somewhat revised from the original edition of 1797.

25. For a discussion of the novel see Tanselle, *Royall Tyler* pp. 140–80. See also David Butler, "*The Algerine Captive*: The Emergence of Native American Fiction in Royall Tyler's Novel"

(Master's thesis, Southern Illinois University, Edwardsville, 1968).

26. H. Milton Ellis, "Joseph Dennie and His Circle: A Study in American Literature from 1792 to 1812," *Bulletin of the University of Texas*, no. 40, Studies in English, no. 3 (15 July 1915), pp. 94–95. According to Peladeau, *Verse*, p. xxiv, Tyler, by virtue of his age — he was eleven years older than Dennie — and his eminence as a lawyer, was the major force in the group. The Literary Club of Walpole, or the Guilford School (since it met often at Tyler's home in Guilford) included, as well as Dennie and Tyler, Jeremiah Mason, Roger Vose, Samuel Hunt, Thomas Green Fessenden, and Samuel West. It also met frequently at the Crafts Tavern in Walpole, next door to the printing shop of Isaiah Thomas and David Carlisle, who owned the *Farmer's Museum*. Dennie, who had joined the *Museum* late in 1795, assumed the editorship from 1796 to 1799, and it was he who was the leader of the Literary Club, says Tanselle. Not all of the contributors were members of the Literary Club, but "much of the copy" was produced in the tavern. See Tanselle, *Royall Tyler*, p. 115.

27. Quoted by Tupper, "Royall Tyler," p. 91. Peladeau, *Verse*, p. xxii, says that Tyler provided most of the poetry, Dennie most of the prose.

28. *The Yankee in London, Being the First Part of a Series of Letters Written by an American Youth, during Nine Month's Residence in the City of London* (New York: Isaac Riley, 1809). For a critical discussion see Tanselle, *Royall Tyler*, pp. 189–205. The last manuscript on which Tyler worked was "The Bay Boy," an unfinished narrative, which Tyler may have begun as early as 1797, and which his wife was preparing for the press in 1825. See Tanselle, pp. 205–9.

29. Written about 1824, two years before Tyler died. "The Chestnut Tree" remained unpublished until 1931. See Peladeau, *Verse*, p. 194. Tanselle, *Royall Tyler*, pp. 136–39, concludes that the poem is flawed by tedious meter (tetrameter), "stock phrases," and a lack of unity — "There is no firm conception shaping the entire work."

30. Montrose J. Moses, *Representative Plays by American Dramatists*, 3 vols. (New York: E. P. Dutton & Co., 1918), 1:433.

31. Odell, *Annals*, 1:256.

32. Dunlap, *American Theatre*, pp. 71–72. According to Moses, *The American Dramatist* (Boston: Little, Brown & Co., 1925), p. 56, Dunlap received his impulse to be a dramatist from Tyler. Dunlap's own first play, *The Modest Soldier*, evidently an imitation of *The Contrast*, was accepted by Halam but never produced, presumably lacking suitable roles for both Hallam and Henry. See Moses, *Representative Plays*, 1:437–38.

33. Seilhamer, *Theatre before the Revolution*, 2:231.

34. Odell, *Annals*, 1:256.

35. Tyler's drama — particularly *The Contrast* and *The Island of Barrataria* — best reveals his ear for the native rhythms of speech. As a poet he was much in the conventions of his age, his diction and syntax tending toward the usual formality of the Augustan writers. Even in native material, as for example, his "Ode Composed for the Fourth of July" (1796), the idiom is a mixture of native and conventional English:

> Thus we dance, and thus we play,
> On glorious *Independent Day* —
> Rub more rosin on your bow,
> And let us have another go.
> Zounds, sure as eggs and bacon,
> Here's ensign Sneak and uncle Deacon,
> Aunt Thiah, and their Bets behind her
> On blundering mare, then beetle blinder.
> And there's the 'Squire too with his lady —
> Sal, hold the beast, I'll take the baby,

[In Peladeau, *Verse*, pp. 47–48]

Perhaps Tyler felt the conventions of language more binding in his verse and fiction (*The Algerine Captive* tends to be written with the journalistic simplicity of Defoe, but without a great deal of native American idiom). In all probability, though, he felt comfortable working in both idioms, but reserved the more earthy regional dialect to signify the lower-class comic character, such as Yankee Jonathan. For a good discussion of literary dialect in American literature see Jules Zanger, "Literary Dialect and Social Change," *Midcontinent American Studies Journal* 7, no. 2 (Fall 1966).

36. Quinn, *American Drama to the Civil War*, p. 66.
37. Louis Kronenberger, *The Thread of Laughter* (New York: Alfred A. Knopf, 1952), p. 202.
38. For example: Lazarus Beach, *Jonathan Postfree* (published 1807); Mordecai Noah, *She Would Be a Soldier* (published 1819); Samuel Woodworth, *The Forest Rose* (published 1825); Cornelius Logan, *Yankee Land* (produced 1834, published ca. 1854).
39. (1) 2.2. Joseph, kneeling to profess his love for Maria, is discovered by Lady Teazle, for whom he had been expressing a "tender concern," and he is forced to concoct a fast explanation. (2) 3.1. Sir Peter, having accused Lady Teazle of an affair with Charles Surface, angrily threatens separation or divorce. (3) 3.3. Charles, being observed by his uncle, disguised as a moneylender, recklessly offers to auction off his entire gallery of family portraits. (4) 4.1. (Really a continuation of the above, but Sheridan manipulates the act division to build another climax.) Charles auctions off the portraits with insolent gusto, to Sir Oliver's increasing horror, but at the end refuses to sell his uncle's portrait, and Sir Oliver, touched by this sentimental gesture, secretly forgives his nephew. (5) 4.3. In this famous screen scene both plot lines merge climactically as Joseph's hypocrisy and Lady Teazle's flirtation with him, and Charles's innocence are all revealed to Sir Peter. (6) 5.2. A minor climax but nonetheless necessary to the denouement, in which Sir Peter throws the scandalmongers out of his house. (7) 5.3. In this obligatory unraveling scene, Sir Oliver's true identity is revealed to the Surface brothers, a concerted effort by Lady Sneerwell and Joseph to malign Charles's character is foiled by Snake's confessions, and Charles, whose former ways are forgiven by all, receives Maria and promises to reform.
40. Tanselle, *Royall Tyler*, p. 61–63, notes Tyler's deficiency in plotting and in providing sufficient action until late in the play.
41. Ernest Bernbaum, *The Drama of Sensibility* (1915; reprinted ed., Gloucester, Mass.: Peter Smith, 1958), p. 6.
42. Allan S. Downer, ed., *American Drama* (New York: Thomas Y. Crowell Co., 1960), p. 2, says: "It is important to read with more care than their aesthetic qualities warrant the earliest plays of the American repertory. At first sight they appear merely imitative of what was currently popular in Germany and in London with a certain amount of Columbianism — speeches celebrating the new nation — thrust upon them. But on closer reading, it becomes apparent that the imitation is of the *form* rather than the attitudes or subject matter of the European originals. Form, after all, is rarely an invention; it is a growth. And the basic forms of European drama, both classical and modern, had slowly evolved through centuries from religious rituals, the Greek festivals of Dionysos, the rites of the Christian church. No such rituals lay in the American past to provide a vehicle for the expression of those truths we held to be self-evident. It was necessary to take what vehicles were available — English comedy of manners, German sentimental drama, French romantic tragedy — and convert them to the use of the republic. For this was to be drama with a purpose, the high, noble, and difficult purpose of making good citizens out of its audiences."
43. Kronenberger, *Thread of Laughter*, p. 62. Comedy, Kronenberger suggests, is dominated by the three principal hungers of man: for money, vanity, and sex, which stem from the cardinal sins of avarice, pride, and lust.
44. Downer, *American Drama*, p. 3.
45. Dunlap, *American Theatre*, p. 67.

46. Although the words of the song have been attributed to Tyler by some scholars, it is more likely a composition of Mrs. Anne Home Hunter, an English poetess, who included it among her *Poems*, 1802. For a summary of the problem of authorship see Tanselle, *Royall Tyler*, pp. 58–59.

47. For a treatment of the Indian character in American drama to 1900, see Richard Moody, *America Takes the Stage: Romanticism in American Drama and Theatre 1750–1900* (Bloomington: Indiana University Press, 1955), pp. 78–110.

48. Constance Rourke, "The Rise of Theatricals," in *The Roots of American Culture and Other Essays*, ed. Van Wyck Brooks (New York: Harcourt, Brace & Co., 1942), pp. 60–75.

49. The term is borrowed from John Harrington Smith, *The Gay Couple in Restoration Comedy* (Cambridge: Harvard University Press, 1948), p. 41.

50. See Elizabeth Mignon, *Crabbed Age and Youth* (Durham, N. C.: Duke University Press, 1947).

51. Mignon, *Crabbed Age*, p. 3.

52. Quinn, *American Drama to the Civil War*, pp. 302–3, cautiously suggests that two Yankees, Jonathan Ploughboy in Woodworth's *The Forest Rose* (1825) and Solon Shingle in Jones's *The People's Lawyer* (produced 1839), may derive from the Yorkshire clown in the tradition of English comedy, but he does not pursue the hypothesis.

53. Francis Hodge, *Yankee Theatre: The Image of America on the Stage, 1825–1850* (Austin: University of Texas Press, 1964), p. 48. For a good sketch of Wignell see Dunlap, *American Theatre*, pp. 82–83.

54. Tanselle, *Royall Tyler*, p. 52.

55. See Marston Balch, "Jonathan the First," *Modern Language Notes* 46 (May 1931): 281–88. Balch, whose article revealed the discovery of the first Jonathan play, feels certain that Tyler had "invented his [Jonathan] from life-long familiarity." See p. 287.

56. Ibid.

57. Ibid. Tanselle, chary of assigning "firsts" to Tyler, says (*Royall Tyler*, p. 58), that Tyler's "use of the song popularized the most familiar and traditional version, which was not published until much later." For the origin of the term "Yankee Doodle" and of the tune "Yankee Doodle," see O. G. T. Sonneck, *Report on "The Star-Spangled Banner," "Hail Columbia," "America," "Yankee Doodle"* (Washington: Government Printing Office, 1909), pp. 79–156.

58. Tanselle, *Royall Tyler*, p. 56–57.

59. Perley Isaac Reed, "The Realistic Presentation of American Characters in Native American Plays Prior to Eighteen Seventy," *Ohio State University Bulletin* 22, no. 26, Contributions in Language and Literature, no. 1 (May 1918) pp. 136–37. Over one-half of forty odd plays by native playwrights before 1787 contained some effort at realistic native characterization. Curiously, after 1789 the Yankee figure is rare for some twenty years. Tanselle, *Royall Tyler*, p. 56–57, interprets this as an indication that Tyler "did not stimulate a tradition of native characters." Hodge, *Yankee Theatre*, p. 6, says the Yankee "had to be literally displayed on a pedestal . . . the stage . . . Royall Tyler's first Jonathan in *The Contrast* (1787) and those that followed for the next thirty years were the projections of the individualist mind which had absorbed the philosophy intellectually and which, in seeing the new American rising everywhere, had presented the character, half in copy of the English country servant on the stage and half as avant-garde expression of American life. But not until the 1820's did the full force of the American political image in Jonathan and his symbolic values present themselves for popular consumption. And then, ironically, it was an English actor in a satirical tirade on American life — *Trip to America* (1824) — performed for English audiences in London, who made American actors aware of the full import of stage exploitation of country Jonathan. From reality to the symbolic life of the stage is the pattern, and we see again the process of myth-making."

60. Hodge, *Yankee Theatre*, p. 6.
61. Constance Rourke, *American Humor* (New York: Doubleday and Co., Anchor Books, 1953 [orig. pub. by Harcourt, Brace & Co., 1931]), p. 4.
62. Hodge, *Yankee Theatre*, p. 60.
63. Rourke, *American Humor*, p. 25.
64. Ibid., p. 50. For a treatment of the Yankee as folk hero see Richard Dorson, "The Yankee on Stage — A Folk Hero of American Drama," *New England Quarterly* 13 (September 1940): 467–93.
65. Dorson, *Yankee on Stage*, p. 491, writing in 1940, lists some twentieth-century descendants of Jonathan, among whom are Jeeter Lester of *Tobacco Road*, and some characterizations of Will Rogers, Bob Burns, W. C. Fields, Lionel Barrymore, and Wallace Beery. To these might be added characterizations of Herb Shriner and Jonathan Winters in the 1960s. Common to all are the Yankee's shiftlessness, homespun humor, naïve-but-shrewd manner, and his basic good-naturedness.
66. Oral Sumner Coad, "The Plays of Samuel Woodworth," *Sewanee Review* 27 (April 1919): 163–75. See also Quinn, 1:292–302.
67. Quoted in Brander Matthews, "The American on Stage," *Scribner's Monthly* 18 (July 1899): 321–33.
68. As Hodge indicates in *Yankee Theatre*, pp. 118–19, *Lion of the West* — later rewritten and renamed *The Kentuckian* — is not properly a Yankee play. The hero, Col. Nimrod Wildfire (Davy Crockett in disguise), who was played by Hackett, is a Kentuckian, or frontiersman. But as such he is a good example of the extension of the original New England Yankee figure.
69. Seilhamer, *Theatre before the Revolution*, 2:214.
70. Ibid., p. 185.
71. Ibid., pp. 235–36.
72. Allan Gates Halline, ed., *American Plays* (New York: American Book Co., 1935), p. 6.
73. Reed, "Realistic Presentation," p. 139.
74. Manly's self-reliance, foreshadowing Emerson's doctrines of a half a century later ("Society everywhere is in conspiracy against the manhood of every one of its members" — "Self Reliance") is seen mainly in his stubborn insistence on defining his personal code of ethics. He is utterly — and provincially — suspicious of fashionable city manners.
75. See Marie Kilheffer, "A Comparison of the Dialect of 'The Bigelow Papers' with the Dialect of Four Yankee Plays," *American Speech* 3 (February 1928): 22–236. Tyler uses literary dialect. He is selective in using only a few distinguishing peculiarities of the New England region (e.g., words such as "tarnal," "meeting-house," and "cute," and idiomatic expressions such as "by the living Jingo!" "kicking up a cursed dust," and "take to my heels and split home, right off, tail on end, like a stream of chalk"). By selecting a few localisms, and presenting them against a background of standard English, Tyler conveys the illusion of Yankee dialect, both with Jonathan and to a lesser degree Van Rough. As Kilheffer shows, many of Jonathan's colloquialisms are "general" and would be as characteristic of the South or West as of New England. But used in the context of the New England rustic, with his references to "home" and his drawl, the general colloquialisms also contribute to the total image of the New England Yankee.
76. Laurence Hutton, *Curiosities of the American Stage* (New York: Harper and Bros., 1891), p. 40, notes that Yankee Hill and J. S. Silsbee had played Solon Shingle in J. S. Jones's *The People's Lawyer* (produced 1839) as a young man, but Charles Burke later developed the part, acting Shingle as a rather shrewd old man. See Hodge, *Yankee Theatre*, p. 214–16.
77. Rourke, *American Humor*, p. 35.
78. The most impressive document in terms of its length and its sermonlike thoroughness reflecting the changing attitudes toward the license of the Restoration stage is Jeremy Collier's *A*

Short View of the Immorality and Profaneness of the English Stage (1698). Collier, a nonconformist preacher, begins with the assumption that the stage should recommend virtue and discountenance vice.

79. See Reed, "Realistic Presentation."
80. Halline, *American Plays*, p. 6, properly calls Dimple a pseudo-Chesterfieldian.
81. Ester Singleton, *Social New York under the Georges* (New York: D. Appleton and Co., 1902), p. 393.
82. Ibid., pp. 373–74.
83. Dunlap, *American Theatre*, p. 67.
84. Jefferson described Washington's mind as "little aided by invention or imagination," and his conversational talents as "not above mediocrity." See *Letters and Addresses of Thomas Jefferson*, ed. William B. Parker and Jonas Viles (New York: Sun Dial Classics Co., 1905), p. 236.
85. Downer, *American Drama*, p. 2, writes, "It would be strange if a new nation which was very conscious that it was the end product of all the progressive forces of a century of extensive theorizing about politics and society . . . would accept without criticism the moral and social values that underlay the theatrical literature of the Old World."
86. Dunlap, *American Theatre*, pp. 86–87.
87. Moreover, there never had been the established sense of class distinction in America, at least as something inherited and, for the most part, inviolable. To be sure, there were and are economic distinctions; but the concern of the haves for the have nots was mostly a republican and Christian obligation. It never stemmed from an aristocratic sense of *noblesse oblige*, as in Europe.
88. Bracketed material omitted in the stage presentation, according to the 1790 edition.
89. For an excellent discussion of Restoration wit and of the Truewit-Falsewit distinction among characters, see Thomas H. Fujimura, *The Restoration Comedy of Wit* (Princeton: Princeton University Press, 1952).
90. See Fred W. Lorch, *The Trouble Begins at Eight: Mark Twain's Lecture Tours* (Ames: Iowa State University Press, 1968).
91. This is a convenient limitation, although justified in that Tyler did use Sheridan as the direct model. But, as Arthur H. Nethercot, "The Dramatic Background of Royall Tyler's *The Contrast*," *American Literature* 12 (May 1941): 435–46, has shown, there was a far broader — though less direct or immediate — influence of British drama, with which Tyler was doubtless familiar through his reading.

3 Three Significant Comedies

1. A Citizen of New-York [William Dunlap], *The Father; or American Shandyism* (New York: Hodge, Allen and Campbell, 1789).
2. *The Oxford Companion to American Literature*, ed. James D. Hart, 3d ed. rev. (New York: Oxford University Press, 1956), p. 209. William Dunlap, *A History of the American Theatre* (New York: J. & J. Harper, 1832), p. 109, says "more than fifty identified plays, twenty-nine of which were entirely or partly his own."
3. George O. Seilhamer, *History of the American Theatre before the Revolution*, 3 vols. (Philadelphia: Globe Printing House, 1888–91), 2:274.
4. Dunlap, *American Theatre*, p. 77.
5. Ibid.
6. Ibid. p. 79.
7. Ibid., p. 80.
8. Ibid., p. 42. See also Arthur Hobson Quinn, *A History of the American Drama from the Beginning to the Civil War*, 2d ed. rev. (New York: Appleton-Century-Crofts, 1951), p. 74.

9. Dunlap, *American Theatre*, p. 50.

10. George Meredith, *An Essay on Comedy*, ed. Lane Cooper (New York: Charles Scribner's Sons, 1918).

11. James Nelson Barker, *Tears and Smiles* (Philadelphia: Printed by T. & G. Palmer for G. E. Blake, 1808).

12. Quinn, *American Drama to the Civil War*, p. 136.

13. Barker's plays include: *The Spanish Rover* (unproduced, unpublished, written 1804), only one act completed; *America* (unproduced, unpublished, written 1805), one-act masque; *Attila* (unproduced, unpublished, written 1805); *Tears and Smiles* (produced 1808, published 1808); *The Embargo; or, What News?* (produced 1808, unpublished); *The Indian Princess; or, La Belle Sauvage* (produced 1808, published 1808); *Marmion; or, The Battle of Flodden Field* (produced 1812, published 1816); *The Armourer's Escape; or, Three Years at Nootka Sound* (produced 1817, unpublished); *How to Try a Lover* (produced 1836 as *A Court of Love*, published 1817); *Superstition; or, The Fanatic Father* (produced 1824, published 1826).

14. The single exception was the Indian play, one of the earliest — and popular from the onset — being Barker's *Indian Princess* (1808). As Moody says, "The nineteenth-century American theatre, on the whole, was a theatre of actors. The audiences looked for the next performance by Forrest, Booth, and Barrett rather than for the next plays by Bird, Stone, or Boker." Indian roles offered these romantic actors what they wanted. See Richard Moody, *America Takes the Stage: Romanticism in American Drama and Theatre, 1750–1900* (Bloomington: Indiana University Press, 1955), p. 188.

15. The biographical material as well as the text of *Tears and Smiles* are found in Paul H. Musser, *James Nelson Barker, 1784–1858* (Philadelphia: University of Pennsylvania Press, 1929).

16. Dunlap, *American Theatre*, p. 377.

17. Ibid., p. 377–78. Barker was particularly sensitive to apathy — or worse, hostility — toward native productions, perhaps because of his own high patriotism as much as his pride as a dramatist. His preface to *Marmion*, written and produced in 1812, although not published until 1816, after the war, is his strongest statement about such hostility and its impact on native drama and native literature in general.

18. For a full treatment of the beau and other native types in early American drama see Perley Isaac Reed, "The Realistic Presentation of American Characters in Native American Plays Prior to Eighteen Seventy," *Ohio State University Bulletin* 22, no. 26, Contributions in Language and Literature, no. 1 (May 1918).

19. The eighteenth-century English theatre, motivated by sentimental considerations of the age, often blurred the more cynical and rapacious outlines of the pure rake of Restoration drama, blending him, as it were, with the fop. For an excellent treatment of wit and the range of characters from Trúewit, through Falsewit, see Thomas H. Fujimura, *The Restoration Comedy of Wit* (Princeton: Princeton University Press, 1952). See also Kathleen Lynch, *The Social Mode of Restoration Comedy* (New York: MacMillan, 1926).

20. Robert Montgomery Bird, *The City Looking Glass*, ed. Arthur Hobson Quinn (New York: Pynson Printers, 1933 [written in 1828]). Dahl says the manuscript is dated July 1829; while correct in pointing out that the play is highly derivative, Dahl is hasty in dismissing it as "little more American than Ben Jonson's *Bartholomew Fair*," as my discussion will show. See Curtis Dahl, *Robert Montgomery Bird* (New York: Twayne Publishers, 1963), p. 44.

21. For biographical information on Bird I have relied on Quinn, *American Drama to the Civil War*, pp. 220–48. Professor Quinn's sources were all primary: the manuscripts of Bird's plays, and a manuscript *Life of Robert Montgomery Bird*, by his wife, Mary Bayes Bird, and the Bird papers — all in the University of Pennsylvania Library.

22. See Quinn, pp. 244–46. In summary, Forrest had paid Bird $1000 for *Pelopidas*. Later Bird agreed to accept that $1000 for *The Gladiator* on condition that Forrest would pay him $2000

more if the play were a success. But it was a verbal agreement, without a signed contract. Bird presumed the same terms were in effect for *Oralloossa* and *The Broker of Bogota*, for each of which he was paid $1000. Again, there was no written agreement, but according to Bird, Forrest owed him $2000 each for these last three plays, or a sum of $6000. (Moreover, Bird claimed Forrest owed him another $2000 for his work in revising John A. Stone's *Metamora* for the actor.) Tragically, the two had been close friends until the squabble in 1837, precipitated when Forrest demanded that Bird repay a loan of $2000, which Bird felt had been canceled out by the unpaid royalties above. That Forrest never sued may be, as Quinn suggests, an indication that Bird was right. But the final trump was Forrest's, for he never allowed any play he controlled, among them Bird's, to be printed, fearful of piracy by other actors.

23. Quinn, "Introduction," in Bird, *The City Looking Glass*, p. ix. See also Quinn, *American Drama to the Civil War*, p. 223.

24. This advance in realism seems earlier evident in American drama than in the novel. Because, for example, Natty Bumpo was not of genteel birth, Cooper was limited by certain social conventions as to what he might allow his hero to do, particularly amorously. While Natty lapses into frontier dialect at times, his speech is more often elevated (or inflated) in keeping with genteel literary conventions. It is hardly realistic. See Henry Nash Smith, "Leatherstocking and the Problem of Social Order," in *Virgin Land: The American West as Symbol and Myth* (Cambridge: Harvard University Press, 1950).

25. That middle-class (or genteel) Americans are more concerned for propriety than absolute morality is a point Norris W. Yates argues in *The American Humorist: Conscience of the Twentieth Century* (Ames Iowa State University Press, 1964).

4 Forty-five Years of Experimenting

1. Noah's historical play, *She Would Be a Soldier*, was still being produced as late as 1848. See Arthur Hobson Quinn, *A History of the American Drama from the Beginning to the Civil War*, 2d ed. rev. (New York: Appleton-Century-Crofts, 1951), p. 152. The long popularity of Woodworth's *The Forest Rose* has been discussed by Oral Sumner Coad, "The Plays of Samuel Woodworth," *Sewanee Review* 27 (April 1919): 163–75. See also Quinn, *American Drama to the Civil War*, pp. 292–303. Logan's *Yankee Land* was performed for twenty years, up to 1854, in cities including New York, Boston, Providence, and Philadelphia. See C. A. Logan, *Yankee Land* (New York: Samuel French and Son [ca. 1854]). The title page of this edition indicates, "As now performed at the principal English and American Theatres." As was customary in such acting editions, casts for various performances are listed by year, the last one being for 1854. Since Yankee actor Dan Marble used this play in London in 1844 (see Francis Hodge, *Yankee Theatre* [Austin: University of Texas Press, 1964], pp. 236–37) and did not return to America until 1848, in all probability *Yankee Land* was published after that time, ca. 1854.

2. J. Robinson, *The Yorker's Stratagem; or, Banana's Wedding* (New York: T. & J. Swords, 1792).

3. Quinn, *American Drama to the Civil War*, p. 131. They were, however, West Indian Negroes, using not "plantation" but "Guinea" dialect.

4. John Leacock, *The Fall of British Tyranny; or, American Liberty Triumphant* (Philadelphia: Printed by Styner and Cist, 1776), in Montrose J. Moses, *Representative Plays by American Dramatists*, 3 vols. (New York: E. P. Dutton & Company, 1918), 1:283–350. Quinn, *American Drama to the Civil War*, pp. 55–56 notes that Ralpho, in Robert Munford's *The Candidates* (Philadelphia, 1798 [written in or before 1770]), was probably the first Negro character in native drama.

5. See discussion of Mowatt's Zeke in ch. 4 for further comment on the stage Negro.

6. John Murdock, *The Triumphs of Love; or, Happy Reconciliation* (Philadelphia, 1795), in Evans, *American Bibliography*, item 29129 (microcard).

7. A. B. Lindsley, *Love and Friendship; or, Yankee Notions* (New York: D. Longworth, 1809). Note the pun on "Notions."

8. There is no record of the performance in Odell, but the published play gives the cast for the performance, evidently its only one.

9. Mordecai Manuel Noah, *She Would Be a Soldier; or, The Plains of Chippewa* (New York: Printed by G. L. Birch for Longworth's Dramatic Repository, 1819), in Moses, *Representative Plays*, 1:629–78. The standard source for Noah's career is a letter he wrote to Dunlap, printed in William Dunlap, *A History of the American Theatre* (New York: J. & J. Harper, 1832), pp. 380–84. The comedy was premiered on June 19 for a benefit, an uncertain beginning, but was repeated on July 5. See George C. D. Odell, *Annals of the New York Stage*, 15 vols. (New York: Columbia University Press, 1927–49), 2:535. It "held the stage for many years, being played as late as July 8, 1848, at the Broadway Theatre." Quinn, *American Drama to the Civil War*, p. 152.

10. See Quinn, *American Drama to the Civil War*, pp. 136–62. Some examples of plays based on native themes are: Barker's *The Indian Princess* (produced, published 1808) and *The Armourer's Escape* (produced 1817, unpublished); Finn's *Montgomery* (produced, published 1825); and Noah's *The Seige of Tripoli* (produced 1820, unpublished) and *Marion* (produced 1821, published 1822).

11. Samuel Woodworth, *The Forest Rose; or, American Farmers* (Boston: William V. Spencer, 1855).

12, Coad, "The Plays of Samuel Woodworth," p. 166. Critics praised the play, as Coad notes, "for the Americanism of its scenery, sentiments and incidents." It appears to have been well received abroad too, for the preface to the 1855 edition claims that the comedy "was produced in London by J. S. Silsbee, who played Jonathan for over one hundred consecutive nights."

13. Quinn, *American Drama to the Civil War*, p. 295, notes that Simpson, who first acted Jonathan Ploughboy, played him as a New Jersey country boy, but that later comedians played him as a New England Yankee. We can assume that Woodworth, who published the play several times, was partly responsible for the revisions in Jonathan's character, but there is the strong possibility that various Yankee comedians influenced these changes by their differing interpretations of the role. Hodge, *Yankee Theatre*, p. 54, views the play as transitional, "being at once a summation of the Yankee's development on the stage up to this point [1825] and a foretaste of what it is to become."

14. Jonathan's repeated epithet, "I wouldn't serve a negro so" and his calling attention to the Negro servant's fondness for garlic ("garlic-chops") reveals a new note in Yankee theatre — the comic abuse of the Negro servant. There is no precedent for this direction in earlier Yankee plays. Tyler's Jonathan, when Jessamy calls him Manly's servant, responds irately, "Sir, do you take me for a neger, — I am Colonel Manly's waiter" (2.2), but Tyler's use of "neger" is clearly only a social distinction here and he goes no further with it in the play.

15. Cornelius A. Logan, *Yankee Land* (New York: Samuel French & Son [ca. 1854]). Hodge, *Yankee Theatre*, p. 142, says that the play was a revision, retitled, of an earlier piece in Hackett's repertoire, *The Wag of Maine*, but thinks that Logan is the author of both.

16. Joseph N. Ireland, *Records of the New York Stage from 1750 to 1860*, 2 vols. (New York: T. H. Morrell, 1866), 2:451.

17. Quinn, *American Drama to the Civil War*, pp. 294–303.

18. The first instance of a Yankee story in fully developed dialect, an important device in later Yankee theatre, occurs in Lindsley's *Love and Friendship* (produced 1807–8 season at the Park Theatre in New York, published 1809). At the conclusion of 1.1, Jonathan, alone on stage, relates an argument he had had with Captain Horner when he first came aboard his schooner "Peggy." See Hodge, *Yankee Theatre*, p. 50.

19. *The Better Sort; or, A Girl of Spirit* (Boston: Isaiah Thomas & Company, 1789). There is a good possibility that author is William Hill Brown, who also wrote (anonynously) *The Power of Sympathy*, the first American novel in the same year. See Richard Walser, "More about the First American Novelist," *American Literature* 24 (May 1952): 352–57. In addition to the evidence Walser cites, we find Mrs. Sententious, in the play, using the phrase "the bettermost genii," which Miss Bourn also uses similarly in the novel. Both characters are alike in being foolishly governed by what is fashionable at the moment.

20. An American [Samuel Low], *The Politician Outwitted* (New York: Printed for the author by W. Ross, in Broad Street, 1789); in Moses, *Representative Plays*, 1:351–429.

21. Dunlap, *American Theatre*, p. 80.

22. Richard Moody, *America Takes the Stage: Romanticism in American Drama and Theatre, 1750–1900* (Bloomington: Indiana University Press, 1955), p. 115, points out that "Low was more intent on exhausting all the comedy possibilities inherent in Humphry than in exhibiting his sterling qualities of honesty, loyalty, etc." Thus Low caricatured his Yankee more than Tyler had with Jonathan.

23. Lazarus Beach, *Jonathan Postfree; or, The Honest Yankee* (New York: David Longworth, 1807).

5 Cultural Maturity and the Flowering of Native American Social Comedy

1. Anna Cora Mowatt, *Fashion; or, Life in New York* (New York: Samuel French, 1854) is the edition used here. The first edition was published in London, 1850.

2. "These articles consisted of sketches of celebrated persons with whom I had been brought into communication, and humorous stories, generally founded on fact. The larger portion of them have since appeared in London magazines. Several were translated into German, and reprinted. Under my own name I at that time published nothing but verse." Anna Cora Mowatt, *Autobiography of an Actress; or, Eight Years on the Stage* (Boston: Ticknor, Reed, and Fields, 1854), p. 184. Of her activities as a hack writer Mrs. Mowatt says: "I also prepared for the press a number of works, the copyrights of which were purchased by Messrs. Burgess & Stringer. They were principally compilations, with as much or as little original matter as was found necessary — book cement, to make the odd fragments adhere together. The subjects of these books were not of my own choosing — I wrote to order, for profit, and to supply the demand of the public." Ibid., pp. 185–86.

3. Ibid., pp. 184–85.

4. Anna Cora Mowatt, *Evelyn; or, a Heart Unmasked* (Philadelphia: Carey & Hart, 1845).

5. Arthur Hobson Quinn, *A History of the American Drama from the Beginning to the Civil War*, 2d ed. rev. (New York: Appleton-Century-Crofts, 1951), p. 315. Mrs. Mowatt does not provide dates in many cases in the *Autobiography*.

6. Mowatt, *Autobiography*, p. 227.

7. Ibid., pp. 21–22.

8. Ibid., p. 37.

9. "My success gave rise to a host of lady imitators, one of whom announced 'Readings and Recitations in the Style of Mrs. Mowatt.' . . . At one time there were no less than six advertisements in the papers, of ladies giving readings in different parts of the Union." Ibid., p. 157.

10. Ibid., p. 213. The locust shell analogy is Mrs. Mowatt's and does not appear in either of Poe's reviews. (*Broadway Journal*, 29 March and 5 April 1845.) In the first, which although it was published after the play had opened was not, by Poe's own admission, based on the performance but upon his study of "the author's original MS," Poe felt that the play lacked "originality or invention." He would have "regarded it as a palpable hit" had it been intended as "a burlesque upon the arrant conventionality of stage incidents in general." He argued, "it will no longer do to copy, even with absolute accuracy, the whole tone of even so ingenious and

really spirited a thing as the 'School for Scandal.' It was comparatively good in its day, but it would be positively bad at the present day, and imitations of it are inadmissible at any day." In his second review, Poe, who admitted being "deeply interested in the question of 'Fashion's' success or failure," and who had thus "been to see it every night since its first production," stood fast on his first judgment, except to admit he was "not quite sure, upon reflection, that her entire thesis is not an original one." He could "call to mind no drama, just now, in which the design can be properly stated as the satirizing of fashion *as* fashion. Fashionable follies, indeed, as a class of folly in general, have been frequently made the subject of dramatic ridicule — but the distinction is obvious — although certainly too nice a one to be of any practical avail save to the authoress of the new comedy." Reviews are published in Edgar Allan Poe, *The Complete Works of Edgar Allan Poe*, James A. Harrison, ed., 17 vols. (New York: AMS Press, 1965), 12:112–21, 124–29.

11. Broadway Journal, 19, 26 July 1845. Quoted in Quinn, *American Drama to the Civil War*, p. 315.

12. Mowatt, *Autobiography*, p. 227.

13. Some of the cities identified in Mowatt's *Autobiography* are: Boston, Providence, New York, Philadelphia, Baltimore, Charleston, Mobile, Savannah, Macon, Montgomery, Vicksburg, New Orleans, Buffalo, Pittsburgh, Cincinnati, Louisville, Lexington, and St. Louis. It is interesting to note the spread of theatrical activity South and West by the mid-nineteenth century.

14. Ibid., pp. 323–31. Mrs. Mowatt includes some of the reviews in this section.

15. She felt that the character offered her "no opportunity for the display of dramatic ability," Ibid., p. 232. She played the role of Gertrude at Charleston, Mobile, and New Orleans, as well as in Philadelphia initially, but wrote, "To be forced to enact the . . . character of Gertrude was a severe punishment" (p. 250).

16. Quinn, *American Drama to the Civil War*, p. 318. Mrs. Mowatt, *Autobiography*, p. 421, writes of her retirement from the stage but does not specify her last role.

17. Quinn, *American Drama to the Civil War*, p. 318.

18. Mowatt, *Autobiography*, p. 301.

19. Washington Irving, *A History of New York* (New York: Inskeep & Bradford, 1809).

20. *Broadway Journal*, 29 March 1845. Quoted in Montrose J. Moses, *Representative Plays by American Dramatists*, 3 vols. (New York: E. P. Dutton & Company, 1918) 2:530.

21. "The customs and fashions which we imitate as Parisian are not unfrequently [*sic*] mere caricatures of those that exist in Paris. For instance, it is the present *mode* not to introduce persons who meet at parties or in visiting, but the custom is intended to obviate the ceremoniousness of formal introductions. Every one is expected to talk to his neighbor; and if mutual pleasure is received from the intercourse, an acquaintance is formed. The same fashion in vogue with us renders society cold and stiff. We abolish introductions because the Parisians do so; but we only take this first step in our transatlantic imitations. Few persons feel at liberty to strangers. Little, contracted circles of friends herd in clannish groups together, and mar the true object of society. As yet, we only *follow* the fashions; we do not conceive the spirit which dictated them.

"So in our mode of dressing. Expensive materials, worn here [i.e., Paris] only at balls, are imported by American merchants and pronounced to be 'very fashionable in Paris.' They are universally bought by our belles, who instead of wearing them at proper seasons, parade the streets in what is meant exclusively for evening costume. Are we not as yet merely a nation of experimenters?" Mowatt, *Autobiography*, pp. 125–26.

22. See chapter 4 for a discussion of Mrs. Sententious in *The Better Sort*.

23. Mowatt, *Autobiography*, p. 203. The veracity of this incident — delighting as it is — is dubious, although audiences then were actively involved and demonstrative. See, William Dunlap, *A History of the American Theatre* (New York: J. & J. Harper, 1832), p. 138.

24. Dunlap, *American Theatre*, p. 138.

25. The prologue was written by Mrs. Mowatt's friend, Epes Sargent, who had initially suggested that she write the play. Mowatt, *Autobiography*, pp. 202, 207–8.

26. Ibid., p. 30.

27. Moses, *Representative Plays*, 2:532.

28. Laurence Hutton, *Curiosities of the American Stage* (New York: Harper & Bros., 1891) is a good source for information about the American stage Negro, containing in particular much useful material about the development of Negro minstrelsy. See pp. 87–144. Richard Moody, *America Takes the Stage* (Bloomington: Indiana University Press, 1955), p. 33 says, "Without the singularly romantic notion of a slave-Negro singing and dancing at his work, smiling and joking even under the punishing strokes of his overseer's whip, Negro minstrelsy would never have had the necessary spark to set it burning through the middle years of the last century." Slavery, as Moody indicates, provided both an audience for the Negro stage image and the image itself.

29. Mowatt, *Autobiography*, p. 203.

30. Ibid., pp. 323–31.

Selected Bibliography

Plays Consulted

Americans in Paris; or, A Game of Dominoes. William H. Hurlburt. 1858.

Americans Roused in a Cure for the Spleen, The; or, Amusement for a Winter's Evening. [Jonathan Sewall.] [1775.]

Armand; or, The Peer and the Peasant. Anna Cora Mowatt. 1849.

Beatrice; or, The False and the True. Oliver S. Leland. 1858.

Benevolent Lawyers, The; or, Villainy Detected. Mrs. Mary Clarke Carr. 1823.

Better Sort, The; or, The Girl of Spirit. 1789.

Broker of Bogota, The. Robert Montgomery Bird. 1824. In Quinn, Arthur Hobson, *Representative American Plays.* New York: Appleton-Century-Crofts, 1953.

Bucktails, The; or, Americans in England. James Kirke Paulding. 1847. In *American Plays,* edited by Allan G. Halline. New York: American Book Co., 1935.

Candidates, The; or, The Humours of a Virginia Election. Robert Munford. 1798. In Moody, Richard, *Dramas from the American Theatre, 1762–1909.* Cleveland: World Publishing Co., 1966.

City Looking Glass, The. Robert Montgomery Bird. 1828.

Contrast, The. Royall Tyler, [A Citizen of the United States]. 1790.

Deed of Gift, The. Samuel Woodworth. 1822.

Disappointment; or, The Force of Credulity. Thomas Forrest [Andrew Barton]. 1767. In Evans, Charles, *American Bibliography.* Item 10554 (microcard).

Disowned, The; or, The Prodigals. Richard P. Smith. 1830.

Downfall of Justice, The. 1777.

Fall of British Tyranny, The; or, American Liberty Triumphant. [John Leacock.] 1776. In vol. 1 of Moses, Montrose D., *Representative Plays by American Dramatists.* 3 vols. New York: E. P. Dutton & Co., 1918.

Fashion; or, Life in New York. Anna Cora Mowatt. 1854.

Fashionable Follies. Joseph Hutton. 1815.

Father, The; or, American Shandy-ism. William Dunlap. 1789.

Forest Rose, The; or, American Farmers. Samuel Woodworth. 1825.

Fox Chase, The. Charles Breck. 1808.

Fraternal Discord. William Dunlap. 1809.

Gladiator, The. Robert Montgomery Bird. 1831.

Glance at New York, A. [Benjamin A. Baker.] 1857.

Group, The. Mercy Warren, 1775.

Henrietta, The. Bronson Howard, 1901.

How To Try a Lover [*A Court of Love*]. James Nelson Barker. 1817.

Hypocrite Unmask'd, The. W. Winstanly. 1801.

Indian Princess, The. James Nelson Barker. 1808.

Jonathan in England. James Hackett, 1828.

Jonathan Postfree; or, The Honest Yankee. Lazarus Beach. 1807.

Julia; or, The Wanderer. John H. Payne. 1806.

Life in New York; or, Tom and Jerry on a Visit. John Brougham. 1856.

Lion of the West, The. James Kirke Paulding, (Written 1830; rev. 1831, 1833.) Edited by James N. Tidwell. Stanford, Calif.: Stanford University Press, 1954.

Love and Friendship; or, Yankee Notions. A. B. Lindsley. 1809.

Love in '76. Oliver B. Bunce. 1857.

Marion. Mordecai M. Noah. 1821.

Marion; or, The Hero of Lake George. Mordecai M. Noah. 1822.

Marmion; or, The Battle of Flodden Field. James Nelson Barker. 1816.

Merry Dames, The; or, The Humorist's Triumph over the Poet in Petticoats and the Gallant Exploits of the Knight of the Comb. John Minshull. 1804.

Montgomery; or, The Falls of Montmorency. Henry J. Finn. 1825.

Musard Ball, The; or, Love at the Academy. John Brougham. 1858.

My Wife's Mirror. E[dward] Wilkins. 1856.

Oralloossa, Son of the Incas. Robert Montgomery Bird. 1832.

Pelopidas; or, The Fall of the Polemarchs. Robert Montgomery Bird. 1830. In Foust, C. E., *Life and Dramatic Works of Robert Montgomery Bird.* New York: Knickerbocker Press, 1919.

People's Lawyer, The. Joseph S. Jones. 1856 (produced 1839).

Politician Outwitted, The. Samuel Low. 1789. In vol. 1 of Moses, Montrose J., *Representative Plays by American Dramatists,* 3 vols.

Poor Lodger, The. William C. White. 1811.

Reconciliation, The; or, The Triumphs of Nature. Peter Markoe. 1790. In Evans, Charles, *American Bibliography.* Item 22638 (microcard).

Sans Souci, alias, Free and Easy; or, An Evening's Peep into a Polite Circle. [Mercy Warren?] 1785.

Saratoga. Bronson Howard. 1898.

School for Prodigals. Joseph Hutton. 1809.

Siege of Tripoli, The. Mordecai M. Noah. 1820.

Self. Mrs. Sidney F. Bateman. 1856.

She Would Be a Soldier; or, The Plains of Chippewa. Mordecai M. Noah. 1819.

Spanish Rover, The. James Nelson Barker. 1804.

Sprightly Widow, The. John Minshull. 1803.

Superstition; or, The Fanatic Father. James Nelson Barker. 1824.

Tears and Smiles. James Nelson Barker. 1808.

Traveller Returned, The. Judith Sargent Murray. 1798. In vol. 3 of *The Gleaner.* 3 vols. Boston: Constantia [pseud.], printed by I. Thomas & E. T. Edwards, 1798.

Trip to Niagara, A; or, Travellers in America. William Dunlap. 1830.

Triumphs of Love, The; or, Happy Reconciliation. John Murdock. 1795. In Evans, Charles, *American Bibliography.* Item 29129 (microcard).

Trust, The. Charles Breck. 1808.

Vermont Wool-Dealer, The. Cornelius A. Logan. [ca. 1854.]

Virtue Triumphant. Judith Sargent Murray. 1798. In vol. 3 of *The Gleaner,* 3 vols. Boston: Constantia [pseud.], printed by I. Thomas & E. T. Edwards, 1798.

Wheat and Chaff. D. Wadsworth Wainwright. 1858.
Yankee in England, The. David Humphreys. [ca. 1815].
Yankee Land. Cornelius A. Logan. [ca. 1854.]
Yorker's Stratagem, The; or, Banana's Wedding. J. Robinson. 1792.
Young Mrs. Winthrop, The. Bronson Howard. 1899.
Young New York. E[dward] Wilkins. n.d. (produced 1856).

Books

Adams, James Truslow. Provincial Society, 1690–1763. Vol. 3 of *A History of American Life.* 12 vols. Edited By Dixon R. Fox and Arthur M. Schlesinger. New York: Macmillan Co., 1927.

Barnes, Eric W. *The Lady of Fashion.* New York: Charles Scribner's Sons, 1954.

Bayard, Ferdinand-M. *Travels of a Frenchman in Maryland and Virginia.* Translated and edited by Ben. C. McCrary. Williamsburg, Va.: (Lithoprinted by Edwards Bros., Ann Arbor, Michigan), 1950.

Bernbaum, Ernest. *The Drama of Sensibility.* 1915. Reprint. Gloucester, Mass.: Peter Smith, 1958.

Blair, Walter. *Native American Humor.* New York: American Book Co., 1937.

Bridenbaugh, Carl. *Cities in Revolt: Urban Life in America 1743–1776.* New York: Alfred A. Knopf, 1955.

Brown, Herbert R. *The Sentimental Novel in America, 1789–1860.* Durham, N.C.: Duke University Press, 1940.

Brown, T. Allston. *A History of the New York Stage from the First Performance in 1732 to 1901.* 3 vols. New York: Dodd, Mead & Co., 1903.

Bruce, Philip A. *Social Life in Virginia in the Seventeenth Century.* 2d ed., rev. and enl. Lynchburg, Va. J. P. Bell Co., 1927.

Burnaby, Andrew. *Travels through North America.* Edited with an Introduction and Notes by Rufus R. Wilson. 1798. Reprint. New York: A. Wessels Co., 1904.

Burnham, Henry. *Brattleboro, Vermont: Early History, with Biographical Sketches of Some of Its Citizens.* Brattleboro, Vt.: D. Leonard, 1880.

Cambridge History of American Literature. 4 vols. Edited by W. P. Trent [and others]. New York: G. P. Putnam & Sons, 1917–21.

Clapp, William, Jr. *A Record of the Boston Stage.* Boston: James Munroe & Co., 1853.

Coad, Oral Sumner, and Mims, Edwin, Jr. *The American Stage.* Vol. 14 of *The Pageant of America.* 15 vols. Edited by Ralph Henry Gabriel. New Haven, Conn.: Yale University Press, 1925–29.

Collier, Jeremy. *A Short View of the Immorality and Profaneness of the English Stage.* 1698.

Cox, James E. *The Rise of Sentimental Comedy.* Olney, Ill.: Olney Printing Co. [published for the author], 1926.

Crawford, Mary Caroline. *Romance of the American Theatre.* Rev. ed. Boston, 1927.

Dahl, Curtis. *Robert Montgomery Bird.* New York: Twayne Publishers, 1963.

Dobree, Bonamy. *Restoration Comedy.* London: Oxford University Press, 1924.

Downer, Allan S., ed. *American Drama.* New York: Thomas Y. Crowell Co., 1960.

Duyckinck, Evert A. and George L. *Cyclopaedia of American Literature.* New York: Charles Scribner, 1855.

Dunlap, William. *History of the American Theatre.* New York: J. & J. Harper, 1832.

Fisher, Sydney George. *Men, Women and Manners in Colonial Times.* 2 vols. 2d ed. Philadelphia: J. B. Lippincott Co., 1898.

Ford, Paul Leicester. *Washington and the Theatre.* Publications of the Dunlap Society Series, no. 8. New York, 1899.

Foust, Clement E. *The Life and Dramatic Works of Robert Montgomery Bird.* New York: Knickerbocker Press, 1919.

Franklin, Benjamin. *Autobiography.* Riverside Literature Series, no. 19 and 20. Cambridge, Mass.: Houghton, Mifflin Co., 1896.

Fujimura, Thomas H. *The Restoration Comedy of Wit.* Princeton: Princeton University Press, 1952.

Gallagher, Kent G. *The Foreigner in Early American Drama.* The Hague: Mouton, 1966.

Genest, John. *Some Account of the English Stage, from the Restoration in 1660 to 1830.* 10 vols. Bath: A. E. Carrington, 1832.

Goodwin, Rutherford [R. G., Gent.]. *A Brief and True Report for the Traveller Concerning Williamsburg in Virginia.* Richmond, Va.: August Dietz & Son, 1936.

Grenville, Vernon. *Yankee Doodle-Doo.* New York: Payson and Clarke, 1927.

Hall, Benjamin H. *History of Eastern Vermont, from Its Earliest Settlement, to the Close of the Eighteenth Century.* New York: D. Appleton & Co., 1858.

Halline, Allan G., ed. *American Plays.* New York: American Book Co., 1935.

Hamilton, Alexander. *Gentleman's Progress.* Edited by Carl Bridenbaugh. 1744. Reprint. Chapel Hill, N.C.: University of North Carolina Press, 1949.

Harrison, James A., ed. *The Complete Works of Edgar Allan Poe.* 17 vols. New York: AMS Press, 1965.

Hewitt, Barnard. *Theatre U.S.A.: 1668 to 1957.* New York: McGraw-Hill, 1959,

Hill, Frank Pierce. *American Plays, Printed 1714–1830, A Bibliographical Record.* Stanford, Calif.: Stanford University Press, 1934.

Hodge, Francis. *Yankee Theatre: The Image of America on the Stage, 1825–1850.* Austin: University of Texas Press, 1964.

Holland, Norman N. *The First Modern Comedies.* Cambridge, Mass.: Harvard University Press, 1959.

Holliday, Carl. *The Wit and Humor of Colonial Days.* New York, 1912.

Hoole, William Stanley. *The Ante-Bellum Charleston Theatre.* Tuscaloosa: University of Alabama Press, 1946.

Hornblow, Arthur. *A History of the Theatre in America.* Philadelphia: Lippincott, 1919.

Hughes, Glenn. *A History of the American Theatre.* New York: Samuel French, 1951.

Hutton, Laurence. *Curiosities of the American Stage.* New York: Harper & Bros., 1891.

Ireland, Joseph N. *Records of the New York Stage from 1750 to 1860.* 2 vols. New York: T. H. Morrell, 1866.

Irving, John B. *The South Carolina Jockey Club.* Charleston, S.C.: Russell & Jones, 1857.

James, Reese Davis. *Old Drury of Philadelphia.* Philadelphia: University of Pennsylvania Press, 1932.

———. *Cradle of Culture.* Philadelphia: University of Pennsylvania Press, 1957.

Jefferson, Thomas. *Letters and Addresses of Thomas Jefferson.* Edited by William B. Parker and Jonas Viles. New York: Sun Dial. Classics Co., 1905.

Journals of the Continental Congress. 1774, 1778.

Kronenberger, Louis. *The Thread of Laughter.* New York: Alfred A. Knopf, 1952.

————, ed. *Richard Brinsley Sheridan (Six Plays).* New York: Hill and Wang, 1957.

Krout, John A. *The Origins of Prohibition.* New York: Alfred A. Knopf, 1925.

Loftis, John. *Comedy and Society from Congreve to Fielding.* Stanford, Calif.: Stanford University Press, 1959.

Lorch, Fred W. *The Trouble Begins at Eight: Mark Twain's Lecture Tours.* Ames: Iowa State University Press, 1968.

Lynch, Kathleen. *The Social Mode of Restoration Comedy.* New York: MacMillan, 1926.

MacMillan, Dougald. ed. *Drury Lane Calendar, 1747–1776.* Oxford: Clarendon Press, 1938.

MacVeagh, L., ed. *The Journal of Nicholas Cresswell.* New York: Dial Press, 1924.

Mason, Jeremiah. *Memoirs and Correspondence of Jeremiah Mason.* Cambridge, Mass.: Riverside Press, 1873.

Matthews, Brander. *Actors and Actresses of Great Britian and the United States, from the Days of David Garrick to the Present.* New York: Cassell and Co., 1886.

Meredith, George. *An Essay on Comedy.* Edited by Lane Cooper. New York: Charles Scribner's Sons, 1918.

Mignon, Elizabeth. *Crabbed Age and Youth.* Durham, Duke University Press, 1947.

Moody, Richard. *America Takes the Stage; Romanticism in American Drama and Theatre, 1750–1900.* Bloomington: Indiana University Press, 1955.

————. *Dramas from the American Theatre, 1762–1909.* Cleveland: World Publishing Co., 1966.

Moore, John B. *The Comic and the Realistic in English Drama.* Chicago: University of Chicago Press, 1925.

Morison, Samuel Eliot. *Three Centuries of Harvard: 1636–1936.* Cambridge: Harvard University Press, 1936.

Moses, Montrose J. *Representative Plays by American Dramatists.* 3 vols. New York: E. P. Dutton & Co., 1918.

————. *The American Dramatist.* Boston: Little, Brown, & Co., 1925.

Mowatt, Anna Cora. *Autobiography of an Actress; or, Eight Years on the Stage.* Boston: Ticknor, Reed, and Fields, 1854.

————. *Evelyn; or, A Heart Unmasked.* Philadelphia: Carey & Hart, 1845.

————. *The Fortune Hunter.* Philadelphia: T. B. Peterson [ca. 1854].

————. *Mimic Life; or, Before and Behind the Curtain.* Boston: Ticknor & Fields, 1856.

————. *Twin Roses,* Boston: Ticknor & Fields, 1857.

Musser, Paul H. *James Nelson Barker, 1784–1858.* Philadelphia: University of Pennsylvania Press, 1929.

Nicoll, Allardyce. *An Introduction to Dramatic Theory.* London: George G. Harrap & Co., 1923. (New rev. and enl. edition called *The Theory of the Drama.* London: Harrap, 1931.)

————. *A History of English Drama, 1660–1900: Restoration Drama, 1660–1700.* 6 vols. 2d ed., reprinted. Cambridge: Cambridge University Press, 1952–59.

Northall, William K. *Before and Behind the Curtain.* New York: W. F. Burgess, 1851.

Oberholtzer, Ellis P. *Philadelphia, A History of the City and Its People.* 4 vols. Philadelphia: The S. J. Clarke Publishing Co., 1912.

Odell, George C. D. *Annals of the New York Stage.* 15 vols. New York: Columbia University Press, 1927–49.

Oxford Companion to American Literature. Edited by James D. Hart. 3d ed., rev. New York: Oxford University Press, 1956.

Oxford Universal Dictionary. Edited by C. T. Onions. 3d ed., rev. New York: Rand McNally & Co., Conkey Division, 1955.

Peach, Arthur W. and Newbrough, George F., ed. *Four Plays by Royall Tyler.* Vol. 15 of *America's Lost Plays.* 20 vols. Edited by Barrett H. Clark. Princeton: Princeton University Press, 1940–42.

Peladeau, Marius B., ed. *The Verse of Royall Tyler: Collected and Edited.* Charlottesville: University of Virginia Press, 1968.

Perry, Henry T. E. *The Comic Spirit in Restoration Drama.* New Haven: Yale University Press, 1925.

Poe, Edgar Allan. *The Complete Works of Edgar Allan Poe.* 17 vols. Edited by James A. Harrison. New York: AMS Press, 1965.

Pollock, Thomas Clark. *The Philadelphia Theatre in the Eighteenth Century.* Philadelphia: University of Pennsylvania Press, 1933.

Quinn, Arthur Hobson. *A History of the American Drama from the Civil War to the Present Day.* 2 vols in one. 2d ed., rev. New York: Appleton-Century-Crofts, 1936.

————. *A History of the American Drama from the Beginning to the Civil War.* 2d ed., rev. New York: Appleton-Century-Crofts, 1951.

Rees, James. *The Dramatic Authors of America.* Philadelphia: J. B. Zieber & Co., 1845.

Reniers, Perceval. *The Springs of Virginia.* Chapel Hill: University of North Carolina Press, 1941.

Rourke, Constance M. *American Humor.* New York: Doubleday & Co., Anchor Books, 1953. Published originally by Harcourt, Brace & Co., 1931.

————. "The Rise of Theatricals." In *The Roots of American Culture and Other Essays.* Edited by Van Wyck Brooks. New York: Harcourt, Brace & Co., 1942.

Sachse, William L. *The Colonial American in Britain.* Madison: University of Wisconsin Press, 1956.

Seilhamer, George O. *History of the American Theatre before The* Revolution [to 1797]. 3 vols. Philadelphia: Globe Printing House, 1888–91.

Sherbo, Arthur. *English Sentimental Drama.* Lansing: Michigan State University Press, 1957.

Sherman, Robert L. *Drama Cyclopedia.* Chicago: Published by the author, 1944.

Sherrill, Charles H., ed. *French Memories of Eighteenth Century America.* New York: Charles Scribner's Sons, 1915.

Singleton, Esther. *Social New York under the Georges.* New York: D. Appleton & Co., 1902.

Smith, Henry Nashe. *Virgin Land: The American West as Symbol and Myth.* Cambridge: Harvard University Press, 1950.

Smith, John Harrington. *The Gay Couple in Restoration Comedy.* Cambridge: Harvard University Press, 1948.

Smith, Solomon. *Theatrical Management in the West and South for Thirty Years.* New York: Harper & Bros., 1868.

Sonneck, Oscar G. T. *Early Opera in America.* New York: G. Schirmer, 1915.

_____. *Report on "The Star-Spangled Banner," "Hail Columbia," "America," "Yankee Doodle."* Washington, D.C.: Government Printing Office, 1909.

Stanard, Mary Newton. *Colonial Virginia.* Philadelphia: J. B. Lippincott Co., 1917.

_____. *Richmond, Its People and Its Story.* Philadelphia: J. B. Lippincott Co., 1923.

Tanselle, G. Thomas. *Royall Tyler.* Cambridge: Harvard University Press, 1967.

Trumbull, John. *The Autobiography of Colonel John Trumbull.* Edited by Theodore Sizer. New Haven: Yale University Press, 1953.

Tryon, Warren S., ed. *A Mirror for Americans.* 3 vols. Chicago: University of Chicago Press, 1952.

Tupper, Frederick, and Brown, Helen Tyler., eds. *Grandmother Tyler's Book, The Recollections of Mary Palmer Tyler (Mrs. Royall Tyler).* London: G. P. Putnam's Sons, 1925.

Tyler, Lyon G. *Williamsburg.* Richmond, Va.: Whittet & Shepperson, 1907.

Tyler, Royall [Dr. Updike Underhill]. *The Algerine Captive.* Walpole, N.H.: David Carlisle, Jr., 1797.

_____. *The Contrast.* Edited by James B. Wilbur. Limited edition with an Introduction and Bibliography by Helen Tyler Brown (Royall Tyler's great-granddaughter). Boston, 1920.

[Tyler, Royall]. *The Yankee, Being the First Part of a Series of Letters Written by an American Youth, during Nine Month's Residence in the City of London.* New York: Isaac Riley, 1809.

Waldo, Lewis P. *The French Drama in America in the Eighteenth Century and Its Influence on the American Drama of that Period, 1701–1800.* Baltimore: Johns Hopkins Press, 1942.

Watson, John F. *Annals of Philadelphia and Pennsylvania in the Olden Time.* 2 vols. Philadelphia: J. B. Lippincott & Co., 1879.

Wecter, Dixon. *The Saga of American Society.* New York: Charles Scribner's Sons, 1937.

Wegelin, Oscar. *Early American Plays, 1714–1830.* 2d ed., rev. New York: Literary Collector Press, 1905.

Wertenbaker, Thomas J. *The First Americans.* Vol. 2 of *A History of American Life.* 12 vols. Edited by Dixon R. Fox and Arthur M. Schlesinger. New York: Macmillan Co., 1927.

_____. *Patrician and Plebeian in Virginia.* New York: Michie Co., 1910.

Willard, George O. *History of the Providence Stage, 1762–1891.* Providence, Rhode Island: Rhode Island News Co., 1891.

Willis, Eola, *The Charleston Stage in the XVIII Century.* Columbia, S.C.: State Co., 1924.

Wood, William B. *Personal Recollections of the Stage.* Philadelphia: Henry Carey Baird, 1855.

Woodward, William. *The Way Our People Lived.* New York: E. P. Dutton, 1944.

Yates, Norris W. *The American Humorist: Conscience of the Twentieth Century.* Ames: Iowa State University Press, 1964.

Journals, Theses, Dissertations, and Manuscripts

Balch, Marston. "Jonathan the First." *Modern Language Notes* 46 (May 1931): 281–88.

Bateson, F. W. "Contributions to a Dictionary of Critical Terms: I, 'Comedy of Manners.' " *Essays in Criticism* I (1951): 89–93.

Bird, Mary Bayes. "Life of Robert Montgomery Bird." Master's thesis, University of Pennsylvania Library, n.d.

Brown, Herbert R. "Sensibility in Eighteenth Century American Drama." *American Literature* 4 (March 1932): 47–60.

Butler, David. "*The Algerine Captive*: The Emergence of Native American Fiction in Royall Tyler's Novel." Master's thesis, Southern Illinois University, Edwardsville, 1968.

Chapman, Bertrand W. "The Nativism of Royall Tyler." Master's thesis, University of Vermont, 1933.

Coad, Oral Sumner. "The Plays of Samuel Woodworth." *Sewanee Review* 27 (April 1919): 163–175.

———. "Stage and Players in Eighteenth Century America." *Journal of English and Germanic Philology* 19, no. 2 (April 1920): 201–30.

Dorson, Richard. "The Yankee on Stage — A Folk Hero of American Drama." *New England Quarterly* 13 (September 1940): 467–93.

Ellis, H. Milton. "Joseph Dennie and His Circle: A Study in American Literature from 1792 to 1812." *Bulletin of the University of Texas*, no. 40 Studies in English, no. 3 (15 July 1915), pp. 9–285.

Ford, Paul Leicester. *Some Notes Toward an Essay on the Beginnings of American Dramatic Literature, 1606–1789.* Brooklyn, New York: Privately printed, 1893. Revised and reprinted as "The Beginnings of American Dramatic Literature." *The New England Magazine*, n.s. 9 (February 1894): 673–87.

Glenn, Stanley L. "Ludicrous Characterization in American Comedy from the Beginning until the Civil War." Ph.D. dissertation, Stanford University, 1956.

Hoole, William Stanley. "Two Famous Theatres of the Old South." South Atlantic Quarterly 36, no. 3 (July 1937): 273–77.

———. "Charleston Theatres." *Southwest Review* 25, no. 2 (January 1940): 193–204.

Hutcheson, Maude. "Mercy Warren, 1728–1814." *William and Mary Quarterly*, 3d ser. 10 (January 1953): 378–402.

Kilheffer, Marie. "A Comparison of the Dialect of 'The Bigelow Papers' with the Dialect of Four Yankee Plays." *American Speech* 3 (February 1928): 22–236.

Levin, Milton J. "S. N. Behrman: The Operation and Dilemmas of the Comic Spirit." Ph.D. dissertation, University of Michigan, 1958.

Lewis, Stanley T. "The New York Theatre: Its Background and Architectural Development: 1750–1835." Ph.D. dissertation, Ohio State University, 1954.

Matthews, Albert. "Brother Jonathan." *Publications of the Colonial Society of Massachusetts* 7 (1901): 94–122.

———. "Brother Jonathan Once More." *Publications of the Colonial Society of Massachusetts* 32 (1935): 374–86.

Matthews, Brander. "The American on Stage." *Scribner's Monthly* 17 (July 1879). 321–33.

Nethercot, Arthur H. "The Dramatic Background of Royall Tyler's *The Contrast*." *American Literature* 12 (May 1941): 435–46.

Quinn, James J., Jr. "The Jonathan Character in the American Drama." Ph.D dissertation, Columbia University, 1955.

Reed, Perley Isaac. "The Realistic Presentation of American Characters in Native American Plays Prior to Eighteen Seventy." *Ohio State University Bulletin* 22, no. 26, Contributions in Language and Literature, no. 1 (May 1918).

Tupper, Frederick. "Royall Tyler, Man of Law and Man of Letters." *Proceedings of the Vermont Historical Society* (1928), pp. 65–101.

Virginia Gazette. 1736, 1737.

Zanger, Jules. "Literary Dialect and Social Change." *Midcontinent American Studies Journal* 7, no. 2 (Fall 1966): 40–48.

INDEX

Adams, John, 9

Adventures of Robin Day, The: novel, 79

Alexander the Great (The Rival Queens), 11

Algerine Captive, The: novel, 12; preface of, 13; plot and themes of, 14

America, 159n*13*

American Company: and Lewis Hallam Jr., 11

American Girl character, the (girl of spirit): Louisa Campdon, 76–77; Diana Headstrong, 94–95; Christine Jasper, 109, 112–13; Adela, 112; Harriet Miller, 115–16; Mira Lovemuch, 118–20; Gertrude, 136–37

American Indian: Alknomook romanticized in drama, 25

American manners: satire of New York beaux, 41–42; Dimple's satire of New York entertainments, 47; Ranter's satire of, 61; Fluttermore's railing at, 70; Barker's satire of, 70–71; Nathan Nobody's railing at, 93; Mowatt's satire of, 134–35

Aristophanes: political satire in comedies of, 44

Armourer's Escape, The; or, Three Years at Nootka Sound, 159n*13*

Atkinson, Joseph: Irish playwright *(A Match for a Widow)*, 31

Attila, 159n*13*

Autobiography of an Actress, 131, 135, 146

Baker, Benjamin A.: *A Glance at New York*, 99

Bangs, Thomas: wrote version of "Yankee Doodle" in *The Contrast*, 31

Barker, James Nelson: *Tears and Smiles*, 62; dramatic output of, 62, 159n*13*; *Marmion* authorship hoax, 63; biographical sketch of, 63–64

Battle of Bunker's Hill, The, 45

Beach, Lazarus: *Jonathan Postfree*, 101; mentioned, 166

Beau character: Rangely, first native American beau, 72–73; Frankton and Worthnought, 73; Bolt, Crossbar, Mossrose, Philadelphia "bucks," 90; Ned Raleigh, regional (Southern), 90–91; Dick Dashaway, regional college fop (Southern), 106; Seldreer, 107; Captain Pendragon, 109–10. *See also* Military character; Rake-fop character

Beaux's Stratagem, The, 6

Better Sort, The; or, The Girl of Spirit: preface quoted, 118; plot summary of, 118–19; theme of native worth in, 120; possible authorship of, 162n*19*; mentioned, 101, 137, 165

Bird, Robert Montgomery: *The City Looking Glass*, 78; dramatic output of, 79; novels of, 79; biographical sketch of, 79–80; argument with Forrest, 159–60n*22*; mentioned, 63

Brackenridge, Hugh Henry, 45, 108

British tradition of comedy, stock characters from: sentimental heroine, 24; lady of fashion (coquette), 25–27; comic servant, 27–28; man of affairs (businessman, etc.), 28–30; father-guardian, 29

Broker of Bogota, The, 79, 165

Brown, David Paul: minor Philadelphia author, 63

Calavar: novel, 79

Candide: satirical narrative, 14

Careless Husband, The, 6

Caridorf, 79

Cato, 11

Centlivre, Mrs.: English actress-playwright, 6

Charlotte Temple: novel, 103

Chatham Theatre (New York City): premiere of *Forest Rose* at, 113

Chesterfield, Lord (Philip Dormer Stanhope): *Letters to His Son*, 27; mentioned, 13

Chestnut Street Theatre (Philadelphia): premiere of *Triumphs of Love* at, 103; played *Fashion* for one week simultaneously with a New York City production, 130

"Chestnut Tree, The": Tyler's long pastoral poem, 15

Cibber, Colley: English actor-playwright, 6

City Looking Glass, The: not published or produced until 1933, 78; in emerging native tradition, 79; plot summary of, 80–82; influence of Elizabethan and Jacobean drama on, 83; double love triangle of, 83; plot structure of, 83–84; theme of filial obedience in, 87–88; antisentimental elements of, 87–88; theme of